Innovative Treatment Methods in Psychopathology
edited by Karen S. Calhoun, Henry E. Adams, and Kevin M. Mitchell

The Changing School Scene: Challenge to Psychology
by Leah Gold Fein

Troubled Children: Their Families, Schools, and Treatments
by Leonore R. Love and Jaques W. Kaswan

Research Strategies in Psychotherapy
by Edward S. Bordin

The Volunteer Subject
by Robert Rosenthal and Ralph L. Rosnow

Innovations in Client-Centered Therapy
by David A. Wexler and Laura North Rice

The Rorschach: A Comprehensive System
by John E. Exner

Theory and Practice in Behavior Therapy
by Aubrey J. Yates

Principles of Psychotherapy
by Irving B. Weiner

Psychoactive Drugs and Social Judgment: Theory and Research
edited by Kenneth Hammond and C. R. B. Joyce

Clinical Methods in Psychology
edited by Irving B. Weiner

Human Resources for Troubled Children
by Werner I. Halpern and Stanley Kissel

Hyperactivity
by Dorothea M. Ross and Sheila A. Ross

Heroin Addiction: Theory, Research, and Treatment
by Jerome J. Platt and Christina Labate

Children's Rights and the Mental Health Profession
edited by Gerald P. Koocher

The Role of the Father in Child Development
edited by Michael E. Lamb

Handbook of Behavioral Assessment
edited by Anthony R. Ciminero, Karen S. Calhoun, and Henry E. Adams

Counseling and Psychotherapy: A Behavioral Approach
by E. Lakin Phillips

COUNSELING AND PSYCHOTHERAPY

COUNSELING AND PSYCHOTHERAPY:
A BEHAVIORAL APPROACH

E. LAKIN PHILLIPS, Ph.D.

Professor of Psychology
Director, Counseling Center
George Washington University
Washington, D.C.
and
Founder and Executive Director
School for Contemporary Education
Alexandria, Virginia

A WILEY-INTERSCIENCE PUBLICATION

JOHN WILEY & SONS, New York • London • Sydney • Toronto

Library of Congress Cataloging in Publication Data:

Phillips, Ewing Lakin, 1915–
  Counseling and psychotherapy.

  (Wiley series on personality processes)
  "A Wiley-Interscience publication."
  Bibliography: p.
  Includes indexes.
  1. Behavior therapy. 2. Psychotherapy. 3. Coun-
seling. I. Title.

RC489.B4P47   616.8'914   77-1771
ISBN 0-471-01881-3

Printed in the United States of America

10 9 8 7 6 5 4 3 2 1

Series Preface

This series of books is addressed to behavioral scientists interested in the nature of human personality. Its scope should prove pertinent to personality theorists and researchers as well as to clinicians concerned with applying an understanding of personality processes to the amelioration of emotional difficulties in living. To this end, the series provides a scholarly integration of theoretical formulations, empirical data, and practical recommendations.

Six major aspects of studying and learning about human personality can be designated: personality theory, personality structure and dynamics, personality development, personality assessment, personality change, and personality adjustment. In exploring these aspects of personality, the books in the series discuss a number of distinct but related subject areas: the nature and implications of various theories of personality; personality characteristics that account for consistencies and variations in human behavior; the emergence of personality processes in children and adolescents; the use of interviewing and testing procedures to evaluate individual differences in personality; efforts to modify personality styles through psychotherapy, counseling, behavior therapy, and other methods of influence; and patterns of abnormal personality functioning that impair individual competence.

Irving B. Weiner

Case Western Reserve University
Cleveland, Ohio

Preface

Attempts to develop a thoroughgoing account of counseling and psychotherapy in behavioral terms have been few and far between. Some counseling and psychotherapy approaches have been partially behavioral; some have been essentially behavioral without recognizing this; and some have attempted to be explicitly nonbehavioral. However, it appears to me that one cannot engage in counseling and psychotherapy without recognizing its behavioral basis, no matter how many verbal, semantic, and conceptual techniques the therapist-theorist may use to avoid it. If we can establish that behavior is our subject matter, then we can all work together to bring under practical and conceptual control the many subtle and far-reaching aspects of personality; this will make possible better theory and technique in the counseling and psychotherapy realms.

Recognizing that a full-fledged account of the complexities of psychotherapy and counseling is not easily accomplished, it is nonetheless an intriguing and absorbing task to try on the behavioral suit as far as it will fit. This is the intention of this book. In grappling with this problem, I have tried to recognize some of the changes of the last few years that have moved counseling and psychotherapy (not to mention other areas of psychology) in the direction of considering more explicitly the subtleties of covert processes, knowing all the while that "covert" and "overt" are semantic splits that can be as misleading as they are heuristic. What we need are not battles over covert versus overt processes (separating behaviorism from all other counseling and therapy approaches on this pivotal issue), but enlightened ways to challenge the behavioral position to look at, experiment with, and try to use and conceptualize data from any reliable source whatever. Narrow behaviorism in all fields—and especially in psychotherapy—has eschewed data from internal events, perhaps dismissing them as not scientifically available, rather than asking how we can bring these subtleties into scientific study.

Likewise, therapists and theorists coming from psychodynamic or other "depth" positions eschew behavioral analysis and definitions in ways that are far from either clarifying their own positions or contributing to rapprochement with behavioral formulations. In my own development as a therapist and theorist speculating about what I was doing, I have always—in practice—admitted any data that seemed available (in terms of replicability, reliability, and so forth) and have tried earnestly, I believe, to communicate to students and peers what I was doing (or thought I was doing) and to bring the whole matter into the open. However, often I was unsure of both the factual basis of what I was trying to do and certainly not too clear about the conceptual basis. With the coming into maturity of the operant movement as the foundation of modern, functional behaviorism (enlarging considerably upon the Pavlovian tradition and the many forms of observation, measurement, and experimentation developed by psychologists in the past 70–100 years), the task of explicating the complexities of counseling and psychotherapy have been made clearer (to me, at least), more functional, more easily communicated, and far more easily researched. Although not everyone will agree with this observation of the role of operant analysis of behavior and its influence on various clinical areas, I believe that it is essentially true and that time will further bear out the validity of the observation.

Working as psychologists, especially in clinical settings, we often overlook contributions from other areas of science. It is difficult enough to keep up with one's own field, much less try to be even superficially conversant with related areas of science. But it is fruitful to ask now and again how others who are concerned with behavior look upon their tasks. I believe that the broad movement known as cybernetics, touching as it does many areas of science and human affairs, provides yet another robust and convincing way of looking at behavior in any context, ranging from internal, physiological, and homeostatic processes, through the study of individual behavior (as in counseling and psychotherapy), to the study of group, community, and societal processes. Eventually, I believe, operant processes and, indeed, all we now consider as "psychology" will be seen as subsystems within the larger cybernetic framework and the study of homeostatic processes, ranging from minute physiological data to larger aggregates of social, institutional, and societal data, will subsume the principles of reinforcement and the study of consequences within this larger framework. In the meantime, I think operant study is by far the most heuristic way of looking at behavior and can absorb us for many years to come, as we have only begun to apply operant analysis to the variety of problems we meet in the clinic, whether working at individual or small-group levels.

Techniques weigh heavily in operant work. In one sense, operant analysis of and intervention in clinical problems is a matter of technique, since the philosophy—if one accepts it—gives rise immediately to the many specific and pivotal forms of intervention. If we take behavior as our subject and define it in terms of functional relationships, then techniques—which are but ways of implementing the functional, behavioral analysis—follow as inexorably as medical technology follows medical and biological knowledge. This is not to say that techniques cannot be misapplied; the onrush to behavioral technology has created, and will continue to create, many technical, clinical, and ethical problems. The application of discoveries is seldom as maturely performed as the conceptual and experimental work underlying the discoveries themselves. We may need decades of applying behavioral technology before we develop a true and useful lexicon of skills; and much of this work must be done in tutorial and supervisory settings with students and tyro therapists. It cannot be accomplished alone by reading research reports or listening to convention papers on behavior therapy.

If technique serves the purposes of defining how one can go about changing behavior in ethical, useful, economical, and personally satisfying ways, then technique becomes very important. But the employment of technique must stem from an analysis of the problem, which includes the input from the patient, however unsophisticated, irrational, or feeling-centered it may be. Techniques are not to be used just because they are available—they are simply means to an end. As long as the counselor or therapist can attend first, with the patient's help, to the problem(s) at hand, the behavioral analysis of the problems and selection of technique(s) can go hand-in-hand to the benefit of the patient and the enlargement of science and technology.

In a real sense, then, this book has very few messages: First, behavioral analysis is called for, since we have nothing but behavior to study (although with great emphasis I reiterate this viewpoint is to be broad, open, and subject to easy challenge from data arising from any reliable source). Second, although techniques are abundant, even embarrassingly rich in variety, they do not need to inhibit patient contributions to his or her problem status and can even greatly enlarge that understanding. They are to be employed with caution and constant feedback as to their efficacy. Third, our study of behavior in the clinical context (referring mainly to counseling and psychotherapy) is a small part of a much larger context that begs for more complete analysis in general systems terms, because of the notion that all systems, be they minute or encompassing, are subject to the same laws and methods of control.

It is unlikely that all these aspirations have been met. My patients have taught me how important it is to recognize that exorbitant expectations can get one in trouble. I hope I can stay out of trouble!

Many people have stimulated me and contributed indirectly to this writing, although I take full responsibility for what is said here. Dr. Norris G. Haring and Dr. Daniel N. Wiener are two important historical sources of influence; my students and colleagues at the George Washington University Counseling Center and the Department of Psychology have provided constant challenges to me to make my ideas clearer and more useful; Dr. Arthur J. Bachrach and Dr. Charles B. Ferster have challenged me in many ways to try to relate clinical practice to behavioral study and analysis. Last but not least, I thank the many patients from whom I have learned more than I have possibly taught them!

E. LAKIN PHILLIPS

Washington, D.C.
October 1976

Contents

COUNSELING AND PSYCHOTHERAPY

CHAPTER 1

What Is Behavior?

Broadly speaking, behavior is anything people do. This includes all activities human beings engage in—acting, feeling, emoting—and many subtle things that do not readily meet the eye. More ideally, behavior is anything that people do that can be somehow investigated, that is, observed, counted, recorded, or measured. Looking at human behavior in this broad perspective has led to a development called *behavior modification,* also sometimes referred to as behavior therapy or behavior change.

Behavior study has shown enormous vitality over the past two decades. Approximately a hundred books, thousands of research and clinical papers, and several national and international journals have been produced (Hoon and Lindsley, 1974). In the 75–100-year history of the profession of psychology, there has probably not been another development comparable in influence and scientific productivity to that of the behavior modification movement of the past two decades (Krasner, 1971).

In addition to the above-mentioned developments, there have been launched many seminars, workshops, and symposia on behavior change, and there has been a highly visible increase in the number of course offerings in graduate and undergraduate training in psychology, social work, and psychiatry (Task Force Report: American Psychiatric Association, 1974; Ayllon, 1971; Gelfand, Gelfand, and Dobson, 1967).

An important outgrowth from this ground swell is the application of behavior principles to counseling and psychotherapy in the clinic (Woody, 1971). Behavioral study of counseling and psychotherapy has probably evidenced a slower growth than is the case for behavioral applications to handicapped populations and hospitalized and institutionalized patients, where the latter comprise "captive populations" with simpler behavioral repertoires and more easily managed routines. The encouragement arising from the behavioral study of more limited populations has spread recently to clients or patients in "free environments" who are largely in control of their own repertoires and behavioral economies but who nonetheless present interesting and sometimes formidable problems. These are the people we see in psychological and psychiatric clinics, in counseling centers in colleges and universities, and in many mental health, outpatient settings. Although there are many good examples of how behavioral methods work with patients in these noninstitutional settings, there is a compelling need to better highlight behavioral methods in the clinic and to further conceptualize the entire counseling/psychotherapy process in behavioral terms. This is a large undertaking and one that must be approached with some caution; and since there are many aspects to this conceptualization effort, one is able to tackle only a few of them in one book.

The use of behavioral methods in the clinic is necessarily a "flexible" or limited or programmatic use. This does not mean that nonbehavioral methods (whatever they may be) are better, or that behavioral methods leave off where nonbehavioral methods take up; nothing could be further from the truth. What it does mean is that one needs to be careful and thoughtful about how, and with what conceptual clarity and accuracy, one employs behavioral principles in the clinic. Actually, one is always dealing with behavior—what else is there but behavior? The problem arises when clinicians and practitioners conceptualize behavioral data in presumptive nonbehavioral terms and overlook the problems related to operationalizing concepts, providing independent tests of their clinical observations, and testing out theories and hypotheses in scientifically reliable and acceptable ways. Also, problems arise when the behavioral practitioner does not pay close enough attention to how he or she uses data from the laboratory or other settings in the clinical practice of counseling and psychotherapy.

THEORIES ARE IMPORTANT

The setting in which behavioral observations and methods are most stringently tested is the clinic—where disturbed and disturbing people are helped to overcome problems in daily living. The strengths and limitations of the laboratory study of behavior are carried over into the clinic, sometimes without sufficient thoughtful application. The main hypothesis we employ when we apply laboratory knowledge of learning and behavior change to the clinic is to assert that the former does, indeed, apply to the practical situation. Not all would agree with this proposition, however. For many years, some psychologists eschewed the role of laboratory study in providing leads for practical applications to clinical and counseling settings; there was a kind of aloofness, a position that laboratory-derived knowledge was "pure" and "above it all" and would only be contaminated if applied.

However, during the past two decades, the rapid expansion of behavioral work—first to institutional settings, later to more nearly "free" environments—has provided incentive for extrapolating from the laboratory, and this extrapolation has proved heuristic. How carefully we make the extrapolation is related to the definition of concepts taken from the laboratory (e.g., the empirical definition of reinforcement based on operant work) and how well the related definitional problems are faced in the clinic setting. For example, when we praise the client (reinforce him) for talking about and acting on certain issues in his life, are we reinforcing him in a manner demonstrably like that used in the laboratory? If so, do we expect and receive changes in the client's behavior comparable to those observed in the more rigorous setting? Or, are we possibly reinforcing a host of other behaviors, because we may be powerless to single out any one, and therefore go for whatever we can get in the way of directed change? Although we may think we are being precise in the clinic—and we possibly are a J.N.D. or two above the precision offered by ostensibly nonbehavioral clinical methods—we are nonetheless beholden to a number of mediational conditions that we can now only recognize in a general theoretical way. The mediating stimulus transformations between patient and therapist are not the same as the laboratory setting in which the subject is placed in an experimental arrangement designed to control independent and dependent conditions. The verbal self-stimulation of the patient, based on the "instructions" received from the therapist, are subject to a host of errors, interpretations, and related mediational stimuli largely under the control of the patient himself (Bachrach, 1966, 1967; Mahoney, 1974). That one can be critical of a too easy conceptualization of this complex transaction does not mean that the behavioral perspective is superficial or too narrow; any other viewpoint will meet the same problems. We must, nonetheless, recognize what we are doing in translating from the laboratory to the clinic and see how much therapists are, so to speak, on their own, and where they have good guidance from more rigorous formulations of behavioral principles.

Caution in arriving at clinical applications of laboratory work may be summarized in the following points:

1. Care is necessary in recognizing that extrapolations from the laboratory to the clinic may pivot on the therapist's own verbal representations of behavioral principles; on how this is communicated to the patient (as a directive, a suggestion, or as a rhetorical question); on the patient's verbal self-stimulation about the therapist's communication and the patient's understanding of how he can translate what he hears into action for himself; and other related communication issues, depending on how finely one wants to analyze them (Bandura, 1969; Bergin, 1969, 1970; Dember,

1974; Kanfer, 1971; Kanfer and Phillips, 1970; Ullmann, 1970; Boren and Coleman, 1970; Ferster, 1972; Yates, 1975; Truax, 1966). It is simply not the case that the therapist represents a stimulus in a modified laboratory sense, gets a reaction from the patient, and then reinforces what is selected for this purpose. The onflowing verbal instructions and communications from the therapist, the impingement of these stimuli on the patient in terms of his prevailing repertoire at the moment, and the often fleeting opportunities for reinforcement of the patient are much more the run-of-the-mill events in the therapist–patient exchange.

2. Care by the therapist is essential in selecting the variables or procedures and their interrelationship for application to the patient's presenting problems. The therapist may select extinction or "time out" in contrast to positively reinforcing the patient's alternative behaviors, as a treatment of choice (Wolpe and Lazarus, 1966; Lazarus and Serber, 1968); or the therapist may attempt to use systematic desensitization. Some techniques (e.g., extinction) may take a relatively long time to show effectiveness and thereby run the risk of losing the patient's perseverance and cooperativeness, whereas others (e.g., a desensitization procedure) may be relatively quick and effective (Lazarus, 1957). Therapists tend to use the techniques they already know, and thus they confine their own repertoires too severely, not to mention delaying the patient's recovery (Thoresen and Mahoney, 1974). Fledgling therapists tend to use techniques they have heard of, read about, or seen depicted on a film; and experienced therapists often "settle in" to using two or three favorite techniques. One does not know from the research literature how different techniques might work on common problems; or how many different techniques could be brought to bear on the same or similar problems! It is relatively easy to test out role-playing during the therapy hour (e.g., helping the patient improve his ability to make anxiety-ridden phone calls to persons in authority), and perhaps less relevant to use only relaxation in the face of authority-derived anxiety reactions.

3. Assessing the outcome of the behavioral objectives is also important. Assessment of outcome in therapy and counseling is always a tricky matter, at best, but one that must always be faced. For example, obsessive behavioral characteristics may be approached via several therapeutic routes: relaxation; negative practice; or verbal explanations of the role of escape or avoidance in maintaining obsessive behaviors (Walton and Mather, 1964; Bass, 1973). These procedures should yield discernible outcome data, such as number of therapy sessions, alternative behaviors learned, and perhaps other data. Also, the "staying power" of remedial efforts must be assessed more carefully, as any measures that place a high option on alternative behaviors may show good results for a time but fade out shortly thereafter.

4. Care is needed in knowing where to enter into a patient's repertoire, and behavioral economy is necessary in order to become effective. This is a difficult problem and one usually not addressed in the behavioral literature. From cybernetics, we learn of the importance of redundant, "vicious circle" kinds of processes where there is no simple causality of a stimulus–response type (Phillips and Wiener, 1966). We often take presenting complaints as "given," not themselves to be analyzed as part of a redundant process; and although we deal with target behaviors, there may be other targets in the recurrent process that are more pivotal. Treating enuresis among school age children can serve as an example: The bedwetting at night is often ameliorated most easily by cutting down on the child's hyperactive behavior before bedtime, as well as on teaching better voiding behaviors. In interpersonal conflict such as that between husband and wife or boss and employee, there are no easy entry points; an approach that reduces the opportunity for conflict can be as rewarding as behavior targeted for change at the height of the conflict itself. One needs to log in such cases not only the target behavior itself, but the whole recurrent process showing how the problem follows a repetitive mold and can be expected to be repeated within a discernible time frame (see Chapter 9).

5. Closely related to point 4, and possibly a corollary, is the importance of recognizing that the therapist has a responsibility to test out ideas he or she has in regard to conceptualizing the patient's problems. Abstract conceptualizations that may sound good and be delivered fluently in a summary on the patient or in a research paper may not be of much value clinically in changing the patient's behavior. One often hears the therapist assert, "The patient needs to learn to relax . . . ," and this may well be the case; but the value of the description or conceptualization arises when the therapist and patient work together on the relaxation to see if the prediction (or prescription) is valid. If the therapist thinks the patient is ". . . too aggressive in dealing with others . . . ," then some ways should be contrived in the therapy hour to directly deal with the alleged aggression (verbally being the most likely way at first). A general rule here might suffice: offer no abstract explanation that cannot be tested directly or indirectly in the clinical setting.

6. The role of "emotions" presents a problem in the clinic not found in laboratory studies, except for those expressly studying a given emotional state or some aspect of same. In the clinical setting emotions abound and relate to virtually every phase of clinical interaction: liking and/or accepting the therapist as a person; accepting the method and viewpoint of the therapist; being willing to try out ideas both in the clinic and in the outside world without too much hesitancy; evaluating the results of intervention in the clinic and in the outside world; and holding steadily to goals and to

work on target behaviors. Emotions usually result in unsteady and vacil-lating behavior; in mood swings; and hitches in motivation, application, and determination. All of these, regardless of clear conceptualizations, limited target behaviors, and the choice of appropriate behavioral inter-vention techniques, beset the clinician but not as much the experimen-talist. The clinician doing counseling or psychotherapy steps into this mainstream of emotional perturbations and first tries to make sense of them but more fully tries to harness and direct them to positive ends. In the laboratory there is more of a stopping of activity to fit the laboratory ends and less perturbation on the part of the experimental subject once introduced to the experiment.

7. Insofar as the results of therapy and counseling intend to "put the client on his own feet . . . ," the work of the clinic is considerably different from the laboratory. The broad sweep of identifying and pursu-ing change on the part of the patient as a result of therapy actually frees the patient from therapy and the constraints associated therewith; he learns to outgrow therapy. No such purpose exists in the laboratory: the experiment serves a useful and limited purpose, and little or no interest is shown in the subject insofar as his or her general problem solving is concerned; that would be, in most instances, inimical to the purpose of the experiment itself (Yates, 1975).

In spite of the limitations on the application of behavioral psychology to the clinic, there are many fruitful applications of these techniques in the literature. Recognizing the limitations on extrapolation will not preclude nor inhibit application but will make clinical practice more sophisticated. Many research possibilities exist in the effort to breach the gap between the laboratory and the clinic: selecting various behavioral techniques for ostensibly the same problem and viewing results; examining the range of problems that can be shown to fall under the aegis of one behavioral technique; attempting to enter redundant processes at different points or junctures in the recurrent process and ascertaining the effectiveness as-sociated with various entry points; and so forth.

FEELINGS AND BEHAVIOR

Recognizing problems in relation to translating behavioral methods from the laboratory to the clinic gives rise to a second problem in relation to a flexible behavioral position: the problem of *feelings*. Do feelings refer to another facet or aspect of the human being? Are feelings also behavior? Are feelings always covert processes? If so, can they be embraced within a behavioral technology of value in the clinic? Do feelings precede behavior?

Issues revolving around feelings have taken up many pages in the annals of counseling and psychotherapy (Patterson, 1966, 1973; Harper, 1959). Yet feelings are seldom discussed in behavioral therapy books and are hardly ever referenced therein. Most nonbehavioral theories of counseling and psychotherapy are based on various notions about feelings, how important they are, their histories, what gives rise to feelings, and the like. Most theories in this domain locate their variables—if they specify any variables in a reliable way—inside the psyche, usually in terms of covert processes that are hard to locate, study, or change. The more elusive the feelings dealt with, the presumed greater importance they carry.

Two general problems in relation to feelings and behavior must be discerned. The first is one of translating the patient's reported (or observed) feelings into behavioral data (who did what, when, where, how, to whom, under what circumstances, etc.), based on the self-reports of the patient. The second and related problem is that of conceptualizing feelings in terms of behavioral processes as a general condition applying to human actions. These are, of course, really two aspects of a basic problem: the role of feelings in a world of behavior.

Many psychologists, mainly those not associated with any behavioral position, will say that feelings are different from behavior and will tend to hold to a fast and hard dichotomy. Supporting this contention is the commonly experienced relationship in therapy and counseling where the therapist has trouble getting the patient to talk about his feelings, getting the patient to discern the relationship between feelings and other behavior, and helping the patient to overcome unwanted feelings in relation to behavior change. Feelings present formidable problems, not the least of which is conceptualizing them in an economical and fruitful way.

Several things may be said in support of the contention advanced in this book that feelings are behavior.

1. Accompanying the patient's statements about feelings are observable behaviors. These include speech, manner of speech delivery, stance, posture, facial expressions, gestures, "nervous" habits such as tics, and many kinds of expressive behaviors. It would be hard to judge feelings (in terms of emotional states) without the accompanying behaviors cited, or other behaviors. Insofar as feelings refer to emotional states (joy, sorrow, etc.), physiological signs accompanying these emotional states are well known (Backrach, 1967; Benson, Beary, and Carol, 1974).

2. The patient's verbal behavior itself labels and assigns possible

causes and circumstances to the reported feelings. Although people do not know clearly why they feel as they do—in most instances of disturbed behavior, at least—they attempt to assign causality as best they can. This beginning attempt is one of value to the therapist, as the therapist can take the causal thread the patient reveals and unravel it in order to come to a more fruitful notion of how the reported feelings fit into a behavioral context. A patient may report that he is depressed. Questions reveal he has had a conflict with his boss, and this, in turn, hinges on the patient being attacked in terms of his competence, revealing a chain of events of importance in explaining the feelings: conflict–boss–deprecation– low esteem–negative feelings–low - motivation - for - work–continued - negative - feelings, and so on. Conversely, the person who has been positively reinforced for good work tends to step sprightly, smile, be expansive, and be willing to reinforce others. No great microscope to the nth power is needed to demonstrate these behavioral tendencies in relation to feelings.

Feelings do not occur in a vacuum; people reveal their moods and feelings in their behavior. An experienced therapist can often tell a patient's general mood and whether the upcoming session will be a productive one on the basis of the behavioral stance, facial expression, and carriage of the patient as he or she enters the therapist's office. Even beyond the clinic, in theatrical, artistic, musical, and other expressive settings, the feelings conveyed by the artist or his product are closely intertwined with behavioral signs: dark blue colors and somber music for depression, lighter colors and greater movement for gaiety, and so on. Without these accompanying behavioral signs, the artist would not be able to get his point across to the viewer or listener, and the artistic expression would fall flat if it depended entirely on some notion of pure emotion or feeling.

Many feelings are, however, hard to locate and to translate clearly into words. One important aspect of a therapist's training is to be alert to "feeling states" revealed by the patient that are not yet translated into clearer terms, and for which the effort to make the translation may take time. Our ability to observe ourselves must be learned (Skinner, 1971) and is largely a social/cultural product; in fact, we learn a lot about observing others from first observing ourselves. However, we do lack tools to observe and assign meaning to feelings in a very real sense. The dentist can do a much better job of locating the source of pain—and, of course, doing something about it—than can the sufferer. The physician asks us, "Where does it hurt?" in order to probe more analytically. Both dentist and physician can, with the help of their probing techniques and technology, locate and tell us more about some feeling states than we can possibly do for ourselves.

Psychologists who use personality tests effectively can also probe and locate feelings more accurately than the reporting patient can. High scores on the psychasthenia and/or depression scales of the MMPI, although based on the patient's self-report, can lead the experienced clinician to tell the patient about his general feelings which are only dimly discerned by the patient. The patient may often remark, "Well, how could you tell that I felt that way?" There is nothing magical about this clinical inference, but it does illustrate how some types of probing can yield useful leads for purposes of changing behavior.

It would be impossible, then, to talk about feelings that do not include or imply behavior. The expression of the feeling in nonverbal ways is behavior, as we have seen; and surely reporting verbally on feelings includes many complicated examples of behavior. Looking, too, at physiological activities accompanying emotion or feeling, we again see many behavioral signs (blushing or facial reddening, agitated movements, inability to focus on a problem, inability to concentrate, inability to communicate verbally, and so on).

Behavior is often shown early in the arousal of feeling or emotion *before* we express the feeling in words—increased pulse and heart rate being a common example. Since feelings in the form of emotional arousal also tend to continue long after the "danger" has passed, the resulting feelings are observed by ourselves and others in terms of the well-known aspects of physical stance, speech, and other signs. We continue to "feel" something long after the provocation itself (the arousing stimulus) has passed, and we continue to react verbally and physically to these feelings as they ripple through our bodies. All feelings have somatic or bodily components; or, conversely, there are no feelings without some bodily registering of them.

What is the meaning of this view of feelings in regard to counseling and psychotherapy? Feelings are simply not separate psychological conditions to be pursued in their own right. Feelings are behavior; feelings are somatic conditions. Therapies that work on feelings devoid of the behavioral context are likely to waste time and to overlook important facets of the person's problem.

People in general, and clinicians in particular, tend to view feelings as one's own private domain, incapable of intrusion by any "outsider." One assumes that even though a person may not be in control of his or her feelings, nonetheless the feelings are *known* by the person in a full, intimate, real, and private sense. This may be true for *some* feelings *some* of the time. However, even "depth" therapies assume that feelings are not readily and fully knowable by the person himself (even though they are "owned" by the person). But they ought to be fully known, the clinician might say; the traditional view here is that of "making the unconscious conscious," which is another way of saying that feelings are to be labeled and brought under deliberate control. But this is not as easy as it seems. The "unawareness of feelings" (or "unawareness of one's behavior") is a complicated issue and one that concerns the experimentalist as well as the clinician, as seen in an experiment by Hefferline, Keenan, and Harford (1959).

Hefferline and colleagues (1959) wanted to condition a response—a minute muscle twitch of the thumb in this case—so fine that the experimental human subjects would not be "aware" of making the response. He used an electromyograph to record the muscle activity of the subjects; while the subjects listened to music, noise or static was superimposed over the music. The noise could be terminated by a muscle twitch, and the subjects "learned" without awareness to turn off the noise and listen only to the music. Later in the experiment when the subjects were told of the details of the study, they were asked to deliberately make the minute muscle twitch of the thumb in order to turn off the noise, and they were unable to consciously make this change in their behavior! The moral of this is that private events may not be such an individual prerogative after all; and even when knowing about some behavior, one cannot then necessarily bring it under deliberate control. However, the physiological processes and learning processes involved were brought under control. These "inner" events were better identified and controlled by "outside" conditioning than they could be by and through "conscious" control.

McGuigan and Schoonover (1973) detail many ways in which subtle physiological process can be measured by proper instrumentation yet remain outside of conscious control or even knowledge. An example is imagery: When persons are asked to imagine that one or the other arm is moving, the corresponding eye (right or left) moves, and subtle muscle changes occur in the "moving" arm. This suggests that what we loosely call imagery and often "imagine" is nonbehavioral or nonphysiological is, on the contrary, derived from a physical base (Bachrach, 1972, p. 54); and that what we need, in order to study and identify such subtle processes, is ever more finely geared instrumentation which places these inner processes more fully within a behavioral and/or physiological framework. Some of the early scientific studies of subtle processes, cited in McGuigan and Schoonover (1973), go back as far as 1954, when the use of biofeedback of low-level muscle activity in relation to relaxation was documented. Perhaps what we register subjectively as inner feeling states is, more realistically and more objectively, a set of subtle, minimal, but often pervasive physiological activities that we can only haltingly identify ourselves, yet which ramify into sometimes far-reaching behavioral consequences.

Being on the lookout for many subtle processes, behavioral therapists should not eschew feelings, which they are often accused of doing. Recognizing that behavior and feelings are one and the same, the therapist knows that only semantically is there a deliberate effort at discerning differences, usually in concession to the patient on a verbal level in order to better understand the patient's plight and what he or she is trying to communicate to the therapist.

Feelings are what bring people to therapy; they are the big impact on the person's awareness, just as they are in the case of physical disease and disorder. The feelings tell one "something is wrong," but they do not spell out the larger circumstances; in fact, feelings may be very misleading in providing information not only on "inner" events but also on the larger context of a problem, as we have seen.

Nor should the behavioral therapist *dwell* on feelings. Feelings are a "getting started" place; they provide a beachhead in order to launch a larger attack on the problem, taking the wider terrain into consideration. Mainly, therapists of a nonbehavioral persuasion isolate feelings and probe them, tickle them, turn them over and over—hence the observed emphasis in depth psychology and depth therapy on psychopathology (which may be a kind of study of feelings gone wild!). Exploring feelings has benefit if it leads to a management of the unacceptable feelings (usually part of the presenting complaint); but as an end in itself, it cannot be very productive and the preoccupation with feelings, per se, tends to reinforce them through the attention afforded them in therapy. In therapies that emphasize feelings for their own sake, there tends to be a bogging down, a preoccupation with the thousands of nuances that feelings afford, all to no practical end; and although the therapy discussions may be endlessly fascinating, they do not culminate in a grip on the feelings that makes for better and more efficient living; the practicalities of behavior change are missed or eschewed.

For these reasons it is not correct to say that feelings cause behavior, as those are inclined to do who follow a philosophy of mental–physical dualism. It is rather the case that certain behaviors tend to lead to other behaviors; chains of responding and circular processes tend to be conditioned to one another, and once in motion the pattern moves toward repetitiveness. If nothing of a corrective nature intervenes, the patterns (chains and circular processes) will continue; and we soon recognize what we ordinarily designate as traits, character dispositions, attitudes, and other global descriptions. In the case of circularity of responding, a very common condition, we note that some stimuli elicit other behaviors and, unless arrested, the repetitive process may lead to untoward results, emotional reactions, strong feelings of unworthiness, and other complications. We then *feel bad* about these untoward results.

In the complexity of therapy, it is better to say arbitrarily that behavior causes feelings. This allows us—therapist and patient—to look at the antecedent conditions, the probable eliciting stimuli that presumably accounts for the unwanted behavior and negative feelings. The question then becomes, "What behaviors were noted prior to the advent of unwanted feelings?" When we look at these antecedent conditions, we learn what the person did or did not do, how he or she interacted with others, what previously reinforced behaviors were in evidence, and so forth that produced the unwanted consequences. We can then bring the feelings under control by changing the antecedent conditions the next time around (keeping in mind the conditions will recur, as they are cyclic and redundant). The behavior of the therapist is especially important in intervention, in changing the nature of the eliciting stimuli, the redundant processes, because the therapist can more easily and readily identify the likely antecedent events, can help the patient focus more clearly and readily on these antecedent conditions, and can thereby increase the likelihood of reacting differently with each new opportunity.

If, indeed, all that one can observe and deal with is behavior, what does one make of those who offer what are presumably nonbehavioral concepts, theories, and therapeutic approaches, based essentially on feelings? Wishing to avoid dogmatism at this point, but putting an emphasis on observations, empirical methods, and testing hypotheses with replicable research, it is difficult to see how any data other than behavioral data can stand up to these tests (Krasner, 1971). Essentially mentalistic theories, with variables located in the psyche, so to speak, may have some common sense and natural language appeal, but they do not weather well in science; and no one today has built a solid, empirical, and testable body of knowledge on such theories. Theory builders in counseling and psychotherapy will object and say that not all propositions in science are hard, rock-bottom, and testable; that many now-respected hypotheses and theories have grown into respectability; that theories and hypotheses need time for testing, for integration into a discipline, and one cannot begin this complex and arduous process with wholly convincing efforts.

Although too many theories of therapy are vague and difficult to test empirically, they may often give rise to interesting side issues and implications. For example, an interest in "body language" has grown up in recent years, arising out of a concern for nonverbal communications in therapy and in other interpersonal processes. One did not need a rigorous empirical or hypothetico-deductive process to arrive at the notion that people express much behavior via bodily processes and patterns. This notion, in turn, enlarged the realm of therapy and brought new data into the therapeutic exchange. If we always pushed first for rigor, we might sacrifice some productive leads and be the poorer for it in the long run! Also, the study of "body language" is an ideal behavioral topic, even though its origins were probably not explicitly behavioral, and probably began as vague and difficult-to-test notions.

A catholic view, then, is called for in regard to the full range of problems associated with feelings in a behavioral framework. On the one hand, one has only behavior to consider; but that does not allow for a rigid and overdetermined stance against what might at first glance seem too vague and "feelings-laden" to be considered. If we are always dealing with behavior, what difference does it make if we start with apparently nonbehavioral concepts and language? We will eventually move on to considering and clarifying the behavioral issues involved, or else we will have nothing. We are a bit like the preschool teacher who wants to teach the children artistic expression: taking only cues from the great artists would overburden the teacher and the children and preclude creativity, since few if any would be able to imitate the exemplars of the past in art. If, however, any start is a start and can be shaped into creative and artistic directions, what difference does it make where we begin? One has only to recognize a start for what it is worth, and go on intelligently from there!

COVERT PROCESSES

Another area in which a flexible behavioral approach is indicated is the recognition and study of covert processes (Mahoney, 1974). Covert processes refer to "private events," which include dreams, images, feelings, memories, and thoughts. Recent events have indicated that more and more behavioral therapists and thinkers are ready, willing, and able to admit covert processes into the behavioral framework, whereas earlier no mediational concepts were allowed. The main issue here is *how* the mediational or covert processes are admitted into the behavioral framework and what conceptual role they play.

If covert processes refer to a mental–physical dualism, if these processes are not viewed in the same way as other behavioral processes, and if they are offered as explanatory fictions or the like, then the use of covert processes will not help us much. On the other hand, if covert processes are integrated into the behavioral framework in terms of behavioral variables, they may enhance and enlarge the scope of understanding complex human behavior and be of much service in the clinic (Mahoney, 1974, p. 29; Skinner, 1974).

Some behavioral therapists have responded to the challenge of covert processes for some time (Bain, 1928; Wolpe, 1958; Wolpe and Lazarus, 1966; Cautela, 1967), and an interest in such covert processes as "thought stopping" and other means of controlling inner processes has been an absorbing one for years. Thought is the covert process, and repetitive thought constitutes the clinical problem in this instance; the two are synchronized, therapeutically and conceptually, by proceeding with behavioral intervention. The intervention might take one or more of several tacks: Aversive stimulation might be used to halt unwelcome thoughts (snapping a tight rubber band on the wrist when the thought occurs); a similar example is the case of the patient starting to engage in the repetitive thought in front of the therapist who, on a signal from the patient, says "stop" forcefully. One might also avoid settings in which the repetitive and unwelcome thoughts are triggered, then move to increase the amount of time gradually that one is free from such oppressive ruminations. Still another technique would be the employment of writing (see Chapter 7). All these interventions in coping with unwelcome covert processes are behavioral ones that might be used as well in overcoming unwelcome *overt* behaviors. For example, if one wished to overcome the overt problem of thumbsucking in an adult, male patient of normal intelligence and typical social skills, one might use the same techniques employed with the covert problem cited above. In such a case, covert and overt would not be viewed as qualitatively different problems; nor would one be viewed as "mental" and the other behavioral. We would seek means of behavioral intervention in each case, submit the problem to the usual behavioral variables, and proceed to observe the results. There would be no fictional explanations, no resort to reifying concepts, no mental–physical dualism; there would be only behavioral problem-solving efforts in either case. In short, the answer to covert problems is not to deny them but to convert them into overt problems as expeditiously as possible.

The overt–covert problem is probably falsely stated in the first place; natural language formulations often get us into trouble because most natural languages are shot through with mind–body or mental–physical dualism—covert and overt being a good example. No such dichotomy exists in nature; some processes are simply harder to identify and control than others, but these differences are on a continuum and are not qualitatively different in nature. The overt–covert problem is first a semantic one; second, it is a clinical problem; and third, it is a conceptual problem. By overcoming the natural language dichotomy between overt and covert we look for intervention techniques to meet the problem, and upon finding successful solutions clinically we can then conceptualize the problem as one of defining and using variables appropriate to the issue at hand.

Although covert processes should (and do) interest behavioral therapists, the study of these processes has prompted no great new findings in the area of behavior change. In fact, clinical results from pursuing covert problems are not very encouraging (Mahoney, 1974, pp. 83–92). It is hard to distinguish between some covert control efforts in the clinic and related "cognitive therapy" approaches (Mahoney, 1974, p. 89), where the cognitive therapies (Ellis, 1969, 1970) tend to use more *verbal* instructions and verbal suasion techniques and to eschew measures of control such as aversive stimulation and other behavioral interventions.

Covert processes are often spoken of as if they were an entity of some kind or a "region" of the psyche, so to speak, that has not been explored. We can actually differentiate several kinds of covert processes: (1) those that are more *somatic* than anything else (e.g., a heavy feeling in the pit of the stomach); (2) those that refer to *imagery* such as one might conjure up when writing a poem, sharing an experience in prose, or perhaps painting a scene; (3) those related to *thinking* and *feeling,* the handling of experience in an evaluative way, and summarizing what we "think" or "feel" in verbal terms; and (4) those more subtle covert processes associated with *biofeedback* signaling changes in blood pressure, brain waves, and so on. Not all these covert areas are equally productive in trying to understand human behavior, and among the types just cited the biofeedback area has proved itself by far the most heuristic in understanding behavior whether clinically, experimentally, or conceptually (Segal, 1975; Birk, 1973; Schwartz, 1973; Sargent, 1973; Peck, 1972; Miller, 1969, 1972).

It is interesting to speculate as to why the biofeedback movement has apparently been so productive whereas other covert probings have not. One possible explanation is that all biofeedback phenomena measure some physiological processes; hence they are more easily subject to scientific testing and scrutiny than (say) imagery or feelings which are not as closely related to discernible somatic variables. Biofeedback data are refined data, far more summarized and cogent than the patient's "raw feelings." There are many ways to measure biofeedback data: light displays, tactile stimulation, auditory signals, and combinations; this give a variety of measurement approaches to the phenomena under study and allows for possibly more interesting and useful empirical findings and clinical applications (Segal, 1975; Shapiro, et al., 1973).

As techniques are developed that penetrate the skin, so to speak, we find more and more recourse to and need for feedback measurements, more research in ways to instruct the person about his own internal condition, and correspondingly less reliance on covert, hypothetical conditions or processes that are mentalistic, reified, or fictional (Skinner, 1971; Mahoney, 1974). Covert processes are real, important, and relevant to clinical work; they must not be eschewed; but they must be incorporated into the main body of behavioral science if they are to serve the purposes intended.

SOME POSITIVE THRUSTS

Thus far we have seen a number of ways in which a flexible behavioral approach is needed, and some ways in which such a practice may be heuristic. A malleable approach is not one of capitulation, nor is it one of eschewing important or difficult problems; it is a plea for leniency, for openness, and above all a challenge to bring elusive and subtle processes into the behavioral context. Having made this point about openness, it is still important to attempt more conceptual clarification of behavioral counseling and psychotherapy; and to avoid pitfalls of a mentalistic sort among many present counseling and therapy practices. In the interest of further study of the counseling/psychotherapy process in a behavioral framework, a few brief thrusts forward need to be taken into consideration. An explanation of these will constitute the rest of the chapter.

Schools of Therapy/Counseling

There are not 6, 14, 20, or 37 or more theories of counseling and psychotherapy; there are only two basic positions: Those counseling and therapy theories that locate variables in the "psyche" and those that locate variables in the environment. Traditional, depth-oriented theories, mainly derived from Freud, locate variables in the hypothetical mentalistic apparatus of the person. It might be possible, in the light of discussions above concerning feelings and covert processes, to extricate many of the mentalistic concepts from limbo; but it might also not be worth the effort, since few if any of the mentalistic counseling theories have, over time, moved toward a more objective status. Although traditional mentalistic theories (McCary and Sheer, 1955; Patterson, 1966; 1974; Harper, 1959) differ in their specifics, they resort to a common base of explanatory principles that tend to promote a mental–physical dualism, locate causal conditions outside the reach of empirical investigation, reify concepts, and promote or rely on fictional concepts and explanations (Skinner, 1971; Mahoney, 1974).

Environmentally related theories of counseling and psychotherapy are, on the other hand, few in number, and have generally been less popular, less well understood. In recent years, environmentally related counseling theories (Bandura, 1969; 1971a; 1971b; Krumboltz and Thoresen, 1964; 1969; Phillips, 1956; Phillips and Wiener, 1966; Wolpe, 1958; Wolpe and Lazarus, 1966; Rotter, 1954) have derived from or been closely related to a learning theory or Skinnerian base, although classical conditioning theory derived from Pavlov has exerted much influence on practices of therapists such as Wolpe and Lazarus. However, in spite of more focus on definable concepts and more conceptual rigor, even the learning-derived counseling and therapy theories often include mentalistic concepts and may be occasionally careless about how and where concepts are located in the behavioral matrix. It is difficult, and probably not an advantage at this time, to promulgate what some might call "whole-cloth" theories—theories that purport to cover extremely wide areas of empirical and clinical phenomena without much integration or rigor. It is more useful clinically and more productive scientifically to deal with limited techniques and interventions, and give them time to become absorbed into the larger behavioral framework (Staats, 1975). Even theories that locate the relevant variables in the environment can sometimes come up against hard times in accounting for how the environment works in the case of long-term and short-term memory, in cases of behavior altered by presumed brain damage (Bach-y-Rita, 1972), and in indicating how the person is part of his own environment. Behavioral theories of counseling and psychotherapy are not necessarily well-paved, well-surveyed roads that can be traveled at will without complications. The main value of the behavioral position as it regards counseling and psychotherapy lies in its ability to pose workable questions and solutions to problems, rather than relegating or explaining away problems on a fictional basis.

Understanding Presenting Complaints

Although a discussion of the early interviews will be taken up elsewhere (see Chapter 3), it is important in the definition of behavior to see how the patient's presenting complaints are conceptualized in behavioral counseling and psychotherapy.

People apply for help—or are induced to do so by others—when, on balance, they do not feel they can handle their problems alone, or when they think that an extra increment of help from another would be welcome and profitable. They come, as one patient put it, "because I hurt more than I feel good. . . ." Because of this imbalance in the negative or problem-ridden direction, the main stance of the presenting picture by the patient is one of worry, distress, emotional upset, unwelcome feelings, and other complaints. The patient is usually preoccupied with these problems and cannot generally see very clearly the larger behavioral picture. If the person could solve his problems—if, on balance, matters were more positive than negative—he would likely do so, or never apply for help. Most people, most of the time, solve most of their problems; the 10 to 15% who end up in institutions and the additional percentage who seek help from outpatient counseling or psychotherapy represent a minority of the population; but they represent also those who choose themselves to apply for aid on the basis of the impasses and burdens they face.

Because of this selection in factors making a person seek help, there is a high degree of preoccupation with pathology and failure in life. This state of affairs is interesting to the therapist, and baffling or formidable cases are even more challenging. The patient is obsessed with his or her plight, and so the two together (patient and therapist) can easily get bogged down is assessing pathology, being preoccupied with feelings, and endlessly searching for some ultimate meaning explaining the whole matter.

If the therapy does not hone in on practical matters—set goals, determine target behaviors, set up agendas, provide for means of immediate feedback to the patient during the interim between therapy sessions—then the therapy can meander for months or years in search of a scenario that will tell the actors what is going on. It is *common* that the early interviews are concerned mainly with presenting complaints, and these are essentially preoccupations with feelings and pathology; it is *essential* that practical exigencies take over as soon as possible so that the early preoccupation with pathology gives way to skill development, positive problem solving and greater behavioral adequacy (see Figure 1).

Figure 1 describes how a behavioral therapy should work to develop behavioral adequacy with respect to the presenting complaint(s); therapies that do not move as steadily as possible toward the skill development and problem-solving portion of the reciprocal relationship may be wasting good time, may risk losing the patient, and contribute less than they should to the patient's present and ultimate welfare. If problems are not solved, then the only thing left to do is to preoccupy one's self with the pathology; the patient, then, must be "very sick" or he would get better sooner! What must be understood here, whether one is a depth therapist or a behavioral one, is that the pathology–adequacy reciprocal relationship is just that—*reciprocal*—which means the more we have of one the less we have of the other.

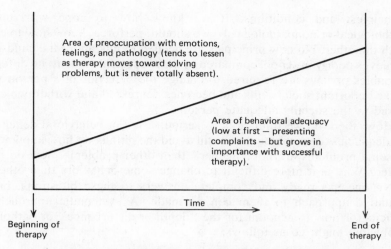

Area of preoccupation with emotions, feelings, and pathology (tends to lessen as therapy moves toward solving problems, but is never totally absent).

Area of behavioral adequacy (low at first — presenting complaints — but grows in importance with successful therapy).

Time

Beginning of therapy

End of therapy

Figure 1. How preoccupation with pathology is reciprocally related to behavioral adequacy, and how the latter increased with successful therapy. However, some aspects of both are always present, even though the balance is tipped in time by the development of skills and an adequate behavioral repertoire.

It is not trite, then, to assert that behavioral psychology is not concerned with pathology (and certainly not preoccupied with it), but is, rather, concerned with assessing the behavioral economy of the individual in the light of his present complaints and his environment opportunities. Melding these considerations is a most challenging therapeutic task for any therapist and one bringing the most satisfaction to both patient and therapist.

Some Tentative Rule Making About Behavior Change

It has been stated above that the behavioral therapist is really not very interested in the study or examination of pathology for its own sake. It is much more interesting and challenging to *solve* problems than it is to be bogged down by them. With an emphasis on changing behavior here and now, as expeditiously and effectively as possible, one needs a way of looking at so-called pathological conditions that do not force one into a consideration of the pathology itself, but allow one a set of guidelines or "rules" to use as a conceptual tool. A set of rules would be useful in emphasizing the fact that pathological behavior, so called, is not different in kind from other learned behavior; both normal and abnormal behavior are learned, and both come under the same set of relevant variables, principles, and conditions. If we know how to cope with one— pathological or nonpathological—we should, perforce, know how to cope with the other. No new principles are needed to talk about the child who achieves poorly in school compared to the successful student; no different variables or laws are required to change the behavior of a person who lacks important social skills and becomes depressed and withdrawn compared to the socially adequate person.

How, then, do we think about "seriousness" of behavioral deficits or inadequacies (or pathology) and still avoid the pitfalls we now know well? If some problems are not "deeper" than other problems, how do they differ? Why is it more difficult to change some behaviors than others?

No one has ready and complete answers to these questions, but a tentative approach to them can be made. A systematic approach to deficits (or how to account for the "depth of disturbance" or pathology problems) might go as follows:

Rule 1.   A given behavior is "pathological" or "serious" to the extent that few or no alternative behaviors exist in the person's repertoire or behavioral economy.

If one were suddenly dropped into a foreign and strange land with no suitable social and language skills, one's chances of survival as a psychological being might be slim. Should such a person survive, his social functioning might be minimal; and, also, if he remained in this hypothetical environment, he might get "worse" in the absence of effective corrective actions. However, he might, conversely, learn the needed social and other skills and "adjust" a little in time. Until a change began to come about, he would presumably be using little of his previous repertoire; and the importance of the adjustments made (how well he adapted) would be determined by how well he learned to function in his new environment.

A child poorly placed in school might show "pathology" in that he would not be able to perform the necessary skills at the needed level and would probably suffer social deficits and emotional complications as a consequence. Actually, the educational and social–emotional skill deficits would probably interact to exacerbate one another. Placing such a child in a different educational environment and/or trying to overcome skill deficits would allow him to "get out of his pathology" and begin to function better in his environment. If no alternative behaviors existed for the child initially, he would be a more "serious" case than if he could command some behavioral adequacy in his environment; the change-over would be the challenging and serious problem.

When a problem is presented to the behavioral therapist by the patient (or someone representing the patient), the therapist thinks of ways to modify the behavior in question. Certain questions would naturally arise:

What resources—that is, what behavioral adequacy—does the patient now display under appropriate conditions? How has the presenting problem been worked on in the past? And to what avail? What reinforcers are now (probably) maintaining the unwanted behavior? What alternatives exist in the repertoire for shifting the reinforcement contingencies? Does the environment hold many possibilities for change? Where are the important environmental changes to be made? Who can make and sustain them? And other questions. . . .

If the answers to these questions are neither difficult nor long-delayed, then the patient can be expected to begin to change in the desired direction under the proper therapeutic auspices. If, on the other hand, the changes will be won only after prodigious effort, the patient is relatively "more disturbed" (or "disturbing") since not as much can be done about his or her plight.

The resource potentials, then, spell out how "seriously" disturbed the patient is. Solving problems is a matter of finding alternatives to the current impasse, and that is a reciprocal matter between the patient and his environment (with the therapist somewhat in charge of managing this reciprocity).

Rule 2. A given behavior is "pathological" or "serious" to the extent that new training to overcome the deficit is needed.

Rule 2 is a subtype of Rule 1. Rule 1 looks to alternatives behaviors in the repertoire; Rule 2 recognizes that new training, an enlargement of the repertoire, or some change in the behavioral economy[1] is needed and that no alternatives now exist in the repertoire sufficient to solve the problem(s). Rule 2 is a more limiting condition subsumed under Rule 1.

One child's deficit in school may simply mean that in arithmetic he has to learn the rest of the multiplication tables," and that will help overcome the deficit. Another child may, correspondingly, need to learn social manners—taking turns, not pushing others, helping others—in order to function well in his peer group. These are both common examples of learned deficits, and the deficits can be overcome readily.

---

[1] The term "behavioral economy" is sometimes used, often interchangably with "behavioral repertoire." Actually the notion of a behavioral economy is more viable in some instances as it recognizes that shifts in the behavioral repertoire may be made without introducing the notion of a deficit in the repertoire. The repertoire as a whole may be adequate (i.e., not deficit), but changes in how the repertoire is used—now one way, now another—put an emphasis on resourcefulness not contained in the notion of repertoire deficits as an explanation for non-problem-solving behavior.

However, if a child has a profound communication problem (speech, hearing, or combinations), the measures necessary to overcome or ameliorate such a deficit may be "serious"—that is, require much effort and many procedures aimed at building a new or greatly enlarged repertoire of behavior with respect to these deficits. In this hypothetical case, perhaps few behaviorally adequate skills would originally exist in the repertoire; they would have to be learned from the basics upward. The deficits would not be ameliorated by simple educational changes or opportunities in the child's everyday world—although such changes would undoubtedly have to accompany more profound efforts. Presumably in this hypothetical case, more extensive changes in the form of special education services, special equipment, special environmental arrangements, and the like would need to be instituted. In fact, unless remedied early, a child with profound speech/hearing and related communication problems would probably become more seriously disturbed with increasing age, as the original deficits would accumulate into social-vocational deficits in time.

The problem of "seriousness" or "pathological state" is, then, a function of alternative resources, ranging all the way from small and easily procured educational/remedial changes to comprehensive environmental and technological changes. The pathology does not exist *in* the person in some isolated sense, but is reciprocally related to what one can do in the environment about the problem. One could find problem areas other than speech and hearing—for example, profound social deficits, chronic depression, and schizoid characteristics that disable one for ordinary social contacts.

Rule 3.   A given behavior is "pathological" or "serious" to the extent that the needed behaviors (as per Rules 1 and 2) cannot be supported by the typical, natural environment, but require an altered or prosthetic environment to develop and maintain the needed behaviors.

Here we look not only to the need for a change in the repertoire (Rule 1), or a more extensive reeducational or therapeutic program to overcome behavioral repertoire deficits (Rule 2), but to extensive environmental changes in order to allow for the overcoming of the deficit (Rule 3). Rule 3, then, becomes an even more specific and specialized example of Rule 2, which, in turn, is a subdivision of Rule 1. With Rule 3, we are recognizing an even more technically prepared set of environmental conditions—perhaps a largely prosthetic one—in order to move toward overcoming or ameliorating the problem condition.

With Rule 3, we might think of instances where autistic children are treated and educated in special environments (very small classes, many one-to-one relationships with adults, the use of primary reinforcers over an extended time before social reinforcers can be used, the use of educational technology to provide for special learning instructions, and so forth). Similarly there is a need for prosthetic environments for the blind, deaf, orthopedically handicapped, institutionalized psychotic, and profoundly retarded.

In all the hypothetical instances, we are accepting the person's deficit as a set of "givens" in relation to the usual environment, but then going on quickly to ascertain how great an environmental change, in the form of prosthetic devices and the like, might be needed in order to gain movement toward a solution to the person's problems. We know in a practical sense that the present state of the arts and sciences involved will not make a person with profound deficits normal; but we know in a programmatic and procedural sense how to ask the functionally productive questions concerning the person's deficit. We learn in time, also, how to improve upon our technology as we face more and more profound problems or deficits requiring ever more profound prosthetic and other changes in the environment. There is not only a reciprocal relationship between the person's deficits and the encompassing environment at a given time, but an even larger reciprocal relationship between the state of technology at a given time and the need for enlargement upon this technology owing to the problems posed.

Psychotic adults may require more specialized prosthetic environments also. The recent advent of token economies in mental hospitals (Ayllon and Azrin, 1964, 1965, 1968) is an important move in that direction. It may be that token economies will be moved out of hospitals and into life generally in circumscribed ways and places, allowing the individual to function more adequately with respect to the larger society.

In a very real sense the behavioral therapist is always asking and always confronted with the fundamental question: "What environmental changes are needed to solve these problems?" The answers may range all the way from the presence of an active, participating, and structuring therapist to profound alternations in the environment. But some degree of environmental change is always called for; it is part of the skill of the therapist and part of the intriguing business of doing therapy that one is confronted with the important questions related to how much change, under what conditions and auspices, and to what ends?

The last point above—that special environments may need to be permanent features of therapeutic effort—recognizes that society and those interested in treatment processes will often be required to work even more gradually and painstakingly in overcoming profound disturbances and difficulties in human behavior. This leads to Rule 4:

Rule 4.   The longer it takes—treatment resources being roughly equal—to overcome a deficit, the greater the "pathology" or "seriousness" of that deficit.

Rule 4, although somewhat less on a continuum than the first three rules, simply recognizes that even when environmental changes of whatever degree of radicalness are achieved, there will still be different amounts of time involved; the longer the time involved, the more difficult the undertaking. This assumes, of course, that we know in a given instance what remedial procedures are needed and can proceed apace. When we do not know for sure what we are about, or when we have legitimate doubts about procedures and have to alter environments a number of times or experiment with prosthetic changes, then the behavior change process will take more time and therefore the "pathology" will be relatively greater.

Classical theories of psychotherapy and counseling, derived as they are from depth psychology, locate the problems of deficits squarely *in* the person; whereas, we now know, the behavioral position locates the deficit in a reciprocal relationship between the person and the environment. All theories of psychopathology that are not environmentally located see various kinds of deficits as outgrowths of more basic faults in the mental apparatus of the individual (birth traumas, basic anxieties, developmental deviations, basic need deprivation, and the like). Even if these theories of a depth type were true, or if they touched on aspects of a general truth, the intervention process would still have to take place in order to correct the original condition with which one is confronted. The only ways in which traditional theories have responded to the problem of amount of deficit, or seriousness of disturbance, have been through the number of hours of psychoanalysis needed to correct the problem, or in response to the particular psychic area traumatized at some developmental level. Traditional therapies have seldom responded cogently to the now recognized, behaviorally derived, *reciprocal* relationship between the deficit on the one hand (as a functional loss) and the environmental conditions needed to overcome or ameliorate the deficit on the other hand.

Contingencies

The heart of the behavioral position is based on reinforcement contingencies; reinforcement is contingent on the organism doing something in, or to, the environment. The animal in its native habitat scratches through the grass and leaves to find food; finding and devouring food and continuing survival are contingent upon the organism's acting upon the environment in such a way as to yield the needed sustenance.

Environmental contingencies may also be "arranged"; that is, the classroom teacher may arrange a free play period for the child contingent upon the child's having finished the arithmetic assignment. The therapist attends to the patient's problems and offers help contingent upon the patient appearing at the designated time and upon the patient giving attention to his or her problem in a manner agreed upon by patient and therapist. All human interactions are implicitly, if not explicitly, a matter of contingencies; in fact, human culture can be described in part as a systematic network of contingencies. There is very little learning or modification of behavior that is not dependent upon some contingency (Bandura, 1965a; 1974), however subtly present.

The use of contingencies can be shown to underlie all behavioral techniques. Ullmann and Krasner (1972, p. 332) make this point explicit, as follows:

"Despite differences in approaches and techniques, we would propose that all behavior modification boils down to procedures utilizing *systematic environmental contingencies to alter the subject's response to stimuli*." (Italics original).

Although contingencies are usually discussed as if they comprised a unitary or homogeneous genre, it is probable that different kinds of contingencies exist and that they may have differential effects on the person's behavior. Simple, direct contingencies in the material environment are legion—for example, turning a key to start the car or to unlock a door—and perhaps most of our environment is made of such stuff. Some other, more complex social contingencies may be described as intermittent or periodic, such as paying mortgage or car payments. One gets to keep and use the article thus purchased contingent upon continuing the payments without serious fault. In this case one is avoiding a longer-range aversive consequence, since the car or house may have to be forfeited due to nonpayment. These kinds of contingencies "ward off" aversive interim consequences before the final payoff of a positive nature is received (i.e., ownership or title to the article). One could, however, lose the momentum midstream in such a case and all investments could be lost at some interim, intermittent point in the series. This kind of contingent arrangement is considerably different from getting a positive, direct reinforcement from each intermittent act, such as purchasing several examples of an article, paying for another meal, or adding to a cumulative bank account.

Another example of closely related social contingency is paying life insurance installments in order to build a reserve in the event of illness or death that would jeopardize the person's assets or increase his liabilities.

This hedge against uncertainty is a common type of contingency in our complex social life, inasmuch as one is obliged to "build for the future" by arranging contingencies that would offset the worst kind of aversive consequence (death, permanent impairment, loss of possessions, etc.). This is a difficult kind of contingency to maintain over time, as shown by statistics indicating that a high percentage of people drop their life insurance within a short period of time after activating a policy. One reason society does not plan more realistically to meet energy resource and other long-term goals is that the daily or interim inputs to such a contingent arrangement cannot be shown to reduce aversiveness enough (in terms of the long-range expected outcomes) to keep the system going. There is momentary relief (reinforcement through avoiding the aversiveness of making the energy sacrifice, or in the case of the individual, making the insurance payments) which tends to dominate behavior; and the long-range, survival consequences remain unheeded (Skinner, 1971). Social and individual planning and problem solving are a complex set of different kinds of contingencies, some operating on an immediate positive reinforcement basis and some operating on the basis of warding off aversiveness on an intermittent basis.

A difficult-to-manage contingency occurs where there is an adversary role played by both parties toward one another. Workmen strike for higher wages; higher wages is an example of positive reinforcement for the workers but represents a loss (or a cost/benefit problem) for management. Management's role is rendered less reinforcing for them (loss of money) if they have to pay higher wages. This seesaw arrangement is a situation where as one party profits the other loses. One's contingent gain is another's contingent loss. Many human interactions are unfortunately structured this way. One aim of therapy would be to recognize these kinds of "adversary contingencies" and try to switch them over to more nearly mutual, positive reinforcing contingencies. In the case of solving marital conflict problems—a common, adversary position one meets in therapy—the adversary role of each participant has to be hopefully switched over to a mutually positively contingent one, which is a challenge for all concerned.

The social contingencies that make most of our relationships reinforcing are probably mutually shared contingencies (McGinnies and Ferster, 1971). Dancing is a simple, clear example; each partner asserts, yields, and invents on the spur of the moment, all of which culminates in a smooth, interesting, esthetically pleasing experience. Complex behavior in traffic is, likewise, a mutually shared contingency that usually requires much structuring and bolstering by means of traffic lights, speed-regulating signs, and lanes.

The practice of counseling or psychotherapy, regardless of one's persuasion, is likewise an example of a mutually shared set of contingencies. In fact, in behavioral counseling or psychotherapy, one tries to make the contingencies more explicit—for example, giving clearer role definitions of both patient and therapist, keeping logs, setting agendas, agreeing on target behaviors, and so on—and the extent to which this can be done and reliably held to may be the extent to which the therapeutic enterprise is a success. The therapist early on should try to note what contingencies the patient may be exhibiting in coming to therapy: "I want to change, but I want you to provide all the guidance and incentive I need," might be a patient's implicit contingency. Some of the questions the wary therapist should ask himself or herself about the patient's contingencies might include the following: "Are the contingencies regulating the patient's behavior potentially under the patient's control?" "When the patient utters complaints about his plight, is he revealing important information about the contingencies under which he operates?" "What new possibilities for contingencies exist for this patient at this time?" "Is the patient using therapy primarily as a means of warding off more untoward consequences in his life, rather than seeing therapy as a contingent opportunity to make positive changes?" And so on. . . . In the therapist's selection of any therapeutic tactic or technique the fundamental question faced is whether this contingent move is, itself, a reinforceable matter.

Behavior Modification Characteristics

One of the reasons the behavioral movement has been so successful is that its viewpoint is quite versatile and flexible. Based on the central notion of reinforcement contingencies, there are a wide variety of tactics and strategies that can be used. All of these have one focus: changing behavior (Kanfer and Phillips, 1970, pp. 16–24). The main characteristics of behavioral methods that make possible the operational versatility for purposes of counseling or psychotherapy may be stated as follows:

1. *Systematic*. The behavioral therapist approaches tasks in a systematic and methodical manner: taking data, using logs, introducing controlled changes, observing results, setting agendas, and so on. This is done under the aegis of an overall behavioral position which identifies variables characterizing the person's behavior in relation to his environment, and attempts systematic changes to bring about desired results.

2. *Empirical*. The variables underlying the systematic procedures are empirically based on reinforcement contingencies as the central consideration. Probably no other area of psychology, and certainly no other

approach to counseling and psychotherapy, has the empirical backing that behavioral principles afford (Reese, 1966).

3. *Identifies target or goal behaviors for change.* The behavioral therapist does not attempt to "restructure personality or character," or "make the unconscious conscious," or do "major psychic surgery," but, with the help of the patient and the picture of presenting complaints, tries to identify reasonably modest goals and use tactics and strategies as economically and effectively as possible to bring about the desired ends.

4. *Uses gradual (successive approximation) steps.* Most changes in behavior come gradually; they are then better incorporated into the whole behavioral economy of the person. Gradual changes take advantage of, and are based on, reinforcement schedules that solidify change.

5. *Identifies and pivots change on observables.* The importance of identifying observables cannot be overstressed: One does not treat "depression" but rather tries to deal with specific examples of unwanted behaviors (slowness in movement, feeling badly, lack of social interests, etc.).

6. *Locates variables in the environment.* Important variables are located in the environment, not in the psyche of the individual; therefore data on the variables can be observed in the patient–environment interactions (and especially in the patient–therapist interactions).

7. *Identifies relevant stimuli.* As the patient reports on his distress, the therapist attempts to tentatively identify what may elicit the problems the patient reports, and tries to identify ways of changing or restructuring significant stimuli in the environment calculated to produce a change in behavior. The therapist is an important part of this stimulus complex and tries to be useful in contingent ways.

8. *Behavior is a function of its consequence.* A close look at the consequences of the patient's behavior in question tells the therapist much about what is controlling the patient and where and how these consequences may be altered. As consequences are changed in the patient's environment (including the environment of therapy)—by his or other's actions—new behaviors can be brought into play. The unwanted consequences must somehow be altered for changes to take place in the patient's behavior (Bandura, 1974).

9. *Emphasizes self-management and self-control.* Contrary to what many think, behavioral therapy is not a one-way, manipulative street where the therapist imposes his "will" on the patient in some blind, authoritarian way. As the patient learns problem-solving skills, he takes over an increasing role in his own self-management; the objective of therapy is to put the patient on his own feet as effectively as possible (Mahoney and Thoresen, 1974).

10. *Emphasizes change*. Change is the important matter; if we really understand behavior, we can change it. The therapist does not seek abstract explanations for their own sake; and "explanation" of problem behavior and how to overcome it is of value only if it produces results.

These descriptive points and the various techniques listed in Chapter 2 help pose for the therapist (and indirectly for the patient) fundamental questions at the outset of therapy: "Is the present repertoire or behavioral economy of the patient in his present environment capable of yielding a basis for the needed change?" or "Will additional new learning and/or a new (prosthetic) environment be required to promote the desired behavior change?" Answering these fundamental questions as early as possible—but keeping open the possibility of revisions in answers—can tell the therapist where he or she stands vis-à-vis the patient–environment complex and can guide the implementation of therapy or counseling along realistic lines.

Self-Reinforcement and Self-Control

Within the behavioral movement there has been a growing interest in identifying self-reinforcement and self-control as an important aspect of therapy or counseling (Ullmann and Krasner, 1975, pp. 585–586; Skinner, 1953:285; Kanfer and Marston, 1963; Goldiamond, 1965; Staats, 1963, pp. 95–97; Mahoney and Thoresen, 1974). Staats (1963, p. 96) covers the issue of "self-reinforced" behavior as follows:

"Each time a response occurs it produces its characteristic stimuli. If this response is followed by a positive reinforcer, it would be expected that the response elicited by the reinforcer would be conditioned to the response-produced stimuli. These response-produced stimuli would therefore become conditioned reinforcers. Thus, the stimuli produced by a response can function as conditioned positive reinforcers and serve to strengthen the response that produces them."

It would now appear that not only what Staats says is true, but another feature of self-reinforcement in relation to "expectations" or "anticipated self-reinforcement" might need discernment. The child who is given a cookie by the parent (Stimulus) eats the cookie (Response) and, in addition, does not spill the cookie over his clothes. The parent says "Good boy, you didn't spill a bit" as part of the reinforcement complex associated with eating the cookie (S^{R+}), reinforcement by parent for child's eating cookie carefully. The child adds to this his own covert response—or he may readily make his response overt—(S^{R++}), adding his own "+" to the reinforcement following the parent's reinforcement (saying, in effect, "I am a good boy—I didn't spill the cookie crumbs"); the child's own self-reinforcement being added to the paradigm of stimulation, responding, and reinforcement afforded by the parent's actions (see Figure 2).

$$S - - - \rightarrow R - - - \rightarrow S^{R+} - - - \rightarrow S^{R++}$$

Figure 2. Showing the Stimulus (S), cookie; the Response (R) of eating the cookie; the Reinforcing Stimulus (S^{R+}) of parent's saying "Good boy"; and the child saying "I am a good boy" (S^{R++}).

The self-reinforcement aspect of the paradigm, leading to "expectation" or "anticipation" of his success on subsequent occasions would, greatly simplified, look like Figure 3.

Figure 3. Showing through (a), (b), (c) how the child "anticipates" on subsequent occasions reinforcement earlier in the process of being given a cookie and being rewarded for his good behavior in eating it. Finally, he "expects" the whole reinforcement paradigm to operate upon hearing the word "cookie", or indeed when he thinks "cookie."

In this presumptive manner the child not only learns "self-reinforcing" behavior but learns to extrapolate ("anticipate" or "expect") particular results from his behavior which have been reinforced previously on similar occasions. He then is in the business of building self-approval, self-esteem, self-confidence, and so on; the absence of these positive reinforcing conditions would similarly account for lack of self-esteem or for its equivocal status in the child's interpersonal environment.

The therapist or counselor aiming to build self-reinforcing capabilities in his patients would be careful to reinforce the patient's efforts, shape them into a more reliable status, and, above all, reinforce the patient's own self-approval efforts as he verbalizes about himself. First comes the environmental reinforcements usually under the aegis of important people in the person's life (those with strong reinforcement value); then it follows immediately that the paradigm can be taken over by the person so that he becomes his own "reinforcing agent," at least in some important aspects of his life. The latter is not an all-or-nothing matter; one is always under the control of important environmental reinforcers and there is a constant feedback or playback between self-reinforcement and external reinforcement that is subject to adjustment, revision, or eventual extinction (Staats, 1975, pp. 183–187).

The paradigm above illustrating self-reinforcement also fits well one way of identifying progress in behavior change. First, the person discerns after-the-fact his unwanted behavior. As the unwanted behavior is more clearly identified and fitted into a general pattern in his behavioral economy and so conceptualized in therapy, the paradigm identifying the unwanted behavior can then be brought under progressive control. To get a change, however, the unwanted behavior has to be identified *earlier* in the sequence. The second step in this corrective process is to get the patient to identify the unwanted behavior about the time it occurs and to interrupt it or reduce its aversive consequences. A third step is to anticipate that the behavior might indeed occur and is clearly associated with given stimuli; so that the correction on subsequent occasions can occur progressively earlier. In time, the unwanted behavior is brought under control before it occurs; hence a behavior change has occurred (see Figure 4).

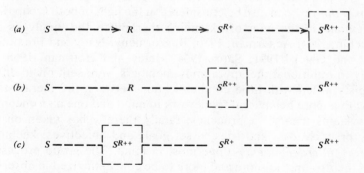

Figure 4. Using the same notations as in Figure 3, here (*a*) shows the therapist first identifying some condition associated with the patient's unwanted behavior (S^{R+}) and the patient's concurrence, (S^{R++}), which is reinforcing to the patient as a matter of labeling an important aspect of his problem; following, (*b*), by the patient's own earlier verbalization of the same phenomena (S^{R++}) (the patient may say, "Yeah, I see what you mean—I do that a lot"); this discernment moved back earlier and earlier in time, (*c*), on subsequent occasions, finally brings the unwanted behavior under control by precluding its occurrence.

WHERE IS BEHAVIORAL COUNSELING/THERAPY GOING TODAY?

As an example of the vitality of behavior change methods, it would be useful to look briefly at where behavioral counseling and therapy methods are going today. There is much ferment, and there are many positive signs of considerable robustness in the behavioral movement.

One active area of growth is in various approaches to *group processes* using a behavioral framework (McGinnies and Ferster, 1971; Staats, 1975; Bandura, 1969; Phillips, 1968; Phillips, et al., 1971; Johnson, 1975), some of which use token economies while others simply structure group processes in terms of behaviorally related variables. Many of these studies can be expected to pave the way for more direct group therapy efforts, where the group acts qua group to reinforce the efforts of its members, and where the group sets goals, assignments, and agendas and generally treats the group process less like traditional individual therapy and more like a unified effort with behavioral objectives. Krasner's review (1971) shows the background of some of these changes and developments in applying behavioral methods to ever-larger settings, as does Johnson's recent work (1975).

An interest in behavioral groups may be taking some of its cues from informal groups, such as Alcoholics Anonymous which, over the years, has touched on some important aspects of group processes in terms of overt behavior, but has not refined nor extended its methodology into other groups (Tharp and Wetzel, 1969; Reppucci and Saunders, 1974).

Family therapy can also be considered in the light of both group therapy process and in the light of extending therapy to the family as a unit (Minuchin, 1974; Ackerman, 1970; Boszormenyi-Nagy and Framo, 1965; Haley and Gluck, 1971; Satir, 1964; Haley and Hoffman, 1968). Previously in traditional therapy, family members were sent off to different therapists, often with little communication between the therapists. Today, with a more behavioral framework in mind and one also encompassing "systems theory" approaches, family therapy has taken on a distinctly practical cast and tries to set goals and objectives, keeping the members' *interdependence* uppermost in mind. The group processes in family therapy appear more and more to be conceptualized in observable, behavioral terms, with many behavior techniques employed throughout (Minuchin, 1974).

Another area of behavioral progress is seen in the development of *instrumentation*. This may include not only biofeedback technology, as we noted above, but the development of devices that help to induce sleep and relaxation. As science develops better techniques for studying internal physiological processes, not only will measurement of these processes be enhanced, but an opportunity for simulating them may accrue. Thus, instrumentation may be able to tap into weak somatic processes with the objective of enhancing or otherwise controlling them so that some state of more optimal health or better psychological and/or bodily functioning may be achieved.

Not only is biofeedback an important consideration but also "augmented feedback" may enhance behavioral control methodology. Simply relying on social reinforcement alone with handicapped learners—to take one important population into consideration—may not be enough to teach the visual–motor and other motor controls needed in learning to trace, copy, draw, or write. A method of providing augmented feedback in a small electric pencil (Bonwit, Phillips, and Williams, 1972) appears to offer a gain in the direction of providing guidance to the motor activities as well as skill improvements that can work in tandem with social reinforcement among handicapped children and adults. Such a pencil can employ visual, sound, or tactile feedback, or combinations of these, and open up reinforcement possibilities due to improved sensory discrimination in the visual–motor areas of performance (Phillips, 1974).

Although *theory development* is gaining in importance among behavioral therapists, most theories are modest efforts confined to limited problems (Staats, 1975, pp. 11–12; Suppe, 1974). Theories are tested not on some grand scale of comprehensiveness but on a more limited basis and on whether, among other considerations, they yield useful empirical data and appropriate clinical applications. The development of assertive training in recent years is a case in point: Assertive training takes the place of many earlier clinical preoccupations with anxiety, shyness, emotional blocking, being-taken-advantage-of, and other problems. The theory is that if adequate, assertive behavior is taught, the previous problems will not have to be undertaken, qua problems, but will yield to the new assertive developments in the behavioral repertoire.

A similar theory-and-practice development may be in evidence in viewing depressive behavior as a matter of social skill deficits (Ferster, 1973). Following some of Ferster's notions, Sowards and Phillips (1975) have proposed that concentrating on teaching social skills will go far in remedying many cases of reactive or exogenous depression seen in outpatient counseling centers and mental hygiene clinics. Thinking along this line has reminded these authors (Sowards and Phillips, 1975) that we do not have a "social curriculum" for children that might be used as a measure of social competence; and at the adult level, the variegated experiences among social skill deficit individuals poses remarkably far-reaching and interesting problems for meeting the clinical demands in regard to coping with social withdrawal and socially deficit behaviors.

Progress is being made in recognizing that many good efforts at behavior change in the clinic may not easily or readily *generalize* to the outside world. Generalization is not a matter of logic—"You learned it here, so why not apply it there?"—but has to be considered as a distinct, and sometimes separate, problem. As Baer, Wolf, and Risley note (1968, p. 97), ". . . generalization should be programmed, rather than expected or lamented." Failure to attempt programming generalization of change made in the clinic to the outside world may account for many instances of presumed change under one set of circumstances that washes out in another set of circumstances. Being sensitive to problems related to generalization will help us discern ever more important features of the environment as it bears on the reciprocal relationship (Kolb, Reubin, and McIntyre, 1971; Schwitzgebel and Kolb, 1974) between patient and environment (including, of course, the therapist or the therapeutic milieu).

Not only are new behavioral techniques (see Chapter 2) being introduced year by year, but there is also an effort to consolidate techniques (Yates, 1975), so that the common elements stand out more boldly among techniques, and so that their effectiveness can be compared in a variety of clinical and other settings within a typical range of problems. A more economical use of all behavioral techniques may result from such consolidation and reconceptualization. Excursions into related areas (Kolb, Reubin, and McIntyre, 1971; Schwitzgebel and Kolb, 1974) may be encouraged through such conceptualization and consolidation.

CHAPTER 2

Behavioral Techniques

In the previous chapter, we have seen a number of ways in which behavioral analyses and formulations may be heuristic. As illustrated, many of the traditional problems relating to clinical and counseling practice may be recast in behavioral terms, and some of the subtle issues of "mental" life can be brought into the behavioral framework. A flexible behaviorism in the clinic pertains to an openness and a willingness to accept subtle and tentative leads; but also a strong responsibility to incorporate these leads into useful behavioral procedures, rather than letting them remain unchallenged or in a state of fictional limbo.

We turn attention now to a large array of behavioral techniques, procedures that offer an extremely wide and versatile approach to clinical problems. Since human difficulties are highly diverse, it is important to have flexibility and resourcefulness in approaching solutions to these difficulties. In treating problems from the behavioral vantage point, it is important to avoid sweeping claims or implied quick results, as is sometimes the case with people who are overly enthusiastic about new techniques and applications. Some types of generalizations about clinical effort and results are probably fictional. One must always be careful to specify the variables involved in etiology or in treatment; to specify how unwanted behavior is maintained; and to specify how a "treatment of choice" is arrived at by the clinician. Solutions to problems in living should attend to the scientific considerations as well as to practical clinical issues.

Not all the behavioral techniques listed and described below are of equal validity; nor is it known at this time which techniques apply best to particular problems, except as now suggested by many rule-of-thumb measures. Some procedures apply more to principles—such as the Premack Principle or Wolpe's Reciprocal Inhibition—while others are less extended but useful techniques to employ in collaboration with the patient on a here-and-now basis.

These techniques may be classified as primarily: (a) procedural (i.e., placing a general emphasis on a technique or procedure that includes nearly all items in the list on one or another level); (b) data gathering procedures (a matter of collecting frequency-of-occurrence information, preliminary to and in conjunction with therapeutic effort; (c) conceptual (a way of looking at a problem or stating how intervention may be conceptualized; (d) active-therapeutic (i.e., resulting in a specific therapeutic or behavior change effort).

These classifications are not mutually exclusive; they are intended to encourage the clinician to think about procedures and conceptualizations and to display a wide variety of techniques. All techniques involve in some way the management of reinforcement contingencies; and all are intended to have a therapeutic impact, although at first this may not be evident, as therapeutic results may be delayed or indirect. Undoubtedly many more behavioral techniques will be brought into prominence in the future; as problems occur in new and different social settings, behavioral approaches will be challenged to meet demands.

Table 1 summarizes the techniques in alphabetical order; the check marks are loosely tied to how the technique is viewed—as a practical intervention, as one requiring the collection of data, and so on. Following Table 1, each technique will be listed and discussed in somewhat greater detail.

ALPHABETICAL LISTING OF TECHNIQUES

1. *Agenda setting.* This is simply a matter of setting an agenda (deciding what will be discussed, imposing some priority on topics) by the patient and therapist. It gives order and meaning to the array of problems the client brings in, and it allows for seeing similarities and differences between problems. The therapist reinforces the patient for cooperation in this way; and the patient is further reinforced by seeing and testing out the relevance and interdependence among the various problems. The therapist might say, ''What do you think about focusing now on these two seemingly main topics and getting some more observations on them next time?'' The patient may agree, demur, or suggest alternatives. Either way the therapy sessions begin to take on some order and purpose beyond just reporting on incidents or feelings.

2. *Assertive training.* This is a large-order type of behavioral intervention, rather than a single technique, whereby the patient is helped to assert himself more effectively. Two types of situations where assertiveness is needed are: First, cases where the patient wishes to achieve some social goal—for example, go out regularly with the opposite sex—but has been too reticent to make consistent effort. Assertiveness might be learned in this instance on a gradual basis: first a ''coffee date,''

Table 1. Alphabetical Listing of Behavioral Techniques and Classification

Technique	Procedural	Data Gathering	Conceptual	Active Therapeutic
1. Agenda setting	✓			✓
2. Assertive training	✓	✓	✓	✓
3. Aversive consequences, avoidance of (or aversive stimulation)	✓			✓
4. Backward (reverse) shaping	✓	✓		✓
5. Behavior cost	✓	✓		✓
6. Behavioral counting	✓	✓		✓
7. Behavioral rehearsal	✓	✓	✓	✓
8. Contingency management	✓	✓	✓	✓
9. Contracting	✓	✓	✓	✓
10. Covert desensitization	✓			✓
11. Cue control	✓	✓		✓
12. Desensitization				
13. Deviation amplifying loop			✓	
14. Deviation counteracting loop			✓	
15. Direct verbal instructions	✓	✓		✓
16. Direct verbal suasion	✓	✓	✓	✓
17. Dream analysis	✓		✓	✓
18. Extinction	✓			✓
19. Fading	✓	✓	✓	✓
20. Fines	✓	✓	✓	✓
21. Flooding (or emotional flooding)	✓	✓		✓
22. Free operant responding	✓			✓
23. Hypnosis	✓			✓
24. Hypothetical other	✓		✓	✓

Table 1. *(Continued)*

Technique	Procedural	Data Gathering	Conceptual	Active Therapeutic
25. Humor	✓			✓
26. Imagery	✓	✓	✓	✓
27. Implosion	✓	✓	✓	✓
28. Increasing interresponse time (I.R.T.)	✓	✓		✓
29. In vivo therapy	✓	✓		✓
30. Labeling				
31. Logkeeping	✓	✓	✓	✓
32. Mass practice	✓	✓	✓	✓
33. Mirror control	✓	✓	✓	✓
34. Modeling	✓	✓		✓
35. Momentary escape/avoidance	✓	✓		✓
36. Moratorium	✓	✓		✓
37. Negative feedback	✓	✓		✓
38. Negative practice	✓	✓		✓
39. Negative reinforcement	✓	✓		✓
40. Overcorrection	✓	✓		✓
41. Overlearning	✓			✓
42. Paradoxical intention	✓	✓		✓
43. Pictures, books, and magazines	✓	✓		✓
44. Positive feedback	✓	✓		✓
45. Premack principle	✓	✓	✓	✓
46. Programmed instruction	✓	✓		✓
47. Punishment	✓			✓
48. Rate-delay-intensity-recovery (RDIR)	✓	✓	✓	✓
49. Reciprocal inhibition	✓	✓	✓	✓

50. Reinforcement (intermittent and continuous)
51. Relaxation
52. Replaying tapes
53. Restitution
54. Reversal
55. Satiation
56. Self-imposed time out
57. Shame-aversion therapy
58. Shaping
59. Skills training
60. Target behaviors
61. Thought stopping
62. Time out
63. Writing (or writing therapy)
64. Zen

then a Sunday afternoon "bike date," and so on. The reticent one would be learning to assert himself or herself by asking for the date, by thinking of conversational topics, by being interesting, and so forth. A second example of the need for assertive training is seen in cases where the patient has been a victim of others' "put down," or has let himself or herself be overrun by another: a case of infringement of one's rights. Assertiveness here teaches the person to stand up for himself, to know and achieve his rights, but to do these things without anger, aggressiveness, or aversiveness; assertiveness is a middle ground between reticence and over-aggressiveness (Wolpe and Lazarus, 1966).

3. *Aversive consequences, avoidance of (or aversive stimulation)*. First there is avoiding aversive (unwanted) consequences of action, as when a person puts on his seat belt in order to turn off the noise. A person avoids an argument with a roommate by not responding (thereby "turning off" discussion/argument) to the quips or challenges. Many aversive social consequences we experience may be "turned off" if we recognize what is going on and if we feel confident in not necessarily engaging in the unwanted events. Conversely, one may use direct *aversive stimulation* on one's self (snapping a rubber band placed on one's wrist) in order to stop unwanted thinking. It acts as a reminder that the behavior in question is to be controlled, the control then turning off the aversiveness (thereby being reinforcing). It may also act as a distraction and mild punishment and inhibit some unwanted behavior (e.g., feeling "nervous" around the opposite sex, thinking "evil" thoughts, etc.) (Kanfer and Phillips, 1970, pp. 117–128; Mahoney, 1974, pp. 90–96). (See below, technique 60, "Thought stopping.")

4. *Backward (reverse) shaping*. Shaping (or "forward" shaping) is a procedure whereby one approaches a problem through successive small steps, moving gradually toward the desired goal. An example would be improving one's dancing, or any skill, by taking explicit, delineated steps, being reinforced for progress at each step, and going on to some higher level of skill. Backward shaping is illustrated by beginning with the *end* product (e.g., a retarded child putting on his shirt) and completing it; starting on the next trial a little further back in the series of steps, until finally the very beginning point is reached. With each successive start, at whatever level of completion, the task is finished. Thus, in putting on the shirt, the arms are put in the sleeves and all but the last act (closing the shirt front) is prepared for the child; he then completes it with a small amount of effort and is reinforced generously. Then the shirt is put back on but not quite as far on . . . and so on back to the very beginning point of first inserting the hand or fist into a sleeve. Each completion session, whether it be one or several steps, is reinforced before going on to the next series of steps. This procedure may apply more to simple behaviors

(e.g., among retardates) than it does to the consultation room. A clinical application, for example, would be having a male patient escort a date to her room in a dorm; followed by an "earlier" step of meeting her in the cafe for coffee; a still earlier step being dancing with her in the cafe; each time completing the series by escorting her to her room. This "exercise" could finally end with a full date from beginning to end (Ullmann and Krasner 1975, pp. 258–259). (See also technique 58, "Shaping.")

5. *Behavior cost.* As the term seems to imply, this technique refers to what it "costs" the patient if he wishes to engage in given behaviors. It is first used as a general term, referring to the contingency involving money or privilege or effort that is necessary before a given behavior is engaged in by the patient. A patient may want a privilege on the grounds of the hospital he or she inhabits; "ground privileges" become contingent upon the patient doing certain things first—for example, keeping the room clean, engaging in school work successfully, or the like. In this sense, the patient "pays for" the privilege in question; it "costs" something. In a similar vein, one can raise the cost of engaging in behavior (a kind of planned inflation); that is, a given privilege is made contingent on an ever-increasing cost. In still a third sense, one may raise the cost of an activity or article so high that the patient will probably not "buy" it—for example, the privilege of engaging in pillow fights in the dorm may come so high that the participants will forgo the pleasure. One might want an expensive new automobile but demur on the basis of expense. In counseling and psychotherapy, behavior or response cost may be associated with paying for missed appointments, adding on costs where there is a failure to perform contractual agreements, or recognizing an increased cost asssociated with any behavior that the therapist and patient agree is prohibitively high and therefore not worth doing (Kanfer and Phillips, 1970; Stolz, Wienckowski, and Brown, 1975). Behavior cost assumes the therapist has the amount of environmental control needed to carry out the contingency involved.

6. *Behavioral counting.* This is simply a case of logging or tallying the instances, in a given time-frame, when a person engages in a given act (smoking cigarettes, biting nails, etc.). Tallying forms a *baseline* against which later behavior changes can be compared, and shows the occasions and the frequency of the behavior in question (people often do not know how frequently they perform some unwanted behavior). Tallying or counting may also give rise to possible methods of spontaneous control which the patient may bring up on his own, once he better discerns the circumstances. Discerning helps to bring the behavior under control. Counting or tallying behavioral events in the classroom where children engage in disruptive behaviors can be very useful to the teacher wanting to bring about a change. In psychotherapy, one patient's tics were

counted under different circumstances during the therapy hour: when discussing vacation plans, when the patient was talking about an anger-producing situation in his office, and when he was listening to a relaxation tape. Figure 5 summarizes these findings and suggests how the therapy hour may yield quantitative and useful data on the patient.

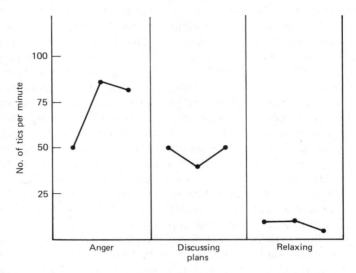

Figure 5. Three one-minute samples of tics by an adult patient in psychotherapy, during one therapy hour, under three sets of conditions (when discussing an office matter that made him angry, during general discussion about vacation plans, and during a 12-minute "relaxation" tape).

7. *Behavioral rehearsal.* This method is simply one of rehearsing under optimal and/or typical circumstances the behavior needed for some critical or test situation. One might, for example, rehearse taking timed tests, and note how fast and accurate one is at the outset, in the middle, or at the end of the testing. One might rehearse roles in social situations—for example, how to ask a member of the opposite sex for something. Rehearsal may at first be a vicarious attempt to solve some interpersonal problem, but it might help solve actual skill or achievement problems as well. It is simply an effort to put into practice the needed or desired behavior. The therapist can often help the patient/client discern specific elements of a behavioral complex or skill that the patient does not first recognize, thus helping the patient move through successive steps to a more skillful rendition of the needed behavior.

8. *Contingency management.* This is simply a name for the skilled management of contingencies from which reinforcement follows. An example may range all the way from a mother saying, "John, you may go out and play after you have learned all your spelling words," to "When the employee has made up his work schedule for the month and indicates the steps and dates inherent in accomplishing this schedule, he may apply for additional leave." This term is also used generally and interchangeably with "behavior modification" (Ullmann and Krasner, 1975, p. 273; Kanfer and Phillips, 1970, pp. 431–432; Haring and Phillips, 1962, 1972). The term is used most frequently in connection with classroom problems but it may, of course, apply to any setting. In a way, all reinforcement practice can be regarded as an example of contingency management.

9. *Contracting.* As the term implies, this is an agreement between (say) teacher and student as to how much work will be done and the contingent terms of the contract. This technique has often been used in school and treatment centers and has been useful in overcoming behavioral deficits and underachievement and in promoting new efforts at self-control. It is used in counseling and therapy in specifying agendas to be worked on, times and places of therapy sessions, and the like (Krumboltz and Thoresen, 1969, pp. 87–129). In some ways, contracting is an extension of contingency management where the two or more participants (teacher, pupil) openly agree on the terms and each participates in evaluating the results. For example, a given amount of work is needed for an "A"; a lesser amount for a "B"; and so on. Some critics of behavior modification practice respond more favorably to contracting than to some other uses of contingency management because of the more open and reciprocal agreements arrived at by the participants. In some ways it is like any contractual agreement, except that it seeks to overcome a deficit in some behavioral area rather than rely mainly on current skills and knowledge.

10. *Covert desensitization.* The "covert" part of this technique refers to a person reading his own inner state, perhaps a feeling of anxiety or unrest, a boiling up of anger, or other discernible (physiological) states. If the individual can sense these physiological and socially related states early (covertly, before they get to be overt and perhaps socially aversive), he can learn to bring them under control. For example, therapists often suggest to people who sense anxiety in social situations that they dismiss themselves a moment to "make a presumed phone call," or lean over to "tie a shoelace," or other actions that distract them from their sense of unrest and give them something to do that can break the tension and introduce new behavior. Much of the relaxation and desensitization (see below, technique 12, "Desensitization") of Wolpe and his followers pivots on teaching the patient to discern early covert (subjectively felt)

discomfort or relief which, then, can be brought under control (Mahoney, 1974, pp. 93–103). (See, also, in Chapter 1, the section on "Self-Reinforcement and Self-Control," pp. 44–46.)

11. *Cue control.* Cues control our behavior to a remarkable extent: Witness the stopping and going on red or green light signals (cues); the parent frowning to the child to stop kicking the chair in front of him. We teach people, in therapy, to look out for cues in the behavior of others so that their own behavior is better controlled. We may ask the patient: "How would you know if she was going to lambaste you when you raised this topic?" and the patient might reply with some cue he had picked up in the person's behavior. Teachers and parents cue their children to both positive and negative behaviors. A cue is an economical way to say "go" or "stop" with respect to some behavior that is momentarily lacking control (Staats, 1975, p. 39). In operant terms, a cue is an S^D (discriminative stimulus).

12. *Desensitization.* This term is associated primarily with Wolpe and his followers (Wolpe, 1958, 1969). It is used in connection with deep muscle relaxation procedures. The patient is lead through successive desensitizing experiences based on a hierarchy of anxiety-provoking events in relation to a given experience. For example, a person who is afraid of riding an elevator may be progressively desensitized in this regard by setting up first a hierarchy of anxiety about elevators starting (say) with a thought about "having to go shopping " as the mildest stimulus the patient can discern in connection with anxiety about riding elevators. A second level, slightly more anxiety-provoking, might be a thought about or the mentioning of a given store where the shopping is to be done; a third level might, hypothetically, be the thought or reminder about shopping on, for example, the fourth floor, necessitating the use of the elevator; and so on to greater anxiety-provoking thoughts. The hierarchical points, beginning with the mildest, are then discussed in therapy until the patient feels little or no concern about this one juncture or point; then the therapist takes the patient progressively through all the points or steps until the patient can discuss the matter of riding an elevator with little or no anxiety. The progressive relation procedures may take several therapy sessions and may have to cover more than one setting of importance to the patient where the use of (say) elevators is an issue. Proceeding in this manner is known as "vicarious desensitization" in contrast to doing the same work in the actual setting ("in vivo"). The therapist may help the patient, through relaxation, to accept, face, and overcome the anxiety associated with the specific behavior in question. (See technique 50, "Relaxation"; also see Chapter 5.)

13. *Deviation amplifying loop*. This term is not often encountered in the behavior therapy or behavior modification literature. However, it is a useful concept, derived from cybernetics, which bears considerably on behavior modification efforts (see Chapter 9). The term applies to the circularity of problems: We all know that problems tend to recur, and it is the recurrent or redundant nature of problems that bothers us as well as the problems themselves. We often say, "if it happened once, that might be tolerable . . . but it happens very often . . . and that's what bugs me. . . ." A "loop" describes the recurrent or cyclic nature of the problem. A deviation amplifying loop describes a problem that, in its cyclic recurrence, tends to worsen or amplify. An example is the inflationary trend where a basic industry, say, raises its prices, then labor follows with a strike or other means to get salary increases, all of which are passed on to the middleman and eventually to the consumer; but with the rising cost of labor and marketing, the basic industry then comes back for another price hike . . . and so on and on. A student fails to study, goes to an exam unprepared, does poorly, feels badly about his performance, looks to diversionary experience and doesn't study, gets another low grade, doesn't study for the next test, and so on until the process drives him out of school. Many phenomena we encounter each day are loop-type processes: the steps we go through to make a car go; the steps we go through in eating, sleeping, exercising, and so on. Some of these remain at a steady level—that is, do not amplify—but when they do amplify (e.g., eating or sleeping to excess), there is often difficulty in getting the system back into a state of equilibrium. Much of therapy is concerned with restoring balance and order in a person's life (Phillips and Wiener, 1966). (See Chapter 9 also.)

14. *Deviation counteracting loop*. In a sense, this loop—a "counteracting" one—is the opposite of the "amplifying" loop. This loop corrects or modifies deviation. If the furnace did not cut off when it reached a given temperature, it would go higher and higher and explode or burn up all fuel (run down) sooner or later. The "cutoff" is a corrective or counteracting aspect of the loop. When driving a car, one counteracts the tendency to run off the road from the natural drift of the car in the wind or from changing surface characteristics of the road. We often say in everyday life that we have to "put the brakes on" or "be sure not to overdo it" and other remarks that imply a counteracting force or effort, which keeps the phenomena in question from getting out of control. Loops often behave as they do (amplifying ones, especially) because no new information or influence enters the loop from outside. The car, going on its own, may drift toward the ditch unless it is corrected by new elements entering the

loop (e.g., the driver seeing the drifting of the car, or the driver seeing another car crowding his space on the road). In therapy/counseling the patient's drift toward undercontrol (e.g., wasting time, overeating, gambling, excessive drinking, other loss of self-control) has to be somehow corrected by and through the actions of the therapist; the therapist is the force from "outside" that corrects the deviation of the relatively closed loop, deviation amplifying behavior of the patient as he risks "going down hill" (Phillips and Wiener, 1966).

15. *Direct verbal instructions.* Common sense and daily social intercourse call for direct verbal instructions frequently. There is no reason why, under some circumstances, direct verbal instructions would not apply in therapy. One patient asked the therapist: "Please tell me if you think this idea is nonsense" whereupon the therapist, feeling concurrence, did make the direct statement. In many aspects of Ellis' therapy, direct verbal instructions play an important and constructive role; and other therapists have noted this value as well (Phillips, 1956; Phillips and Wiener, 1966).

16. *Direct verbal suasion.* If direct verbal instructions can be therapeutically useful so can direct verbal suasion. This is the case where the therapist may say to the patient something like the following:"You know from past behavior and from our discussions that if you do _____ you will come out with an unwanted result—so why beat your head against the wall again?" Often, if a patient does not accept the suasion, he or she will raise a related relevant point that can clear up the matter or show both patient and therapist why the verbal suasion is not useful. In many ways, however, the verbal suasion serves as a stimulus appropriate to some reality in the patient's life (a positive reminder), or as a cue to a possible negative outcome (implying a lack of reinforcement for the patient).

17. *Dream analysis.* Conventional dream analysis is not referred to in this discussion; rather, the dream *report* is, itself, behavior that takes place in the clinical interaction between patient and therapist. The report, in turn, refers to other out-of-therapy experiences the patient has had and about which interpretations, suggestions, and other behavioral controls may be tried out. The dream is a subtle behavior, similar to thoughts, images, and the like, which may be brought into a more behavioral context through verbal discussion, and the dream may occasionally throw light on more easily observed, overt behavior. The dream is not a road to the unconscious; it is simply another area for behavioral consideration that may be more or less useful depending on circumstances. Often the dream captures a "feeling state" or idea or attitude the person may also express in other ways. One patient reported dreaming "All night it

seemed that I was measuring the edge of a table, or cutting cloth along the edge of some object and that I could never get the measurement or the cutting just right'' as he reported on how uncomfortable he was sleeping in a single bed with another person. A woman with a history of sexual promiscuity who had always seemed to leave behind jewelry, articles of clothing, and the like after a love tryst, dreamt that she walked through a grassy field and found several "lost articles" from previous sexual encounters; the dream being connected with a resolve to stop her promiscuity and center her affections on one person. Dreams may signify conflicted situations or they may suggest or confirm resolutions to conflicts. Their value and significance in behavior change depends on a host of circumstances, provided they are regarded in a manner similar to all other behavior. It is possible that one can suggest to the patient that he or she may dream about a given topic that is highly conflictive in therapy at a given time. In such a case the therapist is invoking a kind of verbal instruction or suasion (see techniques 15 and 16 above) which may prompt more consideration about the issues at hand. An example of this kind of therapeutic use of dream reporting occurred in connection with a patient dreaming that his roommate peremptorily used his—the patient's—car, wore the patient's shoes on the wrong feet, and even took food from the patient's plate. The patient had been struggling with the notion that he was being taken advantage of, that he needed to assert his rights more deliberately with his roommate, and with ways in which he might bring under better control the apparent onesidedness of their relationship. The dream report and discussion had the effect of solidifying the patient's acceptance that he was, indeed, being taken undue advantage of and that some remedial effort was in order.

18. *Extinction*. Extinction is a technical term from learning theory; it refers to the gradual loss, through withholding reinforcement, of a given behavior under a given set of circumstances. For example, an animal having learned where to receive food pellets upon executing a given behavior will in time cease to show this behavior and to go to the food box as reinforcement is withheld. The responses originally learned will be weakened (occur less frequently) and may cease altogether. Applied to therapy or counseling, extinction will tend to occur when the reinforcing value of a given behavior is stopped or greatly reduced. Often verbal instructions, as well as arranging changes in the social environment are important in extinction in societal settings. One must recognize that as extinction begins there may be an acceleration of the behavior, so that in therapy settings alternative behaviors are needed to take the place of the original behavior that is being extinguished. For example, if a person has lost a boyfriend or girlfriend, the social reinforcements associated there-

with are missing, and the person suffering the loss may try increasingly for a while to call or see the absent one; recourse to other social contacts is thereby important, although it may not be well received at first by the person, in order to make up for the loss (the behavior that is undergoing extinction).

19. *Fading*. Fading is the gradual removal of a formerly predominant means of reinforcement, allowing a new or different reinforcing circumstance (or stimulus) to take over. One fades out one method of control (reinforcer) in favor of another one. In learning a skill, the tutor gradually fades out his control and turns it over to the pupil; the monitor "fades out" in favor of the learner. It may also be considered as a gradual reduction of cues—a matter of successive approximation; and, in this regard, is the "opposite" of shaping (where shaping refers to the shaping up or building up of response tendencies). In a very real sense, the therapist gradually fades out of the picture and turns the problem solving over to the patient's own control. Any useful therapy results in fading out the influence or control of the therapist or counselor; behavior therapy works explicitly on this objective (Kanfer and Phillips, 1970, pp. 293–295).

20. *Fines*. Fines are penalties, an example of averse control, mentioned separately simply to give them some specific consideration. A fine requires that one give up some positive reinforcement (e.g., money) due to some infractions. Fines may be part of behavioral contracting (see technique where, for example, a patient purporting to lose weight nonetheless gains weight and suffers a fine as a result—paying out money to a "cause" inimical to the patient's personal values—perhaps in addition to losing some positive reinforcement in the form of social approval, ability to wear certain clothes, and so on. In behavioral management, one should be careful not to load on fines when there is already some loss of positive reinforcement (Stolz, Wienckowski, and Brown, 1975).

21. *Flooding (or emotional flooding)*. This procedure is not directly derived from learning principles (in the sense that fading and shaping are) but derives from the practice of some therapists to confront the patient very vigorously and persistently with his problems, or some aspect of the problem the therapist deems important or relevant. A therapist may think that a male patient's reluctance to deal with an opposite sex relationship is due to "homosexual tendencies," and the therapist may pursue this point, hoping to have the patient reach an emotional catharsis in relation to certain (alleged or suspected) critical experiences regarding sex that set the patient in the direction of the present problem. The patient, in effect, is "flooded" with either real or alleged (hypothetical) problems or experiences in connection with the behavior problem under scrutiny at a given

time in the therapy. The older practice of dealing with war neuroses, or "combat exhaustion," in attempting to help the patient—through the use of sodium pentathol or sodium amatyl—face up to and cope with his fears and anxieties from combat, is an example of an earlier, and more specifically applied, use of flooding techniques. The use of flooding assumes that the essential problem and/or important features of the patient's problem are available for direct stimulation through the therapist's verbal instructions. Flooding may constitute a fast and powerful confrontation or it may be executed more gradually (Ayllon and Michael, 1959). Krumboltz and Thoresen (1969, p. 464) give an example of a young woman treated by "flooding sex talk" to overcome certain areas of sensitivity about sexual terms. (See, also, techniques 27 and 55, below.)

22. *Free operant responding.* As the term implies, some behavior is selected that is already present ("freely" available in the repertoire) and reinforced; because the behavior thus reinforced leads to some goal or objective. A child playing the piano fingers a passage in just the right way without being so instructed and the teacher says, "That's it—that's the way to do it." In sports, in skill development, in social interaction, we reinforce, by verbal approval and attention, the behavior of others as this behavior is "freely" emitted. Looking for more mature behaviors among clients or patients, the constantly alert therapist stands ready to reinforce with attention and approval those behaviors that are spontaneously emitted by the person when those behaviors fit in with other goals. An example for counseling or therapy is the following: a patient says, "I've noticed that I get angry with him when he tries to force me to discuss something with him when I'm busy—I now just go into my room and close the door and tell him I'll talk with him later," whereupon the therapist reinforces the patient's report on his behavior with approval and comment as an example of the patient freely finding a solution to one of his interaction problems with another person. The importance of noting free operant responding in the psychotherapeutic situation is to stress the fact that many behaviors of patients are adequate and problem solving and that every problem is not one the therapist has to "work out" with the patient. The therapist's role in reinforcing freely emitted problem-solving behaviors on the patient's part is stressed; this role becomes more important as therapy progresses and as the patient successfully takes more behavior under his or her own control.

23. *Hypnosis.* Hypnosis is, of course, used by many types of therapists, regardless of persuasion, although its history has been associated with more traditional or "depth" therapy. Actually, the more we know about hypnosis, the less it is conceptualized as a separate state, or as an uncovering technique, in the sense of uncovering or peeling off

layers of the unconscious. One can change behavior under hypnosis; current behavior or behavior in the future can be influenced by hypnosis (e.g., in posthypnotic suggestion). Certain cues and social influences, under highly discriminated conditions, may account for much of the behavior we observe under hypnosis. Hypnosis may show how operant control over somatic and perceptual processes can be acheived. The therapeutic role of hypnosis is less popular among behavioral theories, but it is not precluded. The behavioral emphasis remains one of teaching new behaviors, new discriminations, and finding new reinforcers, more than focusing on pathology or alleged original causes. Even if one could prove origins of disturbed behavior, there would still be the problem of teaching new behaviors, and this would put the problem squarely in the arena of learning theory or behavior modification.

24. *Hypothetical other.* This procedure is not a behavioral technique in the strict sense, but it is useful in a verbal way (see, also, techniques 15 and 16, above) to bring some new evaluations to bear on the patient's behavior (calling attention to some stimuli relevant to the patient's behavior not previously discerned). The therapist might say to the patient, "How would you feel if John acted that way toward you?" "What would you say if you encountered others behaving as you say you do?" Or, "Other people could do that to you and you would not mind?—I doubt that!" These are ways of verbally calling the patient's attention to how his behavior affects others by stimulating him to "see" the same behavior performed by others and to reevaluate his own behavior under this hypothetically altered condition. It is a way of "seeing ourselves as others see us."

25. *Humor.* Humor may not be considered a behavioral technique in a formal sense, but it is very useful in couseling and therapy. Humor, in effect, points to new stimuli that may be attended to in a situation; it shades meaning and puts a new perspective on words or the way words represent a situation. Humor may also be used to release anxiety and to serve as an aggressive or aversive stimulus to another person. The counselor who uses humor may thereby help the patient "see" the lighter implications of what he has said or done, and to gain reinforcement when it was absent before (Ullmann and Krasner, 1975, pp. 158–159).

26. *Imagery.* (See, also, technique 10, "Covert desensitization." This is a procedure that pivots on the patient's imagining a tense or a pleasant situation and then using this imagery to bring about overt behavior change (usually a felt and verbally reported greater relaxation). One may also instruct the patient to "visualize" (imagine) conflict situations (e.g., wanting to engage in acting or singing but feeling anxious about being on stage). The purpose of using imagery is, however, to get observable

behavior change, such as being willing to speak before a group, overcoming apprehension associated with entering a room full of people, or overcoming eating excesses. Wolpe's work in this therapeutic area is of great importance. Negative or positive imagery may be considered as a subcategory. The use of imagery is, at first, a vicarious way of approaching a problem area, or a way to bring vicarious pleasant (reinforcing) stimuli to bear on a problem (Mahoney, 1974, pp. 36–41).

27. *Implosion.* This is a term used by Stampfl and Levis (1967) to refer to a very intensive extinction effort to rid the patient of his or her symptoms and distress. The patient imagines scenes allegedly important in the generation of the complaint and often derived from hypothetical psychodynamic interpretations of symptoms. In learning terms, the symptoms or unwanted behaviors (the *CR,* or Conditioned Response, in Pavlovian terms) are reduced by presenting the *CS* (Conditioned Stimulus) without presenting the *UCS* (Unconditioned Stimulus), on grounds that overcoming the symptoms is most rapid if the possible original condition is recaptured in imagery and with strong emotional feelings. Once the patient is led to evoke the strong feelings and anxiety, there follows a diminution in their strength (extinction) owing to the patient not being allowed to escape from the distress but having to face it. The procedure is more intensive and rapid than the gradual desensitization of anxiety procedure followed by Wolpe and many others; the latter procedure seeks to diminish the anxiety associated with any given stimulus, whereas the implosion technique seeks as great an intensity as possible in the extinction process. A quote from Hogan (1966, p. 26) illustrates this point:

"A person afraid of a snake would be requested to view himself picking up and handling the snake. Attempts would be made to have him become aware of his reactions to the animal. He would be instructed to feel how slimy the snake was. Next, he would be asked to experience the snake crawling over his body and biting and ripping his flesh. Scenes of snakes crushing or swallowing him, or perhaps his falling into a pit of snakes would be appropriate implosions."

Implosion and flooding are often used interchangeably. Possibly flooding tends to be used with overt situations—putting a person directly into an actual anxiety–provoking situation—whereas implosion may be more commonly a vicarious (verbal) approach. Both tend to raise anxiety levels, however, and to work from this vantage point (see technique 21), in contrast to gradual, anxiety-reducing approaches.

28. *Increasing interresponse time (I.R.T.).* Here reference is made to the length of time between successive responses or, correspondingly, to a

reduction in the rate of responding under a given span of time. A person seeking to stop cigarette smoking or any other "bad habit" might count the number of cigarettes smoked per day. This is all right, but there is some risk that the person will be concentrating too much on the actual smoking (which he seeks to reduce) instead of concentrating efforts (reinforcing himself) on an increased lapse of time between cigarettes. In the latter case, one might go from a few minutes, to hours, to days between cigarettes; hence the emphasis is shifted from the number of cigarettes smoked to the increasingly longer and longer time intervals between smoking, which, if reinforced, will extinguish or lead to better control of smoking behavior. The same procedural emphasis may be used with overcoming any other "bad habit," such as temper outbursts, drinking, or biting one's nails (Thompson and Grabowski, 1972, pp. 31–36; Lloyd and Salzberg, 1975).

29. *In vivo therapy*. As the term implies, this is the practice of conducting therapy in the actual life situation in which the problem occurs. One might go out on the street with a patient who is made anxious by crowds, or high buildings, or the like, and move stepwise into ways of conquering the anxiety (see Chapter 5). The presence of the therapist in such an in vivo situation is likewise important, as the actual behaviors, and not just in-office descriptions of them, are at issue. One way of contrasting counseling and psychotherapy (which are based on verbal representations of behavior in other settings) with direct intervention in schools, institutions, and the like, is that the latter settings provide amply for in vivo therapy, and presumably all the variables of importance can be brought under some control as a result.

30. *Labeling*. Possibly the first systematic treatment of labeling in relation to counseling and psychotherapy is found in the Dollard and Miller volume (1950) wherein they relate the act of labeling symptoms (or unwanted behavior) to bring the named behavior under control. Labeling can be very helpful, or it can result in a superficial understanding. If the patient has no understanding or knowledge of an act, labeling the act for the patient may have some informational value and thus enable the patient to at least identify the act for what it is (this would be an S^D or discriminative stimulus, in operant terms). For example, to say to a patient whom you (the therapist) feel to be reacting "hysterically" that the present complaint is probably not really heart trouble, or stomach cancer, or some other organically formidable condition, but simply is hysterical or impulsive behavior that is behaviorally open to self-control, is probably a worthwhile labeling. On the other hand, labeling can be very superficial—that is, not lead to any discernible therapeutic action—in the case of calling a person's behavior a "complex" or an "Oedipal" reliving,

or similar labels. The value of the labeling is, in the final analysis, a matter of whether the label specifies behaviors that can be managed, or brought under control, or whether some misapprehension in the assigning of causality (e.g., organic versus functional) can be corrected in a manner to profit the therapy (Phillips and Wiener, 1966).

31. *Log-keeping.* Keeping a log is simply a matter of keeping a brief diary. It is often recommended to the patient as it addresses one to the problem of frequency of occurrence of the unwanted behavior, to the setting in which the unwanted behavior occurs, and to any comments or reactions the patient may have to the incidents themselves, and it provides at least a rough baseline record of behavior. A log is very useful in therapy in that it teaches a patient to observe and report better on himself. It helps to make him responsible for his own behavior and for changing it (shared with the therapist); and it adds precision to the behavior change process. A log need not be copious; brief notes are enough: "Saturday morning I awakened feeling like I could meet the day head-on . . . and I did." Or, "Every time I see that girl, I feel ashamed of myself and wish I had never tried to date her. . . ." Logs may contain either positive or negative items: The switch to the occurrence of more positive versus negative items, over time, may constitute a good index of therapeutic change. Logs are a means to an end, not an end in themselves, although writing down experiences may act as a kind of therapeutic stopgap until the larger issues of a problem can be brought under control. (See Chapter 4).

32. *Mass practice.* This term, like some of the others discussed here, is derived from learning theory. It refers to massing practice, as distinct from distributing practice on a skill, over time. If one is to learn how to type, it is probably better that 15 minutes a day be spent at the task for (say) two months, giving a total of 600 minutes or 10 hours total practice; rather than trying to learn to type by massing practice three hours at a time on three or four occasions. Most skills build gradually and each step in the skill has to be solidified, so to speak, by sufficient practice (assuming reinforcement of the effort). One cannot rush things too much, although the optimal time and the number of practice sessions for any given skill (typing, archery, swimming, playing the violin, learning a new language) is closely related to individual differences among learners as well as to the demands of the subject matter itself. Mass practice therapy has been conducted in which whole days or weekends have been devoted to self-confrontation (sometimes called "marathons") and to interacting with others on an extremely candid basis. It is doubtful if one learns much about himself in this manner; and even more doubtful if one can put into gainful practice the self-observations or "insights" thus learned. Al-

though the hundreds of hours, even thousands of hours, put in by psychoanalytic patients purpose to do "major psychic surgery" on a person, it is doubtful if the high rate of analysis (4–5 times per week) is really any better than a more relaxed schedule (1–2 times a week, even with sessions of a half hour in length) for bringing about behavior or personality change. If one had 50 hours to spend with a patient, one would usually opt for a few initial sessions 1–2 times a week—to lay down a conceptual and interpersonal (i.e., therapeutic) reference point—then spread out the remaining sessions on a 2–4 times a month basis; rather than seeing a patient for 4–5 times a week continually for 10–12 weeks. Mass practice has been used in the treatment of tics and other specific habits (Yates, 1975).

33. *Mirror control.* As the label states, one can use a mirror to help bring about some self-control effort. One patient with tics stated he did not realize that he displayed the tics; he agreed to spend 5 minutes before a mirror several times per day and count the number of times he displayed eye or facial tics. His count dropped from a range of 75–100 tics per 5-minute period down to a range of 5–10 tics, with some 5-minute intervals passing without any observed or recorded tics. The mirror technique helps the person identify the unwanted behavior; it helps provide stimulus control; and the consequences of not displaying tics, immediately available as they are, is reinforcing. Mirrors are, of course, used in teaching dancing and other motor skills; such a technique is not new to the general field of education but it has not been used widely in behavior change efforts of a clinical type.

34. *Modeling.* Modeling is social learning through imitation. The child watches the piano teacher's movements and imitates them; likewise, on the playing field, the coach models the needed behavior. Various verbal, sensory, symbolic, and other processes are used to describe for the person the necessary cues which, in time and under the correct conditions, are imitated (Bandura, 1965b). Modeling is useful in therapy because it is often easier to exhibit social behavior *in situ* than it is to talk about it. It is often easier to observe what behavior one is to follow than it is to have the same behavior verbally described. Many forms of social behavior, especially approach behaviors toward others, can be effectively modeled. Therapists often state verbally what they would like the patient to state; or demonstrate overtly what the patient is later to imitate. We are only on the verge of understanding and using modeling in teaching social behavior, and the areas of counseling and therapy stand to gain much by developments in this important field (Mahoney, 1974, pp. 43–48).

35. *Momentary escape/avoidance.* Although it has been asserted that escape and/or avoidance are the ways psychopathology is maintained, it

is important to recognize how they can be utilized in a controlled way to minimize anxiety or stress. If one is inclined to avoid a class, a speech, an exam, an interview, or whatever, an approved approach to the anxiety problem associated with these events is through a temporary escape, but not outright avoidance. One might, for example, lean over to retie a shoelace, go to the bathroom, make a phone call, or go search for an article in a coat hung in a closet, in order to talk to one's self about the anxiety ("I'm feeling anxious here, but I am not going to be driven off—I will go through with the interview")—and thereby gain a "second wind." This momentary escape or delay in the confrontation enables the person to state the problem verbally and to concentrate on doing what is to be done, in contrast to the redundancy of rumination and reiterated anxiety. The familiar vicious circle has to be broken; new behavior has to be introduced into the situation, and since the whole situation cannot be reconstructed or avoided, the regrouping of effort through momentary escape or avoidance is recommended. In the long run, the ability to conquer the anxiety reaction that clutches one in such circumstances helps to get to the broader problems of sensitivity to certain kinds of self-confrontation; whereas the effort to "get to the basic problem first" is often met with failure, resulting not only in not finding the "basic problem" but in eschewing practical measures that help the anxiety clutch of the moment *and* contribute to the longer-range solutions one needs. In a broader sense, escape and avoidance, although their consequences are similar (they are maintained through reinforcement via anxiety reduction), are topologically different. Escape assumes that one is already in an anxiety-provoking situation (and can therefore utilize the technique discussed here) and must then leave the situation in order to reduce anxiety—people run away from problems, as we commonly say. Avoidance, however, is more complete, and calls not for the staying power afforded by momentary measures, but requires a more gradual approach to the anxiety through relaxation and desensitization, successive approximations afforded by skill development, and the like. In common parlance, however, people tend to use escape and avoidance interchangeably, and no harm comes from this as long as one keeps the topological, the consequential, and the interrupting techniques clearly in mind.

36. *Moratorium.* Declaring a moratorium with respect to the therapy itself or with respect to a relationship between the patient and another person, also discussed in the therapy, may be beneficial. This is posited on the notion that what is going on currently in therapy is not productive, is, on the contrary, redundant, and hence not problem solving, so that a temporary stopping is called for in order to gain a new perspective, shake

down the problem a little more, and see whether with a changed perspective new ideas and procedures occur. There is no intention of stopping the therapy—or the relationship spoken about by the patient during the therapy period—but of changing the pace in such a way that new data may creep into the considerations at hand. A patient who is constantly fighting with a roommate or friend of the opposite sex might be an example; just staying away from the problem—an extended "time out" of sorts—may allow a new approach to the other person, or allow the patient to yield, or perhaps even assert differently, with respect to a given interpersonal issue. When impasses arise between the patient and the therapist, the latter may consider that what is reinforcing the patient is not gainful interaction with the therapist, but a highly redundant assemblage of the problem without making headway. The therapist might say, "I think we've reached an impasse here and I suggest that we not meet for (say) a month or six weeks, with each of us in the meanwhile reconsidering the therapy, making some notes as to what we think has gone wrong (and can be remedied), so we can try to introduce some new ideas for consideration when we meet again." This has to be concurred on by the patient, of course, as to the general idea of the moratorium itself, but also as to its specifics: what to do in the interim, how long to wait before meeting again, making interim notes, and the like. A fresh and productive perspective seems often to result from such tactics, and the resort to a moratorium should not be counted as a sign of failure, but as a resource one may use on occasion.

37. *Negative feedback.* (Also, see technique 44, "Positive feedback.") This is a cybernetic term that refers to information fed back to a controlling agent based on the behavior of that agent as it pursues a goal. An example would be the "positive" or "negative" (i.e., corrective) information fed back to a person trying to get his car out of a ditch. If the driver backed too far, thus miring down further in the ditch, this would be negative feedback ("don't back so far"); positive feedback would contrast with negative feedback by and through some information indicating that slowing down the spinning of the wheels would allow for more traction, thus allowing the driver to get his car out of the ditch. Negative feedback is essentially corrective information indicating that different behavior is required if the problem is to be solved. A therapeutic application would be a person who was trying to lose weight observing—on the basis of keeping his or her own data on food intake—that too many calories were consumed on a given day. Such information would be negative in that a correction (i.e., lessening of caloric intake) was indicated. Instances of negative feedback may range all the way from "you're

stepping on my feet!'' to the election results showing a given candidate has lost decisively.

38. *Negative practice.* In the early days of learning principles applied to skill problems (e.g., typing), it was observed that if a given error tended to persist, it was often useful to deliberately and explicitly practice the error so as to draw attention to it and to show how it was inadvertently performed. One might type "hte" instead of "the" in learning to type. One than would actually type "h-t-e" deliberately, making sure to observe how the incorrect typing was done and/or to pick up any cues as to how this performance was continued, with a view to correcting those conditions (Dunlop, 1928, 1930). The error would be so deliberately and consciously brought under control that its tendency would be curtailed and the correct typing established. In therapy one might ask the patient to deliberately say (or do) an erroneous thing in order to highlight it enough to make its elements discerned. An example could be deliberately mispronouncing a word; or deliberately playing a wrong note in a musical score. We often say that "gets it out of his system in this way" but actually it is not a matter of such a removal, but of better discernment of the context in which the erroneous behavior occurs and in correcting this context and the behavior in question. Deliberately feigning anger with a view to establishing self-control in a social situation might be a counseling application.

39. *Negative reinforcement.* This term is often confused with punishment (see technique 47). Negative reinforcement refers to the *removal* of an aversive stimulus. Thus, fastening one's seat belt, in order to turn off the buzzer (which is annoying), is an example of negative reinforcement. Putting a coin in the parking meter (which may be buzzing when overextended in time) is another example. Household appliances such as stoves often turn on buzzers when a given condition (heat or time) has been reached; hence the turning off of the buzzer is negative reinforcement. In therapy and counseling, one might anticipate an aversive condition (e.g., a child yelling) that can be averted by the mother's behaviors (giving the child a cookie); or a teacher might lift an impediment (a low grade, say) by having the student make up prior work; or a student under pressure to prepare for an exam lest he flunk out of school, might act to get his studying done (work problems, complete lab reports) thereby taking away the aversive consequences of failure.

40. *Overcorrection.* As the term implies, overcorrection is the (aversive) practice of not only correcting some unwanted behavior, but going further to add on other requirements. For example, if a patient in a hospital messes up a dining table, the patient might be expected to clean

up not only that particular table but also other tables. Whether overcorrection is commonly called for is moot; one can overdo the overcorrection and leave a too averse residual if great care isn't taken (Stolz, Wienckowski, and Brown, 1975). It may have greater applicability to slow or retarded learners or those with limited behavioral repertoires, such as hospitalized psychotics, than to typical counseling and therapy cases. However, people sometimes apply overcorrection spontaneously to themselves—one high school student imposed on himself the task of doing ten extra math problems whenever he missed a given type of problem.

41. *Overlearning.* Overlearning is learning something beyond the necessary criterion level needed for adequate performance. It might be that in learning a poem, one could demonstrate his memory by being able to repeat the poem three times without error. Overlearning would consist in going beyond this criterion level. It is not clear that overlearning as a deliberate effort is worth the energy it takes; ordinarily some practical criterion—ability to recall, or repeat some instructions or useful bits of information at a useful time or place—is sufficient; hence, overlearning could be a waste of time. Also, repeated recital of something to the point of overlearning might allow for the occurrence of atypical or conflicting conditions, and possibly distract the learner from his goal, or even allow errors to creep in, thus producing a result the opposite to overlearning. Learning a skill or given behavior is probably best served when it is produced (practiced) in a variety of relevant, functional, and related situations; just to practice something in a humdrum way, in a narrow setting, would ordinarily not be considered functional learning. Counseling applications would be shown in terms of overlearning social skills (e.g., asking an opposite sex person for a social engagement) to the point of functional adequacy.

42. *Paradoxical intention.* This term is not often used in behavioral counseling or therapy, but it refers to a behavioral process that should be made explicit. Literally it means that one behaves in a manner paradoxical (opposite) to the way he feels about something. A boy who is afraid of a dog might try to "scare" the dog in order to control his own anxiety. In conflict theory, one may find the basis for this paradox in behavior. Conflict behavior is characterized by an approach (to a goal) tendency and an avoidance tendency. These tendencies may be shown empirically to cross at some point between a starting point and the goal area. As the organism approaches the crossing point, where the two tendencies are approximately equal, one may be unable to discern clearly when one is approaching or avoiding a goal area, and be unable to observe his own behavior with the larger, approach–avoidance context in mind. Thus, one

may act inconsistently with regard to the way he says he feels or says he is acting, and not know the difference. Paradoxical intention may also be an example of simply learning appropriate assertive behaviors. A counseling application would be to get the socially anxious person to stand up in public and ask a question or make a comment, to overcome his reluctance to deal directly with the anxiety involved.

Paradoxical intention becomes paradoxical *instruction* (Weakland, et al., 1974; Watzlawick, Weakland, and Fisch, 1974) when the therapist takes the tack that the patient is indeed depressed and has every right to be (given his complaints and circumstances), and the therapist wonders aloud how the patient can function at all! It is as if the therapist's paradoxical instructions give the patient the right to be disturbed—thus freeing the patient of the demand on himself to convince the therapist of his, the patient's needs—and allows the patient to then decide if he wants to change, and to begin to experiment with his own responsibility for change. One may also view paradoxical instructions as increasing the aversiveness of the patient's condition ("You certainly are depressed and with good reason") through the therapist's recognition of it and thereby increasing the likelihood that the patient will attempt to move away ("Negative reinforcement," see technique 39) from aversive control through his own efforts. When and if paradoxical instruction works well it is essentially a technique based on negative reinforcement; as the patient increases control over the aversive conditions and develops new and better coping behavior, his actions becoming more under the control of positive reinforcement (problem solving, social skill development, etc.)

43. *Pictures, books, and magazines.* On first glance, it may appear curious that pictures and the like are included. In treating homosexual males, increasing the stimulation of the female form through erotic literature (pictures, books, movies, magazines) may serve as an adjunct to thought control and imagery. Pictures, books, and magazines may serve as controlled stimuli and as reinforcers for certain behavioral objectives in the areas of sexual activity. As well, books may be "assigned" or even spontaneously referred to by the patient which relate to specific problems the patient may display: feeling hurt through the criticism of others, being shunned in social settings such as dances, and feeling unappreciated by others. Passages from some of the works of Ellis (1962), Phillips and Wiener (1966), Wiener and Phillips (1972), and May (1971) may serve as examples. Information received from collateral readings may serve to enlarge upon, reinforce, or further clarify some of the interactions found during the psychotherapy or counseling hours themselves. Any such resources that the therapist and patient respect may be additional sources of help and information.

44. *Positive feedback*. (Also, see technique 37 "Negative feedback.") Positive feedback refers to positive information received by the agent (the behaving person, or even the inanimate object such as a self-correcting furnace) that the behavior just performed is in accordance with a goal, or is to be continued. It is similar in many ways to positive reinforcement. The relationship between positive feedback and positive reinforcement is often so close that there is not much practical advantage in trying to separate them. It is probably true that positive feedback is more often associated with closed mechanical systems whereas positive reinforcement is more often associated with human behavior in open systems where more selection of behavioral tendencies is apparent. For example, in order to learn to drive a car and go smoothly through all the steps, the single step of turning on the key which leads to the starting of the motor is an example of positive feedback. If the motor did not thus start, there would be no positive feedback (but, rather, negative feedback indicating that perhaps the gear shirt was not in neutral, or there was some similar obstruction to starting the car). Positive reinforcement, on the other hand, would be employed more in selecting ongoing driving behavior that was cautious, courteous, and accident-avoiding. In therapy and counseling, positive feedback would be exemplified by information received by the patient from some aspect of his environment (e.g., winning a prize or contest); positive reinforcement would be exemplified by praise from the patient's therapist or peers for having "done a good job." The former— positive feedback—would accrue more from a "general systems" condition (preparing for a contest, entering the contest, winning the contest, and receiving official information on this victory); and the latter—positive reinforcement—would accrue more from the consequences of the prize in the way of social approval, attention, and the like.

45. *Premack principle*. Premack (1959, 1965, 1971) stated that high probability behavior can be used contingently as a reinforcer for behavior with low probability. Conversely, the low probability behavior can be used as a punishing stimulus for high probability behavior. An example of the former would be holding up a child's strong tendency to run and shout (high probability behavior) contingent on his sitting still for a while and doing his arithmetic. Due to lack of more complete environmental control, the employment of the Premack principle in counseling or psychotherapy is more difficult. However, a therapist or counselor may have a patient agree (contract) to hold off playing pool each day (high probability behavior) until he has done his French lesson. The therapist could let the patient complain and emote *after* the patient has attended to the agreed-on agenda or reported on his activities of the past week. People who are orderly and self-disciplined implicitly illustrate the use of

the Premack principle. The principle is another example of the power of contingency management as a hallmark of behavioral technology.

46. *Programmed instruction.* Instruction in some subject matter or field, such as mathematics, foreign languages, spelling, or history, is presented to the learner in small steps that require the learner's participation (working a problem, choosing from among alternatives, reasoning out a sequence, etc.) in the form of choosing and writing (or marking) an answer. The main features of programmed instruction are: (1) It is composed of small, sequential steps, leading progressively to knowledge or skill in some area, (2) Reinforcement is systematically given upon the person's responding (the person learns immediately if he is correct in his answer and is shown how to correct it if needed). (3) The student can work at his own rate; (he can set his own pace for each session with the materials and/or his overall pace for the program). (4) It requires active responding on the student's part and sets terminal objectives (factoring certain kinds of algebra problems, learning a vocabulary of a given number of words, mastering the multiplication tables) (Skinner, 1968). The use of programmed instruction in counseling and therapy is not highly convincing unless one takes the trouble to first work out the "software" of the program itself. One could, of course, adapt it to learning limited social skills, such as cooking a meal, which might have social behavior implications, or learning to dance or play card games. One could program roughly the steps needed in teaching a man to ask a woman for a dance, or to go out to dinner. Wherever a clear sequence is needed and some terminal objective (goal or outcome) is discernible, one could "write" a program of any nature whatsoever, taking care to let the person move at his own pace and build in reinforcement along the way.

47. *Punishment.* Punishment is often confused with negative reinforcement (see technique 39). Punishment refers to the suppression (reduction in frequency) of a given behavior through aversive measures that are applied to the person contingent upon his acting in a given way. Punishment, to be effective, must reduce the frequency of the unwanted behavior. An example might be a child who is spanked for using his hands at the table for eating instead of using common utensils. Many times punishment is in name only: the person's behavior is not suppressed as a result. In such a case, it is not correct to call such measures punishing, because they do not succeed in reducing the behavior in question. Punishment is not a very effective means of controlling or changing behavior; it tends to bring on emotional complications, to encourage the person to fight back, and to produce generally negative attitudes toward the punishing person or situation. Punishment also fails to suggest alternative ways of handling a problem (compared to negative reinforcement

which specifies what is needed in order to deal with the aversive condition). Punishment in psychotherapy is not a welcome practice. Although sometimes therapists use confrontive measures in ways that might appear punishing, there is often specified a way in which the aversiveness can be called off or reduced; this is a better procedure because it allows for the reinforcement of alternatives (Kanfer and Phillips, 1970; Solomon and Wynne, 1953; Holz, Azrin, and Ayllon, 1963; Solomon, 1964).

48. *Rate-delay-intensity-recovery (RDIR)*. Properly speaking, this is not a "technique" but rather calls attention to broad aspects of behavior changes that may be expected to occur. *Rate* simply refers to frequency (see technique 6); *delay* refers to longer time intervals between the occurrence of the unwanted behavior (see technique 28); *intensity* takes notice of how much one is immersed in (dominated by) a given behavioral (emotional) reaction; and *recovery* refers to the "getting-back-to-normal" after an emotional outburst of some kind (e.g., recovery from a temper tantrum or a depressive period). Presumably all these are interrelated or correlated, but in the clinical situation, recourse to knowledge about the intensity of felt reaction and how quickly one recovers is often observationally more apparent to the patient than are the more systematic ways of taking frequency data on events that are troublesome. Rate and delay probably pertain more to limited problems (biting nails, smoking, and other specific, well-delimited behaviors), and apply less to a generally disturbing problem like depression; whereas the intensity and recovery aspects pertain to the more pervasive and often seemingly nebulous emotional reactions such as boredom, failure to concentrate, free-floating tension, depression, and the like. It is, therefore, important that the behavioral therapist be prepared for these more vague emotional reactions and be able to verbalize about them to the patient. As therapy progresses the intensity of emotional reactions (as reported by the patient) can be expected to diminish; likewise, the recovery period can be expected to shorten. Once these more vague conditions are noted, the patient can move on to more precise self-observation, data collection, and self-control measures.

49. *Reciprocal inhibition*. This term was advanced by Wolpe as possibly the main characteristic of his therapeutic approach. It refers to inhibiting a given behavioral tendency by its reciprocal or opposite. Thus, if one is relaxed, he cannot be anxious; the way to combat anxiety is to learn and practice relaxation. One reciprocally inhibits his tendency to bite his fingernails by keeping his hands away from his mouth and face and by employing them in some manual activity. Any behavior one might mention could be shown to have its opposite, or some opposing behavior that inhibits, or makes less probable, the former. As stated, reciprocal inhibi-

tion is widely used in Wolpian therapy, and indeed by all therapists to some extent even though they may not discern or admit it. One might offer a simple catalogue of corrective behaviors by pointing up behavior opposite to the unwanted behavior (Wolpe, 1958).

50. *Reinforcement (intermittent and continuous)*. Reinforcement is the central concept in behavior modification. It has many ramifications in an empirical sense (frequency/timing of reinforcement, amount of reinforcement, and the mixing or compounding of reinforcement schedules). This topic can become very complex and need not concern us here in our applications to the therapy/counseling situation. Intermittent reinforcement refers to reinforcing on some schedule other than every time (or after every response). Reinforcement after each response is continuous reinforcement (symbolically written as F-1, meaning a frequency of one, or after each response). A reasonably accurate representation of the practice of intermittent and/or continuous reinforcement in therapy or counseling may be understood in this way: When the behavior is new, complex, or difficult, reinforcement after each response (or trial, or effort) is indicated; after the behavior in question becomes more stabilized, the reinforcement schedule can be (perhaps should be) thinned out so that the behavior is further stabilized and less subject to extinction. A child may, for example, be reinforced at first after he correctly solves each arithmetic problem in his lesson; but later he may be reinforced only when he has passed an assignment halfway mark, or when he has finished the whole assignment correctly.

51. *Relaxation*. (See techniques 12 and 49, above.) This term has been derived more from Wolpe than from anyone else; he has advocated and built much of his therapy on teaching patients to practice deep muscle relaxation (following Jacobson). Relaxation is opposite (reciprocally inhibiting) to anxiety or "nervousness," and is thereby a useful therapeutic tool. It prepares the patient to withstand aversive conditions, prepares him for more problem solving, and allows him to bring important aspects of his behavior under self-control. Relaxation, as indicated earlier, may be practiced in connection with a hierarchy. One finds the least anxiety-provoking situation in relation to a larger problem and then practices relaxation (and desensitization) around this particular point, going on, later, through succesive steps to ever more anxiety-provoking steps and relaxing at each such point before proceeding. Relaxation in therapy is practiced in relation to almost any problem one can imagine: exam taking, asking an opposite sex member for a date, talking before a group, facing unpleasant thoughts or situations, getting to sleep, eating too fast, losing one's temper, and so on (Jacobson, 1938; Wolpe, 1958).

52. *Replaying tapes*. Although not a technique in the usual sense of the

term, asking the patient to replay tapes at leisure between sessions often proves to be fruitful for the patient. This procedure has been used often by therapists in the author's setting and patients report the following illustrative comments: "Why I never knew I sounded *that* way!" "I missed some things you said and I've thought about them since." "I realize from the tapes how whiny and complaining I sound." The replaying of the tapes serves to highlight important aspects of therapy, acquaints the patient with a somewhat more open view of himself, and serves as a "refresher" for the next session. The therapist could ask the patient to make written notes during the replaying as part of the agenda for the following session(s). Tapes made with couples could also prove beneficial in that each patient could gain a more objective view of how he or she sounded vis-à-vis the partner and how the therapy was managing what are sometimes adversary positions between the participants.

53. *Restitution*. The common-sense meaning here is fairly adequate for the behavioral practitioner: giving reparation, or restoring or making up for some destructive loss. A child damages the toy of another child; the first child makes up the loss by somehow restoring the article (buying a similar toy, repairing the toy, or paying a price for the toy). The child who comes in with muddy shoes "restores" the rug to its original, clean state by "making up his mess." He may be required to go outside, clean his shoes, and reenter the house with clean feet. He is then reinforced for this corrective behavior. Restitution is a much better corrective measure than just scolding or making one feel guilty for his wrong doing. Restitution should be "in kind," that is, should make up the loss in the same amount and kind that was originally suffered. It is also possibly reinforcing to the offender that he can really "make amends" and not have to carry on with guilt from his inappropriate actions. It is a good, clean, corrective measure. Restitution in counseling and psychotherapy can be seen in regard to agreeing that the patient "make up for" in some concrete way his aversiveness toward others (which the patient agrees needs restitution). (See, also, technique 40, "Overcorrection".)

54. *Reversal*. This is a somewhat technical term from operant behavior. It refers to the practice of reversing the reinforcing conditions that presumably lead to a given behavior. For example, a child who has cried too often in nursery school has been observed to gain social reinforcement when he cries, in terms of attention and solicitation of teachers. The teachers may then "reverse" the reinforcing conditions and give the child attention only when he succeeds in coping with his problems and avoids crying. One is, in this case, "reversing" the child's behavior by changing the previous reinforcement contingencies. Reversal may be practiced in therapy by first paying attention to the patient's many complaints (in

order to learn more about them and to understand his social/behavior context), but not continuing to reinforce his complaining, whining, or feeling sorry for himself. In the latter case, the therapist would ignore the complaints or change the topic and then reinforce, with attention and comments, the patient's discussion of positive problem-solving efforts.

55. *Satiation*. Satiation is used in a way not unlike that in common parlance: getting too much of a stimulus, so that it loses its reinforcement value. Satiation of drink, food, sex, or whatever leads to a diminution of the "value" of the article or activity. In psychotherapy or counseling one might regard existential problems as the product of plenty, perhaps over-affluence in society. A more common example of satiation, and one more specific and limiting, would be that having a child who had been caught lighting fires strike matches so much that he "never wanted to see a match again." A father once caught a son smoking and chewing tobacco where-upon the father got a plug of tobacco and made the son chew it until he was ill—"He got enough of that damned tobacco," the father averred. One might proceed to stop cigarette smoking by requiring the patient to smoke almost endlessly until he is repulsed by the smell, taste, and thought of cigarettes. (Also see "Flooding," technique 21 and "Implosion," technique 27) (Ayllon and Michael, 1959).

56. *Self-imposed time out*. This procedure means just what it says: One imposes a "time out" from some attractive but unwanted behavior. The idea for self-imposed time out may, indeed, arise from therapy, from discussions with others working on self-control, or from reading about it. Self-imposed time out implies a good deal of self-control in the first place, such that one can then extend this self-management on to some heretofore neglected area. Examples of self-imposed time out have arisen in clinical practice with people saying "I'll just not eat any more" and then getting up from the table; or with people saying "I've seen enough TV—on to other things" even though the program viewed or the attractiveness of the situation lingers for the person. In everyday life, many of us impose such constraints on ourselves, or, once succumbing to an unwanted but attractive behavior (a kind of "attractive nuisance"), then decide to bring a halt to the activity. Self-imposed time out mostly refers to mild but nonetheless wasteful use of time, self-indulgences in entertainment or recreation, engaging too long in "bull sessions." Students in dorms and other collective social situations often display many examples of spontaneous social activities that take place in lieu of more arduous tasks such as studying or working (Mahoney and Thoresen, 1975). (Also see "Time out," technique 62).

57. *Shame-aversion therapy*. This technique is based on aversive stimulation and attempts to bring the patient's behavior under aversive

control through verbal means (using shame). This method does not necessarily suggest alternative behaviors. It is a "commonsense" method used by many parents to cause the child to give up some unpleasant behavior (e.g., spitting at others), and may have only weak effects on one's behavior (Rubin, et al., 1972). Its use in therapy and counseling may be suspect.

58. *Shaping*. Shaping is a central concept in behavior change. It refers to progressive approximations toward a goal or end result. In animal experimentation, shaping is demonstrated by experimentally inducing the animal to progressively turn more and more in (say) a clockwise direction until the animal is not reinforced with food until it has made the entire 360° turn. This is accomplished by first picking up on a spontaneous turn of a small degree by the animal; the consequence of this is food reinforcement. The animal is then reinforced again, contingent on turning slightly more in the same direction (no reinforcement occurs if the animal does not make the slight turn), and so on until the full circle is completed. Shaping is shown in the acquisition of element and motor skills such as dressing among children, retardates, and others with relative meager behavioral repertoires. Shaping applies, as well, to more complex skills and with more resourceful learners, as in programmed instruction. The application of shaping to therapy or counseling is less clear-cut and more subject to problems of control of stimulus conditions and reinforcement. However, it may be demonstrated in increasing concentration or study time from a few minutes to hours; in all kinds of attention-requiring situations; in developing self-control regarding eating, exercise, and the like; and in the development of social and interpersonal skills (Mahoney and Thoreson, 1975). (Also see "Backward shaping," technique 4.)

59. *Skills training*. Although not a technique, per se, it is a term that points to the importance of skills in one's behavioral repertoire. Many personality, adjustment, and emotional problems are due to lacks in social skills, rather than constituting problem-entities that have to be uncovered or exhumed. The shy person, the emotionally withdrawn person, is often one who lacks functional social skills; hence therapy consists in part in teaching these skills, building new social reinforcers for them, and not in exploring endlessly how these people feel about their inadequacies or how the deficits came to be. There is increasingly good reason to think that depressive characteristics hinge to a great extent on loss of social reinforcers or on the relative absence of social skill development during childhood and adolescence (Ferster, 1973; Sowards and Phillips, 1975). One important part of problem behavior is what we might call "skill deficits." That is, behavior problems exist and are fostered in social situations where people lack the social skills needed to function adequately. When such a

situation becomes chronic, the deficits appear as "depression," or the patient shows other types of emotional problems. Correspondingly, when the deficits can be overcome or ameliorated, the depression lifts and other socially related, functional problems are overcome or improved. Skill training in a general way is, then, an important part of behavior change processes. A good deal of counseling and psychotherapy are given over to promoting social skill development.

60. *Target behaviors*. In a sense this is a behavior technique, with a high degree of specificity, and in another sense it is a broad-based way of approaching problem solving in general. The exact behaviors to be changed are targeted by specifying them clearly, gaining some knowledge of how, when, and where they occur, and addressing change efforts to them. All the behavior techniques described here are dependent to a great extent on specifying the target behaviors that are up for change.

61. *Thought stopping*. Sometimes people are obsessed with unwanted, highly repetitive thoughts, usually of a nonsensical or nonfunctional nature. One patient would look at a ruddy-complexioned person and say repetitively to himself "red cheeks . . . red cheeks . . ." while still trying to carry on a social interaction. Usually repetitive thoughts are inimical to social interaction and to personal tranquility. Several things can be done to stop unwelcome thoughts. A simple procedure is to recognize that the thoughts occur in some settings and not others and to prepare one's self for this by identifying and avoiding certain cues that set off the unwelcome thoughts. A more aversive method may be that of snapping a rubber band on one's wrist when the unwanted thoughts occur. To a considerable extent, repetitive thoughts signal an overly self-centered, self-concerned person who needs to "get outside himself." Building indirect social skills and social alternatives to thinking about one's self can be helpful. A writing method may also be used: One can write down "I know I have this tendency to think certain things in this situation; I will admit this now, but I will not be put down by this tendency; I will go on with my social interaction and not be distracted by the thoughts." Sometimes the therapist's help may be directly enlisted; the patient tells the therapist when the thoughts begin to occur in the therapist's presence, and the therapist then firmly states "Stop." Social control in the hands of others can sometimes be a powerful stimulus to self-control. (See also "Aversiveness," technique 3.)

62. *Time out*. This refers to time out from positive reinforcement. A child is doing something that is unwelcome in a social situation; the child is inadvertently reinforced for this "bad" behavior through the attention it brings him (even though the attention may be critical or aversive). The child can be removed from the social situation in which this reinforcement

or attention is forthcoming, and allowed to return when the unwelcome behavior has ceased; or the child can be permitted to return contingent on his controlling the unwelcome behavior. A smaller kind of time out occurs when we no longer give eye contact or verbal response to another person who is doing or saying something of which we strongly disapprove. We sort of "turn our attention elsewhere," thus connoting that we are not interested (we don't respond with eye contact or gestures or words) in what he or she is saying, or that we may disapprove of his behavior. Perhaps everyone uses a little bit of time-out each day in his or her social interactions. (See also "Self-imposed time out," technique 56.)

63. *Writing (or writing therapy)*. This is simply a matter of using writing, in place of spoken words, to convey problems (writing down one's emotional concerns in contrast to talking about them orally) and to work out solutions. Elsewhere in this book writing therapy is more fully discussed (see Chapter 4). Writing has been a neglected method in the behavior modification field; writing is often more indelible and specific than oral methods. Also, in the face of "binding anxieties," one might write down his concerns instead of trying to think and talk to himself about them (see "Thought stopping," technique 61, above). Writing as a therapeutic measure is relatively specific and economical, and it may provide more self-reinforcement than simply talking about a problem. We usually make things "official" (sign checks, contracts, our name) in writing, thereby rendering them more important.

64. *Zen*. To many, the inclusion of Zen mediation might seem strange in a behavioral context. However, in recent years there has been much effort to try to understand the covert processes characteristic of Zen meditation of various types and to compare these with relaxation and desensitization and other more standard behavioral techniques (Shapiro and Zifferblatt, 1976). One may develop what can be termed covert self-control techniques to a fairly high order of reliability and thereby "clear the mind" of distractions, conflicts, and tensions. All of us resort at times—however imperfectly—to Zen-like control, just as we put to use behavioral techniques without so naming them. Bringing the two areas of self-control—or, rather, the somewhat different conceptual models of self-control—together may constitute an interesting and far-reaching problem for counseling and psychotherapy in the years to come. In behavioral terms, what seems to occur in the Zen conditions—if this term can be applied advisedly—is that one discerns ever more relaxing internal discriminative stimuli out of which some self-control can be developed (Shapier and Zifferblatt, 1976, p. 521). The control of breathing, as it is used in more standard relaxation exercises, may be the key to some kinds

of Zen meditation. Concentration, or the control of attention, may constitute other covert processes one can learn to discriminate ever more finely. Arranging personally effective conditions in which one can then bring about these Zen mediations is also important. In all instances, however, we are perforce dealing with internally discriminated stimuli and perhaps many instances of overtly discriminated conditions without being able to name and conceptualize them easily. This is similar, perhaps, to the ways in which a highly skilled musician coordinates his sense of pitch (internally discriminated) with his handling of his instrument. Where Zen meditation has emphasized internal, covert processes most behavioral modification practice has centered attention on the overtly discerned environment. There is no reason in science or in clinical practice why the two cannot be melded and thereby produce a more fruitful clinical practice and lead to new conceptual considerations in the understanding and control of behavior.

From this list of techniques the experienced clinician may gain an urge to branch out into more versatile behavioral intervention and the tyro therapist may be encouraged to try some behavioral intervention for the first time.

One should not gain the impression that all the techniques lie at the same level of complexity, or that one is as easily employed as another. In counseling or therapy, the choice of technique, or the versatile interplay among techniques, must come from therapeutic planning and careful conceptualizing. One has noted many fledgling therapists "trying out desensitization" with no thought of how it might fit the patient's complaints, just because the young therapists have read about the widely publicized relaxation and desensitization measures.

An exercise one might try is that of formulating a patient's problems clearly, together with possible target behaviors set up for modification, then playing through the list of techniques and selecting several for discussion with other therapists. One might then shake down four or five likely applicable techniques to one or two, based on conceptually clarifying the problem at hand. There should be free and stimulating interplay between technique and problem solving, such that greater clarity of therapeutic means and ends is achieved and more robust clinical skills developed.

Techniques, however, should never be regarded as an "end-all" or "be-all." They are primarily means to ends and the selection of means to behavior-change ends should be based on relevance to the patient and his situations, economy, and the competence of the therapist in implementing the techniques used. The vast range of behavioral techniques are to be drawn on selectively as they increase the repertoire of skills and conceptualizations of the therapist; they are not to be imposed on the patient as a kind of "psychological patent medicine."

CHAPTER 3

The Early Interviews

Many books have been written on interviewing in relation to psychotherapy or counseling. Few of these have, however, looked at the interview as a prologue or as an accompaniment to a behavioral position regarding therapy. Most earlier works on interviewing have looked upon this process as mainly a matter of gaining information from the client, and to some extent as a matter of imparting information. In the present framework, interviewing pursues a more systematic purpose, and this purpose is best illustrated in the phrase joint problem-solving.

All aspects of the therapeutic interview serve a problem-solving purpose. Information is not gathered for the sake of information; since one cannot be sure in advance what information will be most relevant, the matter must remain open. Likewise, information is not exchanged for the sake of the exchange, unless it is put to the problem-solving endeavor.

Interviewing from an older and nonbehavioral perspective sought to uncover causes of a problem in the history of the individual, the most illustrative example being the uncovering techniques of the psychoanalyst. In the present perspective, the causes of behavior—especially complex behavior where the original stimulating conditions cannot be ascertained with any reliability—reside in the *consequences* of the behavior in the environment. The therapist or counselor is or can become an important factor in managing consequences for the patient. The therapist is always geared to look for patient behaviors that are unwanted, that can readily submit to problem-solving efforts, and for behavior that can to some extent be immediately influenced by the therapist or by the patient. The therapist is not just a sophisticated recording device to "take down" or "interpret" the events and concerns (however important these may sometimes be) typifying the patient's life; he is an active participant in remediating these concerns and must always react to the patient with this potential clearly present in his or her behavior.

The basis for the therapist's actions in interviews becomes less passive, reflective, or interpretive, but more selective and discriminatory and reinforcing. The therapist knows in advance how the interviewing might proceed—at least generally in regard to agendas, logs, extra-therapy-hour, assertive efforts, and the like—and what kinds of leverage or contingency management will be needed in order to promote effective problem solving.

Early on the therapist must find some evidence of the main problem presented by the patient (although this is often at first a matter of inference) and the range of problems as well. Unfortunately, patients do not come into therapy with their problems neatly tagged and bundled. In fact, owing to the preoccupation with feelings and the corresponding neglect of the *conditions* under which the feelings occur and are reinforced, the beginning patient often knows little about his problems in the manner needed for efficient therapeutic problem-solving. This makes therapy an intriguing enterprise because as the therapist interacts verbally and makes observations on the patient's nonverbal behavior as well, he or she strikes one hypothesis after another as to what the problem might be (not just named but *conceptualized*), how the problem is maintained (reinforced), and what competing behaviors in the repertoire of the patient might be strengthened or weakened in the problem-solving stance.

It is particularly true in the case of therapy with adults, using primarily verbal/oral face-to-face procedures, that a lot of selection goes into stating and conceptualizing a problem. If one is dealing with children in a school setting, problems are not as hard to identify, name, and remedy. Here one has direct, observational access to the behavior in question and to the environmental conditions. In the case of an adult reporting verbally on his or her problems, the therapist is obliged to take the patient's report at face value (which the therapist may alter in several ways), and the therapist is seldom given much information on the consequences of the patient's unwanted and troublesome behavior unless the word of others (spouse, fellow student, teacher, employer, etc.) is readily available. We have to find out first from the patient how he meets a situation involving distress, how he interacts with others in regard to the distress, and what the consequences are. Some have called these the ABC's of behavior change: The antecedent conditions, the behavior in question (the unwanted, distressful behavior), and the consequences. Often these are complexly intermingled; but the conceptualization of this paradigm as a guide to unraveling some of the features of the problem behavior cannot be denied.

One can, of course, go too far and too long in getting a recital of what's wrong with a patient—from the patient or from others. One can dwell too long on the so-called pathology and, correspondingly, too little on the circumstances or on remedial efforts. Since most patients have not paid very much attention to the circumstances, but have paid relatively more to the distress (the feelings), they are particularly well versed in the latter.

One reason for the existence of so many therapeutic and counseling theories is that these theories have traditionally woven complex causal accounts (almost always hypothetical) of the origins of the complaints (symptoms); and have given very little concern to the environmental conditions[1] and to the consequences of the unwanted, distressful behavior. When the environment is taken more into account, there is less need for hypothetical, causal, historical theories. The proliferation of theories has now become more of a hindrance than an asset (Patterson, 1966, 1973); and the location of the significant variables in the "head" (the psyche, in mentalistic terms) may have made interesting reading in books on counseling and therapy, but it has probably not advanced the science much, nor has it lead to practical advantages for the patient.

Although patients want help in reaching a way out of their impasses and distresses, they are not usually very much concerned about theory or about conceptual accounts of their problems. The conceptual parts are of more value to the therapist and may benefit and guide him in approaching the patient, but this intriguing enterprise should not get in the way of the patient's behavior change. *The therapist should always learn from the patient and be ready to change the conceptualization in favor of the facts and in favor of what works from a practical viewpoint.* Orthodoxy, then, is not welcome; although the behavioral position is reasonably clear about its methodology, particular formulations or conceptualizations of the patient's problems should not get in the way of new evidence. What we as therapists initially think is reinforcing to the patient may not be the case; flexibility is the order of the day in therapy.

The therapy interview is a complex matter, but one has nonetheless to proceed in the best way possible. Given this practical requirement and the likelihood that all patients will appear different in many important ways (although they will also appear to be similar, at least conceptually, in

[1] This point requires some clarification. One may argue cogently that past theories of psychotherapy have included environmental considerations: witness the work of Adler, Fromm, Sullivan, and many others. However, with most of the older and more traditional therapists, the "environment" meant more the interpersonal context, the culture itself, and the effects of child-rearing practices on the behavior and attitudes of the older patient. No one would dispute the relevance, validity, and therapeutic efficacy of these older viewpoints. But "environment" today in the behavioral context signals not only these broad considerations—important as they are in understanding behavior—but many more *specific* issues, such as how reinforcement operates, the importance of reinforcement contingencies as vital aspects of interpersonal relationships, the role of reinforcement in maintaining even unwanted behavior, the role of the therapist in helping to bring about environmental changes by and through changing the consequences of the patient's behavior (or helping the patient accomplish this himself), and the role of the therapist in actively stressing the important role of self-management as it is encouragingly pursued by the patient in his own behalf.

many ways), how then do we move into the initial interviews with some order, purpose, and problem-solving acumen?

The following schema is an outline for the therapist or counselor who wishes to proceed from one behavioral vantage point in dealing with patient's problems in verbal, face-to-face interactions.

Interpersonal, Verbal, Therapeutic
Schemata from One Behavioral Viewpoint

I.   Presenting complaint(s)
II.   Circumstances under which complaints seem to occur
III.   What patient has done about present or past complaints/success of same
IV.   Behavioral log
V.   What patient can now do to improve the situation
VI.   Instances of adequate behavior
VII.   Goals
VIII. Revision and extension of change process

Same Schemata, More Detail

I.   Presenting complaint(s)
   A.   General
   B.   Specific
II. Circumstances
   A.   Time of day
   B.   Home/school/work/free social situations
   C.   Effects of drugs/medicines on complaints (if used)
   D.   Competitive or noncompetitive circumstances
   E.   People: parents/spouses/teachers/peers/boss, etc.
   F.   Repetitive nature of complaints
III. What patient has done . . .
   A.   Patient's own efforts
   B.   Past therapy/counseling
   C.   Success/failure of past efforts/areas of no change
   D.   Did efforts to change depend upon others—parents, spouse?
IV. Behavioral log
   A.   Provides "baseline" data
   B.   Provides current data
   C.   Puts therapy in the present
   D.   Tests patient's resourcefulness now
   E.   Based on actual behavioral data
   F.   Helps patient to see the ABC's of his complaints

G. Emphasizes critical incidences, not history for its own sake
H. Shows patterns, trends, cyclic nature of difficulties
I. Reveals patient's strong and weak points in self-help effort, etc.

V. What patient can now do . . .
   A. Role playing in office
   B. Whole armamentarium of behavior techniques (see Chapter 2)
   C. Special skill development
   D. Whole emphasis on skills and strong points in repertoire
   E. Paying attention to patients in-therapy behavior vis-à-vis therapist

VI. Instances of adequate behavior
   A. Past and present
   B. Problem solving and reinforcing value of past successes

VII. Goals
   A. Original goals (by implication, complaints were goals)
   B. Revised goals
   C. Projected plans to carry out revised goals

VIII. Revision and extension of change process
   A. Follows from revised goals
   B. Leaning-out sessions
   C. Termination
   D. Follow-up

I. *Presenting complaint(s)*. A complaint about unwanted behavior may range all the way from an unspecific "I'm depressed," to "I want to learn to control my temper in my job situations." People report distress rather than specific behaviors to be changed, although the latter may occur with people who have thought about their difficulties and can verbalize them clearly. Often in therapy it is useful for the therapist to write down "complaints" offered by the patient; and then number and note them again as they come up in the discussion. These notes form a kind of "complaint baseline." The following are some transcribed notes taken in the first interview with a college junior who presented himself at a psychological clinic for help with interpersonal problems (with girlfriend, roommate, and a person he worked with on a part-time job).

THERAPIST. Can you tell me what brought you in and what we can work on together . . . ?

PATIENT. Well . . . I . . . . I have this problem with my temper too much—and too often, I guess. With my girlfriend . . . I guess it is too often anyhow . . . she says it is.

THERAPIST. I see. It's been bothering her and maybe you, too—the temper, I mean?

PATIENT. Yes . . . well, yes . . . well, that's why I'm here. I really get too angry at her at times . . . (thoughtful pause, head down toward the floor).

THERAPIST. And the anger and temper has gotten in the way of your relationship with her?

PATIENT. Oh . . . yes, it has. And I also get pretty disgusted—angry, I guess you'd say—with my "roomie" too.

THERAPIST. Has the anger gotten out of bounds there too?

PATIENT. Oh, I'll say it has . . . I threw a chair at him the other evening and cut his forehead some . . . it really didn't hurt him or draw much blood, but I guess it scared us both pretty awful.

THERAPIST. Those are two pretty important relationships for you—the girlfriend and the "roomie"?

PATIENT. Yeah, they are . . . and I wouldn't want to lose either of them (head bowed to floor again, rubbing hands in lap).

THERAPIST. Is this anger a more general problem, also? Are there other instances of how it gets out of hand?

PATIENT. Well sometimes I get mad in a store if a clerk won't wait on me or doesn't get what I want to show me or to let me try on. (Thoughtful pause—raised head to look at therapist) . . . But that doesn't happen very often. . . .

THERAPIST. So . . . it's not as much trouble?

PATIENT. No, but my work alongside of Bill at the restaurant . . . I get pretty upset with him when we're dishing out vegetables to our customers.

THERAPIST. And how does this upset show itself with him?

PATIENT. Well I walked off the serving line the other evening and then balled him out loud and strong—I'm sure the customers heard me—when he came back into the kitchen to see what was the matter with me.

The above-cited notes were from a tape transcription of the therapy hour and, like any verbatim transcript, convey a lot of information about the patient and the therapeutic interaction. The therapist at the same time made the following notes, which would have sufficed without the tape and which would give the therapist or anyone following his protocol an overview of the patient's presenting problems.

Problems—
I. *Loses temper.* "I really get upset with her" (g.f.)
   (a) Girlfriend
   (b) Roommate (no name given)—calls him "roomie." Threw chair—scared patient. self
   (c) Impatience at work—Bill—serves food with him in cafe
   (d) Impatience in stores

Following this same procedure of listing the presenting complaints, additional therapist's notes revealed that the patient was also unable to study effectively (could not concentrate very long, lost track of what he was reading, and tended to study in short, fitful spurts); got into frequent "hassles" with his parents over money and letter-writing; and had been fired the previous summer from two jobs owing to not showing up on time and to losing his temper when given instructions or corrections on the jobs.

Although it is best not to conceptualize too soon, it would appear that a general problem of *self-control* is evident: It shows up in the temper outbursts with several people (we do not yet know the exact provocations, whether they are prompted by verbal remarks by the other person, or what . . .); with study and concentration difficulties; and with a recent history of job-related problems, also probably arising out of temper outbursts.

It would not be amiss for the therapist to say, after the patient and therapist discussed the presenting complaints thus far, something like this:

THERAPIST. It might be possible to characterize all of these problems as examples of loss of self-control, might it not?

PATIENT. Yeah . . . (thoughtfully, looking at the floor again) . . . but why do they occur so much? I guess everyone has some temper now and then . . . but I seem to have too much. . . .

THERAPIST. The why's and wherefore's and specific conditions will have to be ferreted out as we go along . . . but for now, it might be useful just to caption this set of presenting difficulties as possibly representing examples of self-control problems.

There is no diagnosis here, no labeling, no invidious comparisons, no resort to deep-seated emotional and historical problems—not anything but a possibly useful verbal handle on the matter of presenting complaints in a way that suggests gainful ways of working on their solution.

The discussions above took about 20–25 minutes with some exchange between the patient and therapist not reported here relating to the number of college courses taken, the hours worked at the restaurant each week, and similar fill-in but sometimes useful information. At this juncture, the therapist might raise the following issue for consideration:

THERAPIST. Now you've given me a good résumé of some important problems you want to work on here. I think we can do that . . . work on them together to help you overcome them.

PATIENT. Yeah, I sure hope so . . . I just feel I *have* to do something . . .

something now . . . something pretty soon (appeared to have tears in his eyes, and he rubbed them several times while looking at the floor).

THERAPIST. Well, that's our purpose here. I wonder if you could take some notes on your upsets, or temper, or whatever you call it . . . and let us go over them when you come in the next time. Sometimes notes taken in between sessions helps to pin down problems, to get more details on who, how, when, where . . . and like that. We call that a log.

PATIENT. Sure . . . sure . . . I can do that . . . I can . . . I can do that.

This last point anticipates a further item in our schemata . . . getting the patient to keep a log (a kind of "psychological temperature chart") on his "ups" and "downs," and will be gone into more fully below. Introducing it here illustrates how the schemata have to bend and give to meet exigencies and idiosyncrasies in the therapy hour with a given person.

Back to the schemata:

II. *Circumstances* (under which the presenting complaints occur). As everyone knows, complaints (problems, symptoms) do not occur in a vacuum, but are intimately related to other people and special circumstances, and are characteristically related to the individual's repertoire as a result of past learning.

Revealing the circumstances may include such seemingly prosaic conditions as *time of day* (sluggishness in getting started, being late for appointments or classes, being unusually sleepy at given times of the day, not being able to work or study until late at night, and conflicts with other peoples' schedules); situations that arise at home, school, or office, and so on. Especially with children and adolescents, perhaps with young adults as well, the time of day appears to have a strong effect on efficiency and effort; and, failing these efforts, leading to depressive aftermath.

Since drugs and medicines are extremely common these days, people tend to resort to sleeping pills, "pep" pills, and tranquilizers, and have trouble functioning without these nostrums. Among young people, such as high school, college, and university populations, these medications are often relied upon to "get started" or to "slow down" when the person does not pace himself adequately.

Many times anxieties arise in *competitive situations:* speaking in class, taking exams, competing for the attention of a member of the opposite sex, mingling comfortably in social groups, and so on.

Not infrequently, problems become centered in the home, the school, or the job setting, or in "free" social situations where one's responses are not clearly structured; and possibly not all these settings are involved. Behavioral tendencies in reacting to others and in handling others' reactions to ourselves may take on special significance (for better or worse) in particular settings such as at school or on the job. It is not as often observed that people have problems in all situations but, rather, they tend to have problems centered around given types of interactions (asserting themselves in the face of opposition, persevering in the face of hardships, getting up courage to try a difficult problem, etc.); and these characteristics may generalize to other situations, or may be contained under special circumstances only. The important matter here is whether one can use the acceptable and functional behavior characteristic of one situation to solve problems and develop more adequate behavior in other, deficit situations.

It seems almost too trite to mention, but other people do figure importantly in one's problems. Even those problems we tend to ascribe to ourselves, such as depression, low self-esteem, and the like, are learned in association with others. Depressive reactions, at least reactive–depressive conditions, stem almost entirely from disappointments suffered in relation to others—loss of job, poor report on one's efforts by a boss or teacher, loss of a loved one, financial reverses, and so on. Low self-esteem is a kind of summary statement in which a person stamps a lot of his or her behavior with an ''I am a failure'' feeling. Upon examination of the particulars, the therapist may find that a patient so characterizing himself will report he has done poorly on exams, or has done shoddy work on his job, or has found it difficult or impossible to please or be pleased by a spouse or intimate friend. Generalized feelings of low self-worth stem from repeated circumstances where the person has found himself wanting—or at least not living up to his own expectations or behavioral demands on himself.

Of importance here in this discussion of special circumstances related to complaints is the fact that the therapist has to pick up knowledge of these circumstances and analyze them to find out where the loss of reinforcement, or the failure to receive reinforcement, occurs and what can be done about this. It is not enough to report low self-esteem; we know that it represents some failure in the delivery of reinforcement, and we need to know more about these circumstances and how they can be remedied.

An excerpt from a therapy interview will illustrate this last point and draw into focus our discussion of circumstances.

THERAPIST.   You were going to tell me more about some of the circumstances under which you lose your temper.

PATIENT.   Oh yes . . . yes . . . I can think of one or two examples lately. One was with my roommate who I did a favor for—picked up his laundry and some cleaning and some other things—and he didn't want to pay me back for the money I spent until the end of the month which is a long time from now. I said I thought he was being unfair and that he still owed me some money from last month.

THERAPIST.   That was pretty irresponsible of him, you felt?

PATIENT.   Yes, I did feel that way . . . (long pause) . . . I sat and mulled it over like I'm doing now and then I got up out of my chair and let him have it with a good cussing-out . . . (long pause as he wiped his face several times with a handkerchief).

THERAPIST.   Did he seem to think you had a point?

PATIENT.   Yes he did . . . later, though . . . not then. I have let him get away with this money stuff too often.

THERAPIST.   I see. There have been other times when he's owed you money and hasn't paid you? (Pause) You tend not to assert yourself at appropriate times?

PATIENT.   Yes, like I said, he owed me money from last month—it isn't much . . . maybe a few dollars, but I don't like the idea very much. I'm too weak unless I'm angry.

THERAPIST.   How does it happen that you do him these favors and he does not reimburse you? . . . and this goes on . . .

PATIENT.   (Breaking in) . . . Yeah, that's a good question. Why do I do these favors for him, especially money favors . . . (pause thoughtfully) . . . that's a good question.

THERAPIST.   You get pretty angry at him when he disappoints you . . . its not very reassuring or reinforcing to you to have him turn you down when he owes you money, especially when you did him a favor over and above the money part.

PATIENT.   (Shakes his head "yes") . . . (long pause) . . . I just give in when he asks me to do a favor, hoping it will be different this time . . . and (pauses) . . . and it never is. . . .

THERAPIST.   Does he sweet talk you, or promise you something?

PATIENT.   No, not really. Our relationship is pretty fair when we don't have a conflict such as this in our relationship.

THERAPIST.   What if you asked him for the money first?

PATIENT.   I don't know . . . I never thought of *that*. (Pause) I guess I just expect him to be fair and he isn't . . . and that makes me mad as hell . . .

THERAPIST.   But you go ahead the next time and do it all again the same way?

It is apparent from this discussion that one particular circumstance or interaction plays a big role in this young man's problems as he discusses them with his therapist. The patient is being disappointed—nonreinforced in the expected way—by his roommate; and, lacking assertiveness on his own part, the patient lets the roommate talk him into the same favor again. The patient's temper is a reaction to his frustration; the temper is a function of the situation, and if we can change the situation, we can alleviate the likelihood of the temper. The temper does not solve the problem anyhow—it only leads to more guilt and depression on the patient's part—and when the heat of the current situation is past, the patient reverts back to his old behavior and ends up again in the same compromised situation with his roommate. A good relationship with the roommate is thereby impaired. The patient gets no reinforcement from the roommate in this kind of interaction. The whole matter is a redundant, nonproblem-solving impasse. It is the task of the therapeutic interaction to break the impasse and get some new behavior in the situation first by the patient and later by the roommate.

As time went on, the patient learned to be more assertive toward his roommate and either asked for the money in advance of doing the favor or declined doing the favor. In behavioral terms, the interaction between the patient and his roommate took on reinforcing properties—the patient was glad to do the favor and was reimbursed—and the roommate developed more spontaneous respect for the patient and even offered to do some favors for him (taking the patient to the roommate's home for a weekend and letting the patient use his, the roommate's, tux for a special dance). For the patient, learning to be assertive was, among other things, very gratifying (reinforcing), and not only avoided impasses with the roommate, but kept the relationship on a "going" basis and netted a plus in getting some extra favors from the roommate; these were likewise reassuring and reinforcing.

In delineating the circumstances, the therapist and patient worked out the causes of the problem (a redundant pattern of ineffective interpersonal problem solving), helped the patient develop some new behaviors, and increased the repertoire of the patient in several ways in dealing with his roommate. Not recorded here but of interest was the fact that two other problem areas in regard to temper outbursts (involving his girlfriend and an associate on a part-time job) were also remediated somewhat. The patient realized that he lacked assertiveness in the *beginning* of an exchange, that he had to set his own limits more clearly vis-à-vis the other person, and that he had been heretofore a victim of interactions he helped to produce and maintain. His temper had been a short-range kind of letting-off-steam (which is reinforcing in the face of frustration), but it tended to accumulate long-range aversive consequences (guilt, anger, feeling weak and inadequate), which is why he presented himself for therapy.

III. *What patient has done.* What the person has done in the past to solve his problems, and whether they are similar to the presenting ones or not, is of moment to the therapist as an item of information on the patient and as a potential source of reinforcement as the patient works on current issues. It is probably safe to say that most people solve most of their problems most of the time, and that far more people solve problems of a personal nature than succumb to the problems. This is not to deny that perhaps one in ten in our population will have had at least a brush with hospitalization sometime in his or her life, an occurrence which probably represents the lowest decile in problem-solving efforts in the general population. The other 90% of the population solve their problems at least with a modicum of success most of the time. Thus it is realistic to look for past problem-solving efforts on the part of even the most disturbed patient, and to point up these adequacies to people as they work on the more formidable problems. It is useful to take examples of adequacy from their own lives, but it is important to get them to actually use the same behaviors to approach and solve current problems.

In the course of therapy for the young man in the above illustration, it was also shown that he had had some temper problems with his athletic coach in junior high school and with a debate coach in high school. In these instances, the patient had been able to ward off the temper problems partly because the athletic coach was also a boy scout leader for the patient, and the debate coach was occasionally his Sunday school teacher. The additional roles of these coaches tended to modify the reactions of the patient toward them in the critical, school-related situations, and the credibility of being a scout leader and a Sunday school teacher tended to offer other reinforcements for the temper-ridden patient during his junior and senior high school days. The therapy discussion along these points went as follows:

THERAPIST. You mentioned last time that in junior high school you also had trouble with your temper—I believe it was in football or some other competitive sports setting?

PATIENT. Yeah, that was right.

THERAPIST. What do you now think might have happened then to keep the temper from getting out of hand and . . . ?

PATIENT. (Interrupting) . . . Oh, I guess it was because Mr. J.—we called him that—was also my scout master, and I was very interested and absorbed in scouting then.

THERAPIST. I see. It was sorta like saying because Mr. J. was more than one thing to you—coach and scoutmaster—you dare not show your worst side, so to speak, and prejudice him too widely against you when you had the temper outbursts.

PATIENT. I think that was right . . . I remember (pauses, scratches his head) . . . I remember even discussing this with my mother who got after me when I "blew it" in a football game when I lost my temper after being called out-of-bounds by the referee when I caught a pass and was about to run for a touchdown. That was just a junior high school game, but it was very important to me . . . and the loss of the scoring attempt left me greatly frustrated.

THERAPIST. And you reacted with a temper outburst?

PATIENT. I did . . . and I got kicked out of the game.

THERAPIST. Did the coach speak with you then or later about the episode?

PATIENT. He did . . . and my mother did too that evening! She said I would have to stop football and competitive sports if I didn't hold my temper better.

THERAPIST. And what temper outburst had you shown on that occasion?

PATIENT. I took the football and threw it down against the ground, and it bounced off the field and into the bleachers . . . and people laughed and booed me . . . and (pause . . .) I was so embarrassed . . . even humiliated at myself.

THERAPIST. This was a kind of showdown or confrontation you had with yourself?

PATIENT. Yes.

THERAPIST. And with your mother?

PATIENT. Yes . . . oh yes, and with the coach.

THERAPIST. How did the coach handle you?

PATIENT. Well, he moralized a lot, but it got to me . . . and he said I was not only not playing well when I did that sort of thing but I was not using the lessons about fair play and sportsmanship that I learned from him in scouting—he emphasized these things more than ethics or morals, but he could put on the pressure if he wanted to make a point about morals. I guess he stayed away from morals if he thought the person could handle his own behavior, but if it was a difficult situation, or if the guy was out of line very much, he didn't stop from calling on all kinds of powers from fair play on out to what God would think.

THERAPIST. I see . . . he held a lot of persuasive power, playing two important roles with you in your school and personal life?

PATIENT. He sure did!

THERAPIST. How, then, is the present effort to control your temper similar to and different from the one in junior high school?

PATIENT. I don't know for sure, but maybe the coach was a big person to me then . . . an important person I could not get around—what he thought of me was pretty important.

THERAPIST. And today there is no one in your life who is quite that important? (Pause) Not even your boss? Or girlfriend? Or roommate?

PATIENT. I never quite thought of them in this light, but you have a point there . . . I guess I can always get around all these people (pause) . . .

THERAPIST. You mean your girlfriend can be gotten around . . . or replaced if necessary?

PATIENT. Yeah . . . that's not very nice to say, or not a very good way to look at her, but I guess it is part of the problem.

THERAPIST. In other words, there has to be some constraint on your temper tendencies . . . by yourself, or by another person whom you fear and respect so much you will control your temper to please them.

PATIENT. Yes, but self-control in the end is the best thing.

THERAPIST. I am inclined to agree . . . for there may not always be a strategically placed person—a coach, a friend or whomever—to hold you down. You have to do it yourself.

PATIENT.   I know that . . . and that is why I am here.

THERAPIST.   It seems we've said that some things . . . situations make you angry easily—too easily for comfort—and you have let your anger go unbridled. We called that a temper outburst. But in some situations in the past, you felt so much respect and made so much effort to control this tendency when in the company of important people, you went some of the way toward self-control. . . .

PATIENT.   (Interrupting) . . . but it wasn't enough or it didn't stick well enough, and so now I am in the same boat again.

THERAPIST.   We need to see how you were somewhat successful *then* and, while the situations now are not the same, we can relate them somewhat and learn from the past.

PATIENT.   Uh huh (thoughtfully) . . . (long pause). . . .

THERAPIST.   Having some new ideas now?

PATIENT.   Yeah, I'm wondering why I don't think enough of *myself,* and also some of these other people, to control my temper now.

THERAPIST.   That's a very good thought to pause about. . . .

PATIENT.   (Looks up, smiles, pauses) . . . I think I am too sure of being angry or disappointed, and I don't care who gets in my way . . . I just want to have it out—the temper, I mean.

THERAPIST.   And . . . so to hell with everyone else and everything. . . .

PATIENT.   I seem to feel that way at times—at the worst times, I seem to feel that way. . . .

THERAPIST.   Maybe two issues are here—why you feel so angry in the first place, and, how to control the anger so you don't place others in jeopardy, or make yourself look so bad.

PATIENT.   Yeah, there are these two things all right . . . all right. . . .

THERAPIST.   We've seen that you could control your temper in the past, even though the situation and the issues may not have seemed as serious or frustrating as now, but you did then pay attention to others, what they thought of you and the influence they had on you. Today you tend to be superior, we might say, not take others into consideration, and maybe you consider the frustration greater than it is in reality.

PATIENT.   I think I react too strongly when upset . . . or frustrated as you said. (Pause) But I also take things into my own hands too harshly now and really give out with the anger.

THERAPIST.   They are both interrelated—the tendency to be too brittle in the face of frustration and the letting go when you are angry—maybe they are two sides of the same coin.

PATIENT.   They really are . . . (pauses) . . . they really are the same thing.

THERAPIST.   If you are less sensitive, less easily frustrated in the first case, you react with less temper. If you react with less temper, out of self-control or concern for others' thinking of you, then you are less sensitive in the long run.

PATIENT.   They really are related . . . I see that. I think I can see that self-control in the first place—not getting upset so easily—or the threshold things as you said it—is the big thing here. If I don't get so upset, I am not so angry and not as likely to have a temper outburst.

THERAPIST.   That's pretty nearly it . . . (pause) . . . and what about high school and the debate coach and the problems then? What can we learn from them?

PATIENT.   The debate coach was a woman . . . a very pretty teacher I liked a lot . . . (pause) . . . maybe I even had a crush on her.

THERAPIST.   But you also got angry with her too much or too often?

PATIENT.   Or at the debate situation. Maybe she was important, maybe not.

THERAPIST.   For the details—how was the temper shown there? In the debate situation, I mean?

PATIENT.   Well, one evening I really did a good job debating and my partner and I felt we had won, but the judges decided otherwise, and I was really hurt . . . and angry . . .

THERAPIST.   And . . . ?

PATIENT.   And I threw my pencil and cards I had on the desk in front of me on the floor and hit my hand on the desk.

THERAPIST.   What happened then?

PATIENT.   Well, we were on a small stage in front of an audience and the curtains were not completely open and someone pulled them closed before—I guess before my full fury was seen or felt.

THERAPIST.   But it was pretty much a temper and it was seen by some people, wasn't it?

PATIENT.   Oh, yes, and my partner was embarrassed for me and probably for himself too.

THERAPIST.   You then settled down . . . or not?

PATIENT.   No, I got up and stomped—but not too loud—off to the sidelines, off the stage where the debate coach was . . . and I was ready to cry and fight and do anything.

THERAPIST.   The coach was helpful at this time?

PATIENT.   Not too much—I think she was stunned, although she knew I could get mad, because I had gotten mad before at other times.

THERAPIST.   She just didn't expect it here in a real debate with an audience and everything . . . ?

PATIENT.   Boy, I'll say not. I'm even sweating now to think about it and how silly I must have looked.

THERAPIST.   Embarrassment is often an accompaniment of these kinds of situations. . . .

PATIENT.   She called me in the next day before school and said I couldn't debate any more if I could not be a good loser or a good winner. (Pause) She was pretty tough on me. (Pause) The coach never said I couldn't play, but she said I couldn't debate if I didn't straighten up.

THERAPIST.   She had a good leverage that meant self-control or else . . . ?

PATIENT.   Boy she sure did!

THERAPIST.   Do you think—I know it is speculative—that if the football coach had laid down an ultimatum about your playing you would have shaped up sooner in regard to your temper?

PATIENT.   I don't really know . . . I think it might have helped me because I would be scared not to try to help myself, and I would not want to try and fail . . . you know what I mean?

THERAPIST.   I'm not sure—can you spell it out more?

PATIENT.   I . . . I mean if the coach had laid down the law I would have tried to control my temper . . . but if I had failed, it would have been even worse on me—(pause)—maybe it went just as well then, because I was . . . well, maybe . . . well . . . not sure I could control myself.

THERAPIST.   That is a reasonable conjecture, but it is a guess, we both know. (Patient looks at therapist and smiles and nods "yes.") But I am wondering if the other person's trying to help you, even with an ultimatum, is not a pretty constructive thing, because if no one says anything, if everyone lets you get by with the outbursts, then you don't try as hard and then you don't even respect trying.

PATIENT.   Yeah, I see what you mean. I just don't know. . . .

Later information revealed that the temper outbursts did decrease some throughout the rest of the patient's high school career. He became even more absorbed in extracurricular activities of all sorts—debates, athletics, plays, musical events—and was fairly successful, and less frequently on the losing side of contests.

It seemed somewhat relevant to note that his successes with self-control, while certainly not overwhelmingly convincing, were nonetheless aided by the constraints put down by others and by circumstances. In contrast, in the present situation, there have been no constraints put on him by those who could be other than punitive toward him (his boss almost fired him one evening after a temper display but showed no interest in helping the patient learn better self-control). His girlfriend seemed helpless in the face of the outbursts and tended to back off rather than to act more assertively toward the patient.

The present situation was in many ways a repetition of the junior and senior high school days when temper outbursts were common. Other therapy sessions dealt more with what was learned than with the loss of self-control, and emphasized how those lessons and observations might apply today. However, as with many patients, the current demands for self-control were so individually styled and so much related to particular circumstances, that the patient took some time to see how past mistakes and lessons could be profitably brought up-to-date. Some excerpts illustrate this point.

THERAPIST. We talked about how the temper in the past was finally reduced, or brought somewhat under control—didn't we?

PATIENT. Yes, we did.

THERAPIST. And what do you think we learned from that examination?

PATIENT. Well, I'm not sure but I think we could say I did find good reasons to try to control myself better then.

THERAPIST. And the lesson for today?

PATIENT. The same—but I think the situation is enough different now that I am not sure . . . (pause).

THERAPIST. A temper is a reaction to some pretty overwhelming frustration, disappointment, or the like?

PATIENT. True.

THERAPIST. One can experience this frustration no matter what his age.

PATIENT. That seems right.

THERAPIST. And one can have a good way of dealing with the frustration, or one can give in to it entirely with an angry outburst.

PATIENT. And that is what I did then . . . and maybe now . . . too.

THERAPIST. Seems likely . . . (pause) . . . don't you think?

PATIENT. So I have to do better with Carol (the girlfriend), and Mr. M____ (the boss), and anyone else . . . (pause) . . . maybe with Jim (the roommate) too . . . except it is harder with him because he provokes me so.

THERAPIST. Well, frustrations are similar, and provoking people are similar . . . and overreactions are similar . . . and thereby hangs the story.

PATIENT. Yup . . . I think you have a good point.

THERAPIST. What, then, do you think you can *do* in regard to these current situations? (Long pause) You don't have the coaches to warn or threaten or help you . . . but you do have our talks and the ability that comes with more maturity to figure out what you're doing and how you are affected by others. . . .

PATIENT. (Breaking in) I think I have to get on the ball and do more along these lines.

THERAPIST. Like what . . . for instance?

PATIENT. Well I can leave the room when Jim gets on my back . . . and I guess I should try that more . . . and then settle things with him later when I am not so upset and angry at him.

THERAPIST. That may be a good start; although turning away will avoid too much steam being built up right then and there, you may want to be less sensitive to what he says that gets you going in the first place.

PATIENT.   And I have to be more careful with Carol too. (Pause) I can see that she gets my goat when I want to do something and she opposes it, or when I think she is tired of me and is looking after someone else.

THERAPIST.   Some talks with her on those points may make a difference too . . . have you tried that?

PATIENT.   Yes, but mainly when I am angry with her and really not wanting to listen to what she's saying.

THERAPIST.   You got brought around in junior and senior high school by the firm leverage of those more powerful than you—the coaches, perhaps your mother—but now your troubles are with your peers (girlfriend and roommate) and with a boss you do not really have to rely on even if the chips were down . . . and so that throws you back on your own self-control more and suggests all the more how we look upon the problem and how we identify things to do to help you . . . well, they're all the more important.

PATIENT.   Yes, I think I am coming more and more to see that I have to do the things needed and not rely on someone else as a stopgap person for me.

In the therapy with this particular patient, several other issues came to the forefront as the discussions continued. The patient was able to discern more ways in which he had coped fairly well with problems and with some applications to the present situation. He said in one session, following the sessions reported above, that he felt he had probably done better in the past than he had allowed, and that he did a lot more positive things than he heretofore recognized. He had graduated with honors from high school and had done well in athletics and debate despite his temper outbursts. He was fairly popular with his peers—he held a class office and was accepted into several small hobby and social groups in his class. He felt pretty good about these accomplishments.

Problems today have histories, and although these histories do not need to be ferreted out in great detail, or over long spans of time, it is useful to get some problem-solving instructions from the past and update them in terms of current issues. It is also important for the patient to see clearly how he has worked productively in the past to try to solve problems.

Further aspects of the current review of past problems, in relation to presenting complaints, will be addressed below.

IV. *Behavior log.* With the use of the behavior log in therapy or counseling, one begins to make the change effort a current one, and the emphasis is placed on the day-to-day and week-to-week observations and attempts at change made by the patient. The logs are kept by the patient and are brought into the discussion each time with the therapist.

The log is simply a brief record of what the patient notes to be important in his or her daily life, including both positive and negative items. We often say to the patient that it is "a kind of emotional temperature record" that states the "ups" and "downs" of daily life. It may be regarded as a kind of baseline of self-observations by the patient, as well as a beginning point for change. The patient may speculate about what he thinks the cause or causes are for the reported feelings or behavior, but the observational record is most important. People need to gain better self-observation, if change is to be economically promoted.

The log has a number of values that might be summarized briefly:

1. Provides baseline data on incidents, persons, typical problems, frequency of occurrence, etc.

2. Provides current data that can be compared forward or backward in time with what the patient has reported or has actually done or may do in the future.

3. Puts the whole emphasis in therapy on problem solving in the present.

4. Tests a patient's resourcefulness now; tests a patient's willingness to participate in actual change efforts by reporting on and working on important aspects of his or her behavior.

5. Is based on actual events; feelings are included but related more specifically to events. One useful procedure here is to get the patient to state what the antecedent events may have been, a good description of the behavior in question, and the consequences of the reported behavior for the patient and/or others.

6. Emphasizes and gathers therapeutic momentum around critical events, not around history or feelings for their own sake.

7. Shows patterns, trends, and the cyclic nature of difficulties. Most problems recur and the log is a very economical and pointed way of bringing this redundance into focus. The fact that the unwanted behaviors tend to recur serves as a kind of confrontation to the patient (and perhaps to the therapist) that specific efforts at self-control are needed and that only passive talking about problems may not make them go away.

8. Shows the patient's strong and weak points in self-help efforts. The therapist then learns better where shaping may be required, what reinforcers might apply most relevantly, how confrontation may be useful, and how well the patient can establish a pattern of getting along on his own. The feedback to the therapist here is obviously great and therefore it is important to the patient's welfare.

9. Puts the patient into the business of changing his behavior from the very outset; and these changes then reinforce more change and build confidence.

The patient we discussed above in relation to his temper outbursts kept a log. The log showed how frequently the patient took offense at what others said—even when only "kidding" was involved; how vain the patient was in assuming that no one could challenge him or his intentions; how arrogantly the patient blamed others for his ills; how much he was dependent upon others in many trivial situations for his own self-esteem; how brittle was his self-confidence and self-esteem in a variety of situations.

One log made at the fourth or fifth interview related to an incident the patient brought in concerning an argument he had with his girlfriend. The log said:

"Big argument with Carol Tuesday evening. She won't go with me to S_____ this weekend; I blew up at her. She left me and has not been willing to talk with me for five days."

This log was, first of all, a pretty good record of what had happened between the patient and Carol, his girlfriend; it was typical of confrontations he experienced; and it started him thinking about how vulnerable he was to not having his expectations fulfilled by others. The log brought up some other issues that had gone on in his life the past week before the therapy hour, namely, that he had had an abrasive encounter with a clerk at the post office, that he had hung up on a friend he was trying to get some money from over the telephone, and that he had slammed the door and broken a glass window in a burst of anger at his work.

The log helped the patient and therapist to center on what appeared to be the main issues: the provocations, certainly; the matter of controlling temper outbursts; and the resultant depression, guilt, and remorse that followed them. Logs helped the patient articulate better what the antecedent events were, how the strong temper outbursts followed a pretty clear and predictable course, and how the consequences tended to be the same (guilt, alienation from others, resolve to try to do better, and a depressive aftermath).

Writing down incidents of the type cited above in the log served to bring home to the patient how often he walked right into the same problem and how thoroughly caught up he was in the problem of self-control. The value of the log in boldly stating a problem and its aftermath served better to clarify problems than any pronouncements, interpretations, and admonitions offered by the therapist. Had the therapy stopped abruptly after the fifth to seventh interview, the patient might have carried on his own therapy with some degree of success based on the accuracy and thoroughness of his note-taking up to that point.

The log served also to remind the patient of some of his past behaviors in regard not only to the problem of temper, but also the more favorable and assertive experiences he had had. The log serves as a reminder of the past and as a readier for the future.

After a while, the patient may be inclined to drop out the log keeping or to greatly reduce its detail. We have seen some patients start out with several pages of logs and end up with just a few words on a 3 × 5 card toward the end of therapy, or with no notes at all. In the case of dropping out note-taking altogether, the patient usually has distilled his problem situation down to a few economical and conceptually valid points and can then operate well in discussing them verbally. The log is, of course, a means to an end—better self-observations and reports in the interest of changing behavior—and not an end in itself.

Although the above discussion concerning the third item in this therapeutic schema (What patient has done in past) goes into fairly great detail during the second to fifth interviews, as the log keeping became more articulated, the references to the past dropped out, emphasis on the present increased, and the log provided direction for therapy week by week (the patient was seen for a total of 18 sessions, each on a weekly basis). By the fifth session, the log was the main verbal focus of therapy and remained so for another five or six sessions.

One could conduct therapy almost entirely by and through the use of the log and leave out any review of the past, except for that which came up as an adjunct to the points from the log itself.

Several times in the log keeping by the patient with the pronounced temper, the patient was encouraged to write out a statement such as the following: "Although I know I might lose my temper when I speak with _____, I will admit in advance that I am angry, and will then try to control myself, have a conversation, and make my point without the outburst." This procedure worked well with the patient on several occasions, especially where he could see a meeting or confrontation coming; where the confrontation and disputation were thrust upon him unexpectedly, it was as if he did not have time at first to prepare himself for this much exercise of self-control. In time, however, writing down the preparatory statement did bear fruit, as it has for many patients; and with greater self-control being practiced, the need for the "first aid" writing diminished (see Chapter 2, technique 63).

Many other patients using writing of preparatory statement have reported excellent progress in self-control, when used as part of their log keeping. One patient, a 25-year-old female office manager, used to become preoccupied with worry about her boyfriend and their stormy relationship, to the point of having to leave the office for several hours or for the remainder of the day after she got "into her snit." She wrote down the following statement: "I can expect to become worried about my relationship with Paul, and although that preoccupies me greatly, I will admit here and now that it is ungainful of me to spend my time this way—I will talk with Paul later and right now get back to my work." A 35-year-old engineer who had been used to slipping into preoccupation when unable to do calculations, learned how to control this distraction by writing down some such statement as the following: "I do not like to do these calculations, and I often get upset with them to the extent that I have to leave my desk and work for hours; although I feel like leaving, I will not give into this feeling, but will admit it's unpleasantness to me and then get down to the job and get it done." After about four or five "writings" of this type, the patient brought the preoccupation and distraction under control and even learned to enjoy doing the calculations (which became an important part of his job). He also boiled his lengthy original statement down to: "I must not be distracted—I must do my work."

We turn attention now to the next facet of the schema.

V. *What the patient can now do to improve the situation.* The log is the running core of the therapeutic endeavor; but it will fade out as the structure of the therapeutic interaction is established. Once the log is understood and followed, the important issues revolve around the manner in which the patient learns to take an ever-increasing role in self-management.

What the patient can do to aid himself will probably revolve around a number of specific objectives. In the case of the young student reported on above, self-management issues took the following course of events, as revealed in tape recorded interview excerpts:

PATIENT. It seems to me I have to do more to control my temper with Carol—you know we had that problem last week about my getting mad at her when she wouldn't go with me over a weekend . . . and then she wouldn't talk to me for several days after I blew up at her.

THERAPIST. Yes, I recall. I agree with you that an active effort to control the temper is strongly indicated.

PATIENT. I have to see her again tonight in regard to some lab reports we have to prepare together—I called her and she is willing to meet with me.

THERAPIST. How, now, do you think you can and will handle things tonight when you see Carol?

PATIENT. Well, I'll just try to be calm all the time . . . not raise any burning issues or old problems . . . and see how it goes.

THERAPIST. And if it goes well . . . ?

PATIENT. Just enjoy it I guess . . . (long pause) I could ask her out to dinner next Saturday night. . . .

THERAPIST. If the coast is clear with her?

PATIENT. Yes.

THERAPIST. And what if she's guarded and restrained?

PATIENT. It would be a good thing just to let the next date ride for now, I guess . . . although I am impatient to go out with her again.

THERAPIST. That's a good observation on your part—the noting of impatience. This is the culprit—if you can hold back on the impatience to go out with her—or to test out her willingness at this time—you may be doing two good things: helping yourself to better self-control in the face of pressures and cultivating a better relationship with her.

PATIENT. And the two go together well.

THERAPIST. Yes, indeed.

PATIENT. Well, I am to see her at her apartment at 7:30 and we can get our lab work done in an hour or two . . . and I can start to go home and maybe hesitate and ask her if she wants to go out for a beer or something.

THERAPIST. So far . . . so good—what next?

PATIENT. If she wants to go, I can play it cool and not push any in the conversation for another date. I guess if she won't go out for the beer, I can just cool it until next time I see her.

THERAPIST. That sounds pretty calm to me—you can do it that calmly, I assume?

PATIENT. I really think I can . . . I really must. I have a lot more to lose than anytime before if I don't.

THERAPIST. I would tend to agree.

PATIENT. Then, if she won't go out for the beer, or if I don't have an opportunity to try another date on her, I'll just have to wait for another time.

THERAPIST. That's good reasoning! And when would the next time come?

PATIENT. Oh, probably pretty soon. I will probably see her for tennis on Saturday, or I could drop by her place after I get off work Friday night about nine.

THERAPIST. That all sounds pretty good. The issue now is carrying it out.

PATIENT. That's right.

THERAPIST. And what about some other relationships where you might have a tendency to exercise impatience? Can you think of some other self-control arenas to work on?

PATIENT. Well, I'm still having some trouble with my boss. I have to talk with him about a summer job if he will have me.

THERAPIST. When and how can you see him and find out?

PATIENT. I go in for my paycheck this Friday night—I can speak to him then, I guess.

THERAPIST. Is that a good time—for you? For him?

PATIENT. I guess so . . . it's OK for me . . . and I suppose for him.

THERAPIST. Do you feel the need for any rehearsal on this?

PATIENT. It would be a good idea . . . (long pause) . . . Ahem: I could say, "Mr. Morris, I would like to work part time for you this summer."

THERAPIST. What might he then say?

PATIENT. I think he would probably agree . . . he likes me in spite of the trouble I've given him.

THERAPIST. You might be prepared for his saying "No." What then?

PATIENT. I would ask him why he felt that way, agree to try to hold my temper . . . and just handle it that way.

THERAPIST. Well that is a good start—let's see what we see! Any other areas of a similar nature where you should try out your new self-confrontation?

PATIENT. Well, my "roomie" is leaving to go home for the spring vacation period and he'll be away for a week or ten days . . . so there's nothing in that department for a while.

THERAPIST. You mean you won't have any interactions with him for a while.

PATIENT. That's right.

THERAPIST. Well, you have enough to do to cope with Carol and your boss . . . all that's a big order for you. Maybe the roommate needs no attention just now.

PATIENT. That's kinda the way I see it.

Subsequent interviews showed that the patient did, indeed, work things out better with Carol, and the boss said he would take the summer job proposal under consideration and give the patient an answer within a week. A later interview with the patient indicated that he and Carol were getting along much better and that the crisis in their relationship seemed to be passed. Later, the boss said he would hire the patient for the summer if business indicated the need, leaving a loophole of sorts. The patient continued to work well on controlling impulses to temper outbursts and reported he had very few provocations with anyone during the ensuing few weeks of therapy. He left therapy at the end of the spring term "in pretty good shape" as he put it.

VI. *Instances of adequate behavior.* This aspect of the schema can be briefly summarized in a few statements from the patient as to how he managed some trial situations during the last few weeks of therapy, thereby indicating his improvement. These are brief excerpts from his logs and from the recorded interviews:

1. "Well, Carol and I are getting along well now."

2. "Carol and I are planning a week at the beach this summer after school is out."

3. "I found out today from Mr. Morris that I can have the summer job but the amount of time will not be more than 15–20 hours per week."

4. "I got a disturbing letter from my mother about some business

reverses my dad had and I first felt I should write them a 'blast' for being dumb and careless, but as I thought about it, I didn't. I wrote a more sympathetic letter.''

5. ''My roommate tried to borrow some money from me again and he wanted to borrow my hi-fi set for a party at his girl's house and I said ''no'' to both without getting anxious or angry.''

These indications of change were spread over several interviews and fed back strong encouragement to the patient as to how his self-control efforts paid off.

VII. *Goals*. Discussing goals at this point may appear inconsistent— should they not come at the start? Yes, ordinarily we think of setting goals at the start, and the presenting complaints are—in reverse application—a set of goals: behaviors to be overcome. More explicitly, however, goals in this part of the schema refer to more positive ongoing, and more far-reaching, plans and efforts: a kind of putting the results of the therapy into perspective and envisioning more positive efforts in the future that have less to do with immediate anxiety, anger, and the like.

The patient in question here set up some goals in terms of educational objectives; and he and Carol were beginning to discuss the possibilities of marriage. He felt he no longer wanted to work in restaurants for his livelihood while in college, but was willing to take a lesser-paying job that was more to his liking—working in the college library. He gave some consideration to going to graduate school in library science and talked with several librarians about future possibilities.

VIII. *Revision and extension of change process*. Little effort with this particular patient was expended in this direction in an explicit way; the statement of goals and their pursuit constituted the patient's revising and carrying on with changing his behavior. This item in the schema is sometimes seen as a more explicit one when some further crisis occurs in a patient's life or when some aspect of the therapy has not proven as useful as expected. One patient who came through therapy with many constructive changes a short time after therapy lost her husband in an automobile accident and had to revise her otherwise hard-won and functional plans for her own further education and the management of her household and small children.

The schema followed here gives body and direction to therapy. The therapist can keep in mind issues, past and present, that may need to come into focus, and can keep ahead of the patient in the sense of the general structure that therapy follows, although the details are always in the hands of the patient.

CHAPTER 4

Writing as a Useful Therapeutic Technique

The use of writing as a therapeutic technique has probably been over-looked by most people. It is a "natural" in one sense; we usually make things formal or official by and through the use of writing: signing checks, endorsing contracts or agreements, and, of course, the wide variety of formal and informal communication where writing is the major channel used.

Writing as an adjunct therapeutic technique has been around a long time. Some therapists have used writing when the patient or the therapist were away on a trip, or ill, thereby precluding the usual meetings. Some-times writing has been used in the sense of note-taking by patient or therapist, serving as a reminder of things to discuss; or as a way to emphasize some central theme in therapy. But seldom, if ever, has writing been used as the main medium, or the only medium, of communi-cation in therapy. Brief exchanges in vocational counseling have some-times used writing, including printout of test results, plus profiles or recommendations, but these have been very short interchanges and usu-ally directed to a very finite goal.

We have used writing techniques in three ways in the Counseling Center at George Washington University. One writing procedure, refer-enced briefly in Chapter 2, has been a kind of stopgap procedure. A second usage has centered around behavior logs. The third use has been a more extended and involved use of writing. Each of these will be de-scribed now.

WRITING AS A STOPGAP MEASURE

Many times patients present compelling anxieties and depressive states that require immediate action, a kind of stopgap measure that is of value before the longer-range, more mature solutions to problems can be worked out.

The stopgap measures are those we have described as "first aid," but this is not to demean the measures.

A patient comes in for the therapy hour stating that she cannot concentrate on her job, that she goes off into "faraway" states, on occasion experiences short, piercing headaches, or somatic pains or discomforts. She reports that this distress is recurrent and unpredictable, and that it seems not to be related to any specific events in her life or in the immediate environmental constellation of people, work, or her own thoughts. The patient characteristically reports that she has "tried everything" to cope with the distress: telling herself there is nothing to be afraid of, that she should "not let things bother her," and so on through a number of similar cliches. If the distress is very compelling, these measures will not offer relief. The patient regards herself as "untreatable," or perhaps feels that the therapist "doesn't understand" and therefore cannot be of help. It is important to suggest an immediate measure that relieves current anxiety and tension, something that is not strictly a placebo (Fish, 1973; Phillips, 1975), and a measure that also paves the way for or contributes to longer-range measures.

When people face anxiety they may try to deal with it in a variety of nonfunctional ways, such as the following:

1. The negative feelings are barely acknowledged for what they are (usually after the fact); the person feels that the anxiety should not occur; the feelings are unwelcome and by ignoring them it is hoped they will go away.

2. The person does the same thing each time the distress appears, even though to no avail. It is a case of redundant nonproblem-solving; yet, not knowing how to change matters in the face of anxiety, the same behavior recurs.

3. The patient feels trapped in the same situation—locked in—and fails to recognize and change small items in the distress picture that might be altered; hence the redundancy continues.

4. The patient fails to locate the reasons for the distress in the current environment or in relation to his recent behavioral history; and tends to look for remote historical causes which lack the specificity to really anchor the distress to details of present time and place.

There may well be other ineffective efforts to control the unwanted anxiety and tensions. What do we do when we, as therapists/counselors, face such an array of problems? We probably slip into similar redundant processes; most human beings do until they learn more suitable measures.

The therapist must face the fact with the patient that larger or more extended relief from distress cannot be brought immediately under the patient's control; and even though relief may be down the road a distance, immediate measures should not be overlooked. The first order of business is to get a clear indication to the patient that the unwanted anxiety and emotional pressure can be brought under partial control by the patient himself. Writing this down is the best way to make the self-reference statement clear and plain.

The patient should be instructed to stop for a moment and *write* down: "I am experiencing this anxiety (shallow breathing, restlessness, and so on, naming the features as well as possible) and, although I do not know what causes it, I need not be distracted or distressed by it; I simply admit that it occurs . . . and go on with my business." This is an introductory statement by the patient to himself. It helps to admit, detail, and dismiss (temporarily) the unwanted anxiety; then the patient can return to the gainful duties before him such as studying, working, or interacting socially.

This simple writing procedure *reverses* the "errors" cited above by the patient admitting the fact—rather than overlooking it—that there is compelling distress present. Admitting the distress is present, although not fully understood, can allow one to put the distress aside momentarily and then get on with the business at hand. The writing breaks the redundancy, helps solve the problem of the anxiety-as-distractor (rather than anxiety in relation to other or larger issues), and temporarily puts the anxiety aside, allowing the person relief and an opportunity to return to his work.

In allowing for some reduction in anxiety, the writing is thereby reinforcing, taking the place of the usual reinforcement by escape, avoidance, and withdrawal, all of which simply maintain the pathology. In effect, the reinforcement contingency regarding the handling of anxiety is changed 180°.

Just thinking about distress to one's self may not have and usually does not have the same outcome as writing it down. Why not? First, because the writing is "official," indelible; it takes time and requires attention. Writing is also a matter of *doing something* other than emoting over the unwanted feelings; it may be reciprocally inhibiting the anxiety. Writing offers an "out," a relief from the binding anxiety, and relief from the redundant issues of problem–anxiety–distress–distraction–further anxiety. The individual who stops to write something down is more likely to remember his effort and can retain a record of having done the writing. Writing forces one to enter into a different set of activities, compared to "just thinking about the matter."

Writing has been employed with (1) obsessive–compulsive individuals who were "pinned down" (to use the word of one patient with this kind of complaint) by the tendency to count steps, "adjust" wall sockets and plugs, and the like; (2) very anxious individuals who were easily distracted from work at a desk (studying, writing); (3) persons ruminating over arguments about alleged wrongs against them; and others. It is common for a person willing to try the writing, when in a clutch, to gain enough relief to then be able to engage in other behaviors of a more useful nature.

The technique is explained to the patient as "what to do until maturity comes," that is, as a step in the direction of controlling the anxiety, but not one necessarily solving larger problems. As the person gains relief from the distress, other problem-solving efforts can be brought into play more directly, and other aspects of the problem examined. There is no implication here that the first-aid measure is only dealing with a superficial symptom of a "more basic problem," but rather that the first-aid measure is one that is necessary, timely, relieving, and effective. Because the immediate writing does not solve more ramifying issues is no reason to eschew it.

BEHAVIORAL LOGS

Behavioral logs of some types have been used by many therapists, even some early psychoanalytic therapists (Herzberg, 1941). Generally the instructions to the patient in this connection were to take notes on himself as he tried out specific measures suggested by the therapist (see reference to logs throughout Chapter 3). Although the earlier therapeutic measures involving note-taking may have been useful ones, the more extended use of written logs revolves around the following points:

1. Logs teach the person to observe himself better. "Know thyself" might be replaced by "observe thyself," and may be essential to self-knowledge.

2. Self-observations and logs form a kind of frequency data on given characteristics and, when begun early in therapy or before therapy, serve as a baseline. Some therapists we know have even asked patients to keep logs *prior* to the first interview (between the time of making the first appointment and the actual therapy session).

3. Writing things down helps one to remember them and provides grist for the therapy mill at a later time.

4. There is sometimes a therapeutic value (relief, at least) in writing down facts about one's self, even though at the time not much can be done about the issue at hand. It tends to fill out the details in one's life and renders them more available for later reference in therapy.

5. Similar to forming a rough baseline, writing forms a record on the occurrence of problems, their dimunition, and the advent of new or different problems.

6. Logs give a structure to therapy sessions: The patient prepares for work on given topics and assumes more responsibility for taking relevant

actions; also he gains in responsibility and reliability in keeping track of his own behavior. The patient feels like he is "in business for myself" as one patient put the matter.

7. Logs are characteristically brief but act as prompts to the discussion of more wide ranging issues.

8. Logs are a means to an end—better and more active participation—and should not become ends in themselves. Logs taper off in frequency when the patient and therapist reach an easy, productive, and ongoing discourse that is relevant to and productive of behavior change (see Chapter 3).

If one sees a patient once a week, or even more often, there is, of course, considerably more time between sessions than during sessions. There are many distractions to therapy (distractions and competing behaviors); thus the log helps to ferret out the most important facts about one's behavior and helps keep a consistent view of these facts. Therapy tends ordinarily to be somewhat vague and aimless; the log helps to reduce these competing tendencies and to accelerate therapy and make it more practical.

Most patients do not mind using logs, once they see some advantages (which they often spontaneously mention). In a college population, and also with older persons who tend to be somewhat introspective, the log keeping is a natural extension of other aspects of their lives (writing letters, reading, keeping lists and notes on activities, or diaries). Its value, however, is not restricted to highly verbal people. Informally, various therapists have tried out log keeping to advantage on high school students, older adults, institutional inmates, school dropouts, and vocational school youth and young adults.

Good log keeping is a powerful means of reinforcing the patient for helping to build a participating and relevant therapy, and an equally strong self-reinforcement because of the obvious interrelations between the logs, the therapy hour, and consequent behavior change. There is hardly a more natural bridge between the therapy sessions and the outside, real world!

WRITING AS THE TOTAL THERAPY ENTERPRISE

The two writing activities cited and discussed above can be used with any kind of therapy, although they have their greatest relevance and application in a behavioral context. Writing therapy as a total enterprise could also apply to any other therapeutic persuasion (e.g., analytic therapy, or gestalt therapy), but is unlikely to be so used because writing therapy plays down the alleged importance of face-to-face interactions between patient and therapist. Traditional therapies pivot much of their theoretical value on this relationship and especially on certain aspects of the relationship such as transference and unconditional acceptance. However, relationships may harbor many distracting, competing, and even defeating features. There are many unspoken, unanalyzed, and poorly understood aspects of interpersonal face-to-face relations that counteract therapeutic change. These have not been closely examined, but could be studied around such topics as what the patient liked about the therapist, what was disliked or annoying, and, similarly, what the therapist's reaction was to the patient. Some therapists will not accept, or continue with, patients they ''don't like'' whatever that means in more precise terms.

One may have heard patients discussed, as persons—not only as patients—by therapists from widely different persuasions, and there appear to be many personal, value-laden, and even derogatory characterizations of patients by therapists. The therapist in such freewheeling discussions tends to forget therapy qua therapy and dwells more, as laymen might, on the personal characteristics of the patient, good and bad, with no particular relevance for therapy as a professional enterprise. These kinds of therapist behaviors may militate against therapeutic success more than we ordinarily recognize. Even when not articulated, the therapist's covert descriptions of patients may implicitly be more negative than positive.

A look at standard practices in writing psychological reports shows how negative the descriptions of patients can be. Many adverse characteristics are cited: repressed hostility, subliminated aggressiveness, paranoic tendencies, to name a few. These are more than labels; they appear to describe traits or more or less permanent characteristics of the patient and also motivational states. Psychological report writers tend to outdo each other in ascribing and assigning ever more complicated, negative, and hidden features to a person.

If a rule were established that required all therapists to tell the patient what the therapist had written or said, therapists might be more positive in their descriptions of patients. The more the patient is seen in a bad light, the more he or she needs help, and the more the therapist can see himself or herself as a saver of this person. This is a practice not unlike the common one of running down the other person in order, relatively speaking, to build up one's self.

The writing therapy procedure is built on a more candid and straightforward communication with the patient and on a greater respect for the patient's capacity to view himself in clearer light and begin to act to change things. As a result of this candidness, the patient is charged with the responsibility of viewing his or her own behavior more objectively, which leads to a concern for the circumstances that influence the patient adversely, knowledge of which can lead to specific change efforts and to positive feedback.

PROCEDURE FOR WRITING THERAPY

Getting patients for writing therapy has been accomplished in two general ways: first, by announcing in a college newspaper that a study of writing therapy was about to be undertaken (Phillips and Gershenson, 1976; Phillips, 1976), whereupon criteria for accepting writing therapy candidates was employed to select from among the candidates; second, by mentioning the possibility of writing therapy among new applicants for therapy in a university psychological clinic. There are undoubtedly selective procedures operating in each instance that are not fully comprehended. In fact, all therapy practices undergo some selection as to who gets into therapy, who gets what kind of therapy or therapist, who stays in therapy, and other related issues. It is very likely in a large community-based counseling or mental health center that the number of people who finally go through a period of therapy and participate in a follow-up study comprise a small percentage of those who apply, possibly as low as 15–20% of the original number of applicants (Phillips, 1956; Phillips et al., 1967). People fall by the wayside or are selected out by a host of factors at each juncture among the many that must be crossed: originally calling for an appointment, appearing for an appointment, continuing on beyond the first three to five interviews, continuing on beyond the tenth or twelfth sessions (often a "critical" period), terminating on basis of mutual agreement by patient and therapist (rather than prematurely), being available for follow-up studies, replying to follow-up studies, and displaying reasonable objectivity in assessing one's own progress in a follow-up study (Phillips et al., 1967). We can now only recognize that selective factors are continually operative and try to be humble about our results. Thus far in studies of writing therapy, there has been less attrition in a college or university therapy population than among "regular" therapy clientele (Phillips and Wiener, 1966; Phillips and Gershenson, 1976).

Once selected, patients engaging in writing therapy are given a coded notebook in which there are some specific suggestions to be followed. These include specifying a regular time for writing, limiting writing to an hour, and encouraging the person to be as candid as possible in reporting on himself and in replying to the therapist's discussion. The patient is replied to by the therapist before the next (weekly or semiweekly) appointment. The writing therapy sessions may be continued beyond the confines of a semester or whole school year, or they may, as we have done, be limited to ten to twelve sessions (Phillips and Gershenson, 1976). However, any therapist using writing as the main therapeutic medium may make changes that seem useful to both patient and therapist.

Characteristically, early writing therapy sessions are relatively long and involved, and usually rambling. The person may write as fast as possible and fill five or six notebook pages in an hour. As problems become better defined and as the replies of the therapist help to specify and delimit the actions apparently needed, there is more objective reporting on the part of the patient and less emotionalism and rambling. One difficulty with previous writing efforts of patients—before the present procedures employed in writing therapy were elucidated—was that the patients wrote for almost endless periods of time, tending to repeat themselves unnecessarily and unproductively, and not coming to terms with procedures calculated to remedy the problems thus reported. Lengthy writing tended to be too complaining and too self-reinforcing.

Upon receiving the notebook from the patient (the notebook is kept in a locked file when not in the hands of the patient or therapist), the therapist reads the protocol and writes numbers in the margins covering a statement or passage or word written by the patient. This numbering is later referred to by the therapist so that the specific situation responded to can be clearly designated for the patient's benefit the next time writing is done. Such numbered replies by the therapist may range from 5–6 replies in a brief protocol, to 15–20 for more lengthy or involved writing. It is economical not to reply to everything the patient writes and, of course, to try to subsume related topics under one reply where possible.

The therapist's responses may fall into several categories, although these have not been rigorously defined: asking the patient for more information on a topic; asking the patient if the topic under discussion is the same as, or similar to, one discussed earlier (this would apply only where more than one protocol had been received from the patient); asking the patient if he or she had tried or considered trying a different tack in coping with the situation at hand; making specific suggestions to the patient as to what might be the nature of the problem; and, of course, suggesting one or more actual tacks that may be taken by the patient. The therapist nearly always asks for, and gets, feedback from the patient as to how the therapist's suggestions worked. It is incumbent on the therapist to try to come up with workable suggestions so that a functional structure is provided for the patient and problems move toward solution rather than just being endlessly bothersome and fretted over.

As with any therapy, there is both forward and backward movement, hits and misses in defining and delimiting problems, and some sessions are far more encouraging and helpful than others. Most writing therapy can be moderately successful to successful in 5–10 sessions; seldom have sessions gone beyond 12–15, and then usually by special arrangement. The natural structure of the semester or the school year helps to delimit time for most high school, college, or university students; in private practice arrangements, writing therapy has seldom gone beyond one year (where writing sessions occurred an average of two times per month).

A sample protocol is provided in Figure 6. In this instance, the patient's protocol is replied to by the marginal numbers and some underlining of words or phrases to give it a more specific emphasis. The second part of Figure 6 provides some indication of the therapist's reply to the patient's protocol.

I have decided to choose the first twelve weeks of an average freshman at the ▬▬▬▬▬▬▬▬▬ as my topic for the day. After being immersed in new environment for three months one can make some very obvious observations.

1   *Wasted*, that's all I can say about my past few months. I've wasted a lot of time, precious time doing nothing. But, then again doing nothing is something. The effort I put in is not worthwhile, for

2   *I get nothing in return*. I feel very unsatisfied, unfulfilled. I have found nothing meaningful. My work means nothing to me. I get nothing out of it. It's not what

3   I want from life.

There has been only one redeeming factor to my existing here that is a someone I have met. Her name

4   is ▬▬▬. We have a very strange or odd relationship, so we like to call it. Let me present the facts. She has a boyfriend back home. (a senior in college, she is also a freshman)

Reply by therapist to first writing of Mr. _____.

You made a very good start in getting down to details about your life and concerns! Each point in your protocol will be replied to by way of the numbers in the margins. Feel free to ask questions, make comments, etc.

As to your first point, what have you done during the time wasted? Was the waste mainly in connection with scholastic pursuits? Social life? Etc.? We need details here.

Your second point states that you get no pleasure from what you do; the effort does not pay off. What would you consider more rewarding? What happens that is not rewarding that leads to your saying "I get nothing in return"?

What do you want from life (point 3)? Give some specifics. Let us then see how these may be worked toward; how you fail to get what you want as of now.

The redeeming factor—a girlfriend (point 4)—is most reassuring; perhaps there are more rewards than you count accurately! What do you like about her? What do you share together? Let us have more on this general topic, with a view to how you might consider upgrading this aspect of your life.

Figure 6. First writing therapy protocol of a university freshman (note underlining and marginal numbering).

Recent research (Phillips and Gershenson, 1976) indicates that the number of words used varies considerably from person to person, and from session to session by the same patient, but the overall trend from writing therapy session 1 to the last session (10) shows a considerable drop in the number of words used by the patients. The therapists' writing, on the other hand, shows a fairly steady word rate throughout the sessions.

Writing, because of its formality and specificity, seems to have an edge over oral exchanges in terms of efficiency in time, and possibly, also, in terms of more effective outcome from therapy. In the Phillips and Gershenson (1976) study, although patients were paid a "student's hourly rate" for writing, only one of the 17 failed to go the full number of sessions provided (11). In most oral therapy, the dropout rate is considerably higher; and, since most therapy is not conducted on a necessarily brief or time-limited basis, it tends to produce more dropouts along the way if there is no clear-cut end in sight.

ADVANTAGES OF WRITING THERAPY

Some advantages have been implied in the above discussion. Summarized, the advantages of writing therapy might be as follows:

1. It provides easy scheduling of writing for both patient and therapist.

2. Since the amount of writing that can take place in an hour is more limited than the number of words that can be spoken, the hour seems to provide a constructive limitation on communication.

3. If writing is, indeed, a more "official" and/or formal presentation, it may require more judgment and sifting of information and thereby result in a more succinct and relevant presentation.

4. The amount of general emoting and rambling appears to be less than with oral therapy; there is, therefore, less "junky" behavior to deal with and one can get down sooner to the business of changing the behaviors in question.

5. It provides a continuing record of all transactions between therapist and patient (compared to the hours it takes to transcribe a 50-minute oral therapy hour).

6. It can be read and reacted to by the therapist in 15–20 minutes, or less time when the therapist has become familiar with the patient's problems and writing; and this reply can be scheduled at any time convenient to the therapist before the patient's next writing.

7. The continuous record of the communication provides a ready reference base for both therapist and patient in subsequent writing.

8. Despite its brevity, writing therapy may provide more "catharsis" for some emotional distress than talking does; and having read previous writings helps diminish the need for subsequent coverage of the same ground.

9. Writing lends itself to a more contractual basis for communication than does oral transaction: time, place for writing, answering questions, following suggestions, carrying out plans, all being examples.

10. The therapist can react to whatever writing he or she deems appropriate; "time out" procedures, by ignoring some writing and, correspondingly, putting an emphasis on other writing, is easier with written protocols. In this same context, reinforcement may be more specific and concrete and may have more relevance to given behavior change efforts.

There are some limitations to writing therapy, which might be stated as follows:

1. It fails to pick up nuances of social interaction between patient and therapist which may be important.

2. It may allow for too much passage of time before a serious or critical problem is noted, thus ignoring or losing the opportunity for timely strategic action.

3. It may appear too impersonal and cold to some.

4. It loses the advantage of immediate social problem solving and social reinforcement.

Despite these disadvantages—some of which can be ameliorated, overcome, or precluded—the advantages of writing therapy seem to make it a useful therapeutic tool in many settings and for many patients. Just who can profit best from writing is still a moot issue. We do not know, of course, who profits best from any therapy (except perhaps for retardates and similar patients in well-structured settings profiting more from behavioral techniques than from any traditional ones).

The issue of training tyro therapists may be approached through writing therapy. In the case of writing therapy, the novice therapist has time to respond thoughtfully to the patient's writing, can get supervision easily regarding how to respond to the patient, and can measure his or her steps more deliberately than is the case with therapy conducted first in the heat, hurry, and confusion of face-to-face interaction. Informal tryouts of writing therapy with novice therapists indicates they like to use it, and they find it helpful in thinking more clearly and specifically about patient problems. Writing helps the fledgling therapist to see the importance of structuring the patient–therapist interaction in functionally useful ways.

It might appear at first that writing therapy is intended only for the verbally facile. However, this is not the case. Informal use of writing therapy has been conducted with vocational school trainees who were high school graduates and who ranged in age from 20 to 30 years. Qualitative results showed that of 12 participants in writing therapy, all felt that the writing was helpful in solving school-related and social problems, and all but one elected to engage further in the writing at the close of the fall semester.

High school dropouts, all of whom were underachievers, showed an interest in writing, and reported that it helped them sort out their feelings and their vocational and educational plans. No formal follow-up was done on this group, as there was no way to accomplish this with any reliability. Although their written self-expression was often unpolished and ungrammatical, they did not hesitate to express themselves candidly.

A prison population of 20 inmates was given a chance to engage in writing therapy over the course of a four-month period. They volunteered participation in the project and were given time to go to a library once a week for an hour where they completed their writings. A group of graduate students under the supervision of a therapist responded to these protocols. Eighty-five percent of the time the inmates appeared for and engaged in writing. Several of them began to develop plans for part-time study while still inmates, some made outside contacts for post-prison employment, and several asked for vocational and educational batteries of tests in order to think and plan about fields of work that they might pursue in prison and again upon discharge. These developments came after variable periods of time in prison when they had previously let their free time lie fallow.

A recent study of a more formal nature was conducted among undergraduate students at the Counseling Center, George Washington University. The study included 16 volunteers, chosen on the basis of an original population of 42 volunteers, who appeared for 11 writing sessions of one hour each over the semester's time. Pre- and post-tests using the MMPI and the EPPS were used, with the post-testing coming within one month after the end of the writing therapy sessions. In addition, raters read and judged the writing therapy protocols. The writing therapy clients themselves rated their progress; and a study was made of the number of words written by each client and therapist for each session.

Results of this more formal study warrant some confidence in writing as a sole therapeutic technique (Test, 1964; Phillips and Gershenson, 1976). The test–retest data on the standardized tests (MMPI and EPPS) indicate through analysis of variance that there were significant before–after test protocol changes on each test used; that the gains were in the direction of more assertiveness, more social ascendence, and a lessening of ruminative, subjective, and socially isolated or retreating behaviors. Ratings of protocols by the writing therapy clients themselves and by independent raters indicated the clients made gains in solving personal problems and showed an increase in confidence in social relationships. The economy of the method was shown in that the clients wrote on the average less than 1000 words per one hour writing session for 11 sessions, while the therapists' replies contained less than 300 words on the average (see Figure 7). The therapists' writings tended to change very little from the

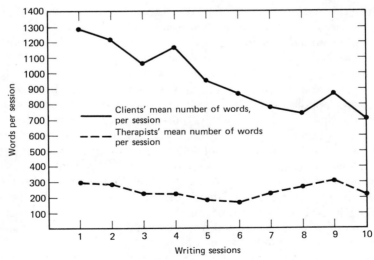

Figure 7. Number of words per writing session, one through ten, for clients and for therapists.

first to the tenth writing sessions, while the writings of the clients decreased steadily, from the first to the last writing session, from about 1300 words to about 700 words. The protocols present a working paper for research on a variety of topics related to writing as a therapeutic measure and, of course, do not require lengthy transcriptions (typically about four hours for a 50-minute interview), nor as many words (4000–6000 words transcribed in a "typical" 50-minute interview).

People are usually willing to write down their thoughts, feelings, and concerns, and to be relatively objective about their experiences, at least in a setting that affords equally candid replies of a helpful nature. Writing can apply to nearly any population of people that is at least semiliterate, and can lend candor and specificity to what are often rambling and misty communications of an oral, face-to-face nature.

CHAPTER 5

Therapeutic Supervision in a Behavioral Framework

Supervision is a topic not often dealt with in the behavior therapy literature. It appears to be the assumption that research reports, therapy protocols, and general discussions of various techniques will suffice to instruct the tyro therapist. We all know, however, that nearly all psychotherapy and counseling cases present unusual or unexpected problems, and that falling back on principles and techniques, while of inestimable importance, will not fully instruct the beginning therapist or counselor.

The main tack taken here in an effort to help fledgling therapists is to "keep structure" with the patient at all times. This may sound like a flowery phrase—keeping structure—but it really refers to a number of practical and useful procedures when supervising the new therapist about his or her therapeutic activities with the patient or client. Some of the ways the phrase "keeping structure" can apply are the following:

1. Asking questions of the patient if you do not know what he or she means by a given statement. Questions may, of course, be asked in a variety of ways; there is no implication that there is a single, correct way. Questions may be phrased indirectly such as, "Are you saying_____?" or, "I hear you saying that you feel so and so about him—am I reading you correctly?" Direct questions may also be proffered without preempting the patient's verbal productivity.

2. Responding often enough to the patient's remarks to leave the impression with the patient that you (the therapist) understand, follow, or perhaps even concur in what the patient is saying. To remain silent for long periods of time—except under unusual circumstances—may leave the impression with the patient that you do not know or care what is being said, that the patient is not saying much of consequence but maybe later something of importance will follow, or other contributions to vague communication.

3. Relating what the patient has previously said—or what you may think has been said—to the present context, that is, tying loose ends

together: "You said earlier that you feel a given way about the relationship and now I think I am hearing some additions or deletions to that earlier statement—am I on the target with you?"

4. Introducing topics if this seems to be of some value in the course of the therapeutic discussion: "I've not heard you say much about your broader relationship with John although you refer a lot to him in passing, it would seem."

5. Pointing out an inconsistency or contradiction in what the patient has said. These contradictions may refer to actual conflicting feelings about someone or something, or they may represent inconsistencies the patient has not faced or grappled with effectively. At any rate, the inconsistencies should be explicated as they relate ultimately to the development of self-control and self-management.

6. Encouraging the patient to talk more about a given topic or to continue to express feelings (if, say, the patient is crying, or visibly angry), not meaning to reinforce these responses with abandon but intending to reach a larger context in which the discussions, feelings, angry statements, and the like may fit, and to indicate it is permissible to deal with such topics in therapy. The encouragement of the expression of feeling is often the sine qua non of therapy, especially in the beginning, and the behavioral therapist stands as ready as any other therapist to deal with feelings. However, the behavioral therapist wishes to move on to a fuller appreciation of the larger context and not simply deal interminably with feelings as an end in themselves.

7. Holding to an agenda (if one is used or if one has been agreed upon) so that there is not too much rambling or vagueness. It is usually permissible to say to the patient, "Now how does all this story relate to our main purpose here?" Or "How can you tie that in to what we've agreed to work on?" Quite often if a patient has talked for five to ten minutes with no input from the therapist, a transcribed protocol will probably show that a number of topics have been covered, contradictory statements issued, and perhaps rhetorical questions asked as well. If the therapist does not punctuate an otherwise long monologue with some opinions, comments, or questions, neither patient nor therapist knows where the discourse is leading, nor what it means for the main therapeutic undertaking.

8. Offering hypotheses or conjectures—openly identified as such—to the patient and asking for the patient's opinions on these conjectures. There is much in complex human behavior, especially in a therapeutic exchange, that even the most skilled therapist has trouble identifying in some meaningful way. To act always as if you, as a therapist, knew exactly what the patient was saying, or to act as if the patient's verbal

discourse was always clear, is to mislead all concerned. Entering into a complex verbal recital with summarizing or conjectural statements, reasonably pinpointed, is an attempt to add clarity and direction to the therapy; it will not inhibit the patient's productivity nor preempt the patient's individuality in expressing himself. Hypotheses proffered by the therapist may often stimulate the patient to think differently about his or her behavior and lead into productive channels for behavior change.

9. Suggesting that the patient try this or that activity in order to clarify a problem, attempt a solution, or tax the patient's repertoire. Such a suggestion may become an agenda item. Whenever the discussion in therapy can lead to a viable out-of-therapy effort of some specific sort, this livens up therapy, gives it specific objectives that can be evaluated, and permits the patient to be reinforced not only by the therapist but by his or her own efforts which are all the more useful if the out-of-therapy effort proves to be productive. The real and abiding answers to therapy problems lie in their practicality in daily life, not in their apparently rational or irrational perspective in therapy alone.

10. Asking the patient to react to what you have said; asking for candid comments by the patient. As a therapist, offer the conjecture provisionally, but get the offering into a two-way communication stream; do not let the suggestion remain one-way, allowing yourself as therapist to be viewed as too authoritarian, or as assuming that your "interpretation" is preforce correct. Don't let the patient get by with some such statement as "If you think so, then you must be right" or other negative remarks by the patient. The therapist is probably never right simply in the abstract, but only when and if the patient gives corroborative evidence in his or her life.

11. As a therapist you may be able to say anything to a patient if you say it in the "correct" way. One can confront the patient candidly by making comments rhetorical, by asking questions, or by suggesting that the patient may be implying something different from what has been said. For example, one might say to the patient whom the therapist considers very hostile: "Has anyone ever told you that you come over as pretty angry or hostile?" Or, "Sometimes people interpret a statement like you have just said as very challenging." And so forth. Too often a therapist, especially a conventional therapist, will express opinions or feelings about a patient that the therapist has been unwilling or unable to voice directly to the patient. This is an unwelcome condition, since the therapist isn't being candid with the patient and the patient is not receiving the help needed from the therapist.

12. No topic is too tender, too pat, or too trivial to be reacted to by the therapist if the latter thinks the topic (or some related comment) can be of value in the therapy. Sometimes the most casual comments lead into

highly productive matters; and sometimes seemingly trivial comments cannot be reliably so judged until they are explored more fully.

Most fledgling therapists are afraid of their patients. Time and time again, young therapists hold back confusingly in the face of angry statements by the patient, or in the face of seemingly perplexing symptomatology or complaints, thinking that what the therapist may say or do can drive the patient up the wall, cause the patient to "explode," or create a kind of "emotional chinook" confrontation for the therapist to face. It is true that one may have to treat a potentially explosive situation gently, especially early in therapy; but as a relationship forms and becomes reliable and predictable, the therapist has a large amount of leeway that should be capitalized upon, explored, and used in ways that enhance the therapist's reinforcement and analytic powers.

Other than advice to the tyro therapist to "keep structure," additional points may revolve around several steps which consist in large part in turning the therapy and the self-control over to the patient. These steps do not necessarily follow 1, 2, 3, . . . , but the steps in one or another form are needed in therapist–patient exchange. Even well into therapy, the steps in any order may be reinvoked, since altered definitions or programs may arise now and again in the course of therapy. These four steps are, then, variously and certainly taken but their order is flexible. (See also Chapter 3, "The Early Interviews.")

1. The first step in dealing with a problem or problems the patient faces or reports is to *name* or label the problem and to state the conflict. Naming provides a handle—"That must have been a pretty angry outburst." Or, "You generally feel depressed after a fight with your wife, do you not?" Labeling is not equivalent to a diagnosis but rather provides a clear communication base between the therapist and the patient. If each, therapist and patient, know what the labels mean and what behavior is referred to, then it becomes easier to keep logs, collect frequency information, relate the named behavior to its context, and finally to appreciate the importance of the behavior so labeled as it recurs (or diminishes) over time in the patient's behavioral economy.

2. A second and equally important step is to delineate times and places where the unwanted (or named) behavior occurs, and how this behavior represents a conflict in the patient's life. It then becomes possible to relate the named behavior to a recurrent context—in contrast to what the patient intends, wishes, expects—such that the antecedent conditions, the behavior itself, and the observable consequences (the ABC's) are combined into a usable package. Whenever the therapist can get a hold on the patient's behavior—and help the patient do likewise—the therapy

then has substantative data with which to cope. Intervention then becomes a matter of dealing with the feelings that influence selecting and applying appropriate tactics and strategies.

3. Given these two important steps it then becomes feasible to set up programs to begin to cope with the unwanted (named) behavior in the therapy discussions, and to project and weave these programs into the patient's natural environment; getting back information at least from the patient as to how the program is working and thereby submitting it to change where indicated. This step, that of trying out the efficacy of behavior change efforts, should begin as soon as possible after the initial therapy contact, and may begin even with the first interview (or between the first and second interviews). (See the final verbatim protocol in this chapter, pp. 138–150, of a first interview with a 27-year-old female patient). Getting into the change effort in this practical way shows more clearly whether the earlier formulations are useful; it demonstrates the likely redundant nature of the patient's complaints; and it enhances both the patient's and the therapist's comprehension of the patient's plight and the shared change effort.

4. This step is one of gradually turning over the control of his or her life to the patient. The therapist may need to refer back to the earlier steps, to reinforce an agreement (or contract) or to solidify patient efforts; but essentially the therapist's role is a diminishing one when and as the first three steps are found to be productive. Even if there are setbacks or new exigencies in the patient's life, the reiteration of the first three steps will provide a basis for conducting the therapy, will help the patient gain confidence in the behavioral procedures utilized, and will further show the patient and the therapist that seemingly new problems can be referred to previously tried and useful solutions (Kazdin, 1972, 1974).

A SUPERVISORY CASE FOLLOWING THE SECOND INTERVIEW

The following supervisory exchange between the therapist and the supervisor took place following the second interview between the patient and the therapist. The therapist had begun consultation with another supervisor who immediately went on an extended leave of absence, hence the present supervisor took over these duties.

The patient was about 30 years of age, a female, single, a professional-school student at a nearby university. The patient presented a number of complaints having to do with underassertiveness, with low self-confidence, with feelings of constriction in public areas (especially while driving her car on busy streets during heavy traffic), and with longer-range career plans.

The supervisory hours were recorded, the first one following the therapist's second interview with the patient, and the second recorded supervisory session following the fourth therapist–patient interview. Comments are provided for the reader so that some indication can be given as to what the supervisor had in mind during the recorded session, and to further structure the supervisor–therapist interactions. There are, of course, many, many responses the therapist can make to what the patient says, and equally as many comments the supervisor can make regarding the therapist's behavior. If we try to follow strictures relating to keeping the structure clear and keeping the therapy gainfully in pursuit of goals, the *exact* comments, except for misread meanings and gross omissions, may not be of vital importance. The main thrust in these supervisory sessions is to help the therapist keep track of what is transpiring between herself (also a female, about 37 years of age, and a graduate student in clinical psychology) and the patient, to keep the therapist from becoming bogged down in emotional details that might better be referred to their context, and to help the therapist gain and maintain confidence that a good therapy program is in order.

The comments refer mostly to the early structuring of the therapy in reference to presenting complaints, how the complaints can be localized in terms of time, space, and other persons, and something about what the patient has heretofore done about them. As such, these comments pertain mostly to the first two steps cited above and far less to the third step; hardly any at all this early in the therapy refer to the fourth step. The reader might also consult the schema stated in Chapter 3—"The Early Interviews"—in order to see further how the comments by the supervisor fit in with the larger schema that presumably encompasses all of therapy. Other comments lay at an immediate action-level between the therapist and the patient and do not easily fit into either the steps, broadly conceived, nor the schema found in Chapter 3. All supervisory periods were recorded and lasted between 25 and 30 minutes only.

Objective: Identifying and describing presenting complaints.

SUPERVISOR.   One of her presenting complaints is her fear of driving? Is that right?

THERAPIST.   Right.

SUPERVISOR.   I see—what about that?

THERAPIST.   It sounds like she has a fear of, a fear of being in crowded places, her greatest fear comes at the time of rush hours. She can't stand to drive on freeways. She can drive on two lane streets and that's about all she can take.

SUPERVISOR. Small roads?

THERAPIST. Right. That's about all she can take. She manages to drive about once a week. Even on some other transportation, she's been taking cabs and buses . . . she can hardly stand it during rush hours. She said she felt like literally screaming.

SUPERVISOR. You mean in driving or as a passenger?

THERAPIST. When a passenger, too—both.

SUPERVISOR. On a bus?

THERAPIST. Right.

Trying to further define presenting complaints.

SUPERVISOR. What if she's walking in a crowd on a street?

THERAPIST. I don't know. I didn't ask her that. But she did say she has never been able to handle crowds.

Offering an hypothesis that is purely conjecture at this time.

SUPERVISOR. I wonder if she's angry about having to cope with crowds. If there's a lot of people around, then you have to wait your turn—having to stand being shuffled aside. I wonder if it is so displeasing that she is basically angry and she may be more preoccupied and angry because she's forced to deal with the situation. You might ask her that question.

THERAPIST. OK. It's an interesting hypothesis to me—the anger. She did report being disturbed about competitiveness at school in a large class of 150 students.

Return to conjecture about anger, coupling it with other items.

SUPERVISOR. People often get lost in a crowd which may mean they lose their bearings, or their place, or individuality; however, they might express it, they are angry at being made so anonymous and helpless, you might say. It's an hypothesis only at this time.

THERAPIST. She avoids tall buildings, too.

SUPERVISOR. Does she work in a tall building?

THERAPIST. I didn't ask her that, I don't think so. I think she would have told me if she did. When she goes to places like the Capitol, she feels like it is going to explode or fall on her. At the Mormon Temple she almost passed out. She said she worries about the fear beginning to spread.

Suggestion about how to begin to cope with some complaints.

SUPERVISOR. She's recently avoided the Capitol and places like the Mormon Temple; now I wonder if there are any tall buildings on Pennsylvania Avenue where she could make a beginning attempt to cope, as part of a desensitization operation? That might be something to consider.

THERAPIST. (Shakes her head "Yes.")

Presenting ideas for therapist to consider and possibly use with patient.

SUPERVISOR. When I raise these questions I don't mean you should go work on them right then, but possibly discuss them, get around to them, with her.

THERAPIST. (Shakes her head "Yes.")

SUPERVISOR. Let's say you pick a tall building downtown, and walk down the street toward the building from here, maybe on the other side of Pennsylvania Avenue, as a beginning desensitization effort. How about the building where you see her?

THERAPIST. I see her on the 11th floor!

SUPERVISOR. Does that *bother* her?

THERAPIST. I didn't ask her. I think not.

Possible confrontation as to what presenting complaint means.

SUPERVISOR. All right, ask her if that bothers her. It may not because she's coming there for something that she wants. But find out if that building bothers her or ones down the street, whichever the next tallest one is.

THERAPIST. I see.

Mainly a practical procedural suggestion for the therapist.

SUPERVISOR. Walk down the street talking about it "in vivo." Say "Well, we are walking around here with people and how are you feeling?" and she'll tell you. But keep the normal social activities going, keep walking, keep interacting with the environment. Then maybe pass the building a time or two. Go down the street and back a few times. I've done that with several patients who had similar problems, not only with fear of tall buildings but with anxiety around traffic at rush times, and many people about.

THERAPIST. OK, I can try it with her.

Any suggestion merits feedback.

SUPERVISOR. Give me some feedback on that issue, please. What other problems does she present?

Getting some goals stated by the patient.

THERAPIST. Well, I asked her what she wanted from the therapy. She said, "If I could make decisions about what I want . . . to be the one that's in control instead of these external forces. . . ."

Asking about her assets—an item to build on in the therapy.

SUPERVISOR. She's lacking self-control and likely assertiveness. Wherein *is* she confident and assertive?

THERAPIST. I don't know just where. I don't think she knows what to do with her life. She's got a kind of confidence about going to professional school, and also a very good job with the Council. She's getting B's instead of A's. She said it shakes her values after a while, being in school. She feels there are no clear-cut issues, you have to see things on both sides and the competition bothers her . . . and so on. She didn't make out well in terms of the competition for a job this summer. She was an "abstractor" at $140 a week instead of getting another job paying more. She doesn't get to go to lunch with her peers, she complains.

Helping therapist to see adequacy—not just disturbance—with the patient.

SUPERVISOR. So she's pretty adequate in some areas but not in others. (Pause) Is there any way she can mingle with her peers and maybe get included in the lunch invitation? Or just amble along?

THERAPIST.   No, it is more the case that a memo goes out saying people are invited out to such and such a lunch, at such and such a place.

SUPERVISOR.   I see! Kinda formal?

More on presenting complaints; may tie in later with other items.

THERAPIST.   She's left out which fits in with the feeling of loneliness and difference—fear of crowds, tall buildings, and so on, which allow her to feel different.

Trying out an assertive role on the patient (but on the therapist too).

SUPERVISOR.   And also the competition. She could learn to assert herself and say "Look, I am a student here, too, even though I am doing abstracting—what are the chances that I might be included?"

THERAPIST.   Yes, she might.

SUPERVISOR.   Find out if there is some person, or two or three friends or acquaintances, to help her get included in these little social gatherings. She appears underassertive about herself. We can help her discern things she could do, herself, to change this. We can try some assertive training in these types of situations.

Ideas must check out with patient.

THERAPIST.   OK. I'll discuss it with her and see how she views it.

Summarizing discussion, listing items to work on; very useful for therapist and for patient.

SUPERVISOR.   We have, then, two or three good problems. One is asserting herself where social situations are concerned. Another, dealing with the feeling of anxiety she experiences with high places or crowds. Another is possibly handling school and career-related problems.

THERAPIST.   She's not identified or worked on these problems as specific issues. She felt that she is working in order to go to school, and working takes up all her time, and she didn't have any real chance to sit down and think about herself or explore what other possibilities there might be for her. She hasn't observed herself very accurately.

Reiterating possible objectives and procedures.

SUPERVISOR.   True enough! Well, right now professional school is the main thing for another year or two. We can build these therapy objectives into this context, if she concurs.

Observing another positive behavior to use in therapy.

THERAPIST.   Yes, I feel we can. Previously she had a job she liked which was writing legislation. This may be a key for the future—after professional school.

SUPERVISOR.   She may want to return to writing legislations, after professional school. We can work with her on the pros and cons of this choice and other choices, as time goes by—while we're also concentrating on the immediate anxieties.

THERAPIST. I think part of her distaste for the things she's doing in professional school are these areas that she's not interested in.

SUPERVISOR. Yeah, but she has to take courses in them. All students have that problem, more or less.

Another possible application of a therapy procedure already considered; helps unify the therapy.

THERAPIST. Exactly. Can we discuss how assertive training would be helpful, even there?

SUPERVISOR. People need assertive help when they do not stand up for themselves or their rights. Say she knows one of the girls who goes out in this luncheon group—she might get to know this girl better and indicate that interesting discussions must take place in their group and see if the other girl takes her up on a subtle theme like that.

THERAPIST. At least she has the chance to learn to be assertive here.

Patients often discount therapy suggestions at first; therapist must "roll with the punches" then.

SUPERVISOR. She might say to you, "Oh, it's impossible," and if she does you can learn better how she regards this assignment. You may then want to revise your strategy toward the patient.

THERAPIST. Yes, I can see that.

A brief discussion of how the therapist might think about assertiveness as a general therapeutic measure.

SUPERVISOR. Another place where people need to learn to assert themselves is where they are specifically taken advantage of. Now, there's a whole group of procedures in assertiveness we can use, but right now it's safe to say she can learn to simply assert herself in regard to some specific social situation such as we've described.

The therapist need not have raised this question.

THERAPIST. I gathered that she's not clear about therapy or its objectives. I said "Do you feel therapists are a ripoff," and she seems to say "Well, not as yet." She was willing to give it a go. But her boyfriend feels her emotional problems are silly and therapy is a waste of time.

SUPERVISOR. How much therapy has she had before?

Interesting to know but not of much immediate value now.

THERAPIST. When she was 12 she had several sessions for fainting and depression, and then I think it was in 1969 she had six sessions at another clinic.

SUPERVISOR. But not long-term?

THERAPIST. No, not in any long-term sense.

SUPERVISOR. Did she figure those therapy sessions were beneficial to her?

THERAPIST. As I remember from the chart—I didn't speak to her about that—but beneficial enough that she got over whatever hump it was that was bothering her at the time.

Probably of more importance, especially if detailed more.

SUPERVISOR. You might ask her what she thought was beneficial about previous therapy, how it helped her or failed to, whether situations then were similar to now.

THERAPIST. I can cover that with her.

This is probably not a new problem (see summary of problems above); therapist must see similarity.

SUPERVISOR. She says here (referring to notes taken by therapist) she almost passed out when she was in some crowds, so there are either new problems along these lines or reactivation of old ones.

THERAPIST. Yes, possibly.

SUPERVISOR. Now she's under tension around exam time which is common enough. Is she still in school?

THERAPIST. No, she's not. She's had similar problems which coincided with the beginning of this job as a librarian, beginning just as she started therapy a couple of weeks ago.

Pretty similar to problems identified above, but need to be made clearer.

SUPERVISOR. I see, she had some problems adjusting to the new job and being with new people, not unlike the pressures from school work and classes.

Can't be sure this is very relevant—can't change her "middle-childness."

THERAPIST. Yeah. That's what it seems like. She's a middle child—if that's important—and that just seems to be the image that I had—she doesn't know where she fits. She's not in first place, not in last. "Where is the place for _____?" seems to me the question that I hear coming from her.

SUPERVISOR. Perhaps so, but that's remediated by taking some appropriate actions to solve problems. What are her chances of getting a library job next year? Could she make more money on a different job, if funds are needed?

This issue need not be postponed for a year; it is better considered for the following semester.

THERAPIST. I would assume that will be more feasible next summer after another year of school. She's got a pretty good head on her shoulders, and certainly not willing to be a grind. She said other people were studying nine hours a day while she averaged about two or three.

Another summary statement; helps to keep therapist on top of problems, to conceptualize.

SUPERVISOR. I would say, in summary, you report she has three main problems to work on. One of my ways of getting new behaviors from patients that you don't necessarily have to follow but I am just suggesting it—in case—is to kind of structure the discussion and say "Maybe we can draw from our last discussion three problem areas, like asserting yourself, apprehension about feeling anonymity in crowds," etc., and I guess included here is the feeling of being "put down," put out, left out. A third problem area related to school and career matters. Actually the first two are very closely related, maybe two sides of the same coin.

Again, asking for feedback from therapist (which also includes same from patient).

If there are three main problem areas, you might be concerned with building some kind of program for her, with her, and include them on *our* agenda next time. Suggest things to be done. Activities become a very important subject because of the sharing between the therapist and the patient; it is important to know what the patient feels and thinks and can do . . . and so on.

THERAPIST. Yes, I can see these are important.

Letting the therapist know what he or she has obtained; reinforcing therapist's work; moving on . . . in the therapy.

SUPERVISOR. You've got here a lot of information. She's given you two whole pages of single-spaced typewritten information (the therapist prepared these notes following a taped interview with the patient). You've trained her well on self-observation so far and she's given you very good information. Now, distilling the information down into several large units which you are concerned with—and that doesn't mean that there won't be other topics spinning off of these or new ones coming up—is a useful way to work with her.

THERAPIST. When you mentioned the three areas did you mean fear of driving as one of them?

Some retructuring needed here.

SUPERVISOR. Yes, I did intend to include fear of driving, fear of coping with some social situations, anonymous situations . . . tall buildings . . . crowds . . . driving—they could sort of all be put succinctly under one.

Perhaps not a separate problem, maybe an offshot from underassertiveness.

A second problem—her anger—she can cope with in several ways by saying, "Well these people on the road are the same as I am. They may not like my being here and I don't like their being here but we're all here so it's senseless to be angry." In other words, cope with the anger which then might release some of the anxiety. Then maybe try to relate that with her concern about tall buildings, etc. If you want to, you can walk down the street with her a couple of blocks down Pa. Ave. . . .

Perhaps an in vivo effort would be beneficial, and likely very informative to patient and therapist.

THERAPIST. (Interrupting) . . . Yeah, use about 15 minutes every session just to do that.

SUPERVISOR. Maybe, and I would go out early in the session so you and she have time to talk about it—don't wait till the last 15 minutes. And if walking along she gets apprehensive, then stop a minute, talk a minute, and then walk along again.

The patient is still more into pathology and less into remedial effort; therapist must "roll with the punches" a bit more.

THERAPIST. Right. To review briefly, I did give her the relaxation tape but she said she would put it onto another tape, and she wants to record her dreams and her experiences around her fears and feelings and so on. She is keeping a log. I also gave her a questionnaire to fill out just about all kinds of past history that the clinic had given me.

SUPERVISOR.   Any question about your procedure?

THERAPIST.   No, not just now—there's plenty to work on though. . . .

SUPERVISOR.   That's good! Full speed ahead.

An excellent observation to be followed up on . . .

THERAPIST.   Yeah, and some of the anxieties I've noticed were not as acute as they had seemed before. A previous therapist who did the intake on her said to me that she (the patient) was a very angry young woman, very anxious and upset in the beginning, demanding "You've got to give me something for these anxieties." None of that was evident in these sessions. Maybe just beginning work on specific issues is, itself, reassuring and therapeutic.

Helps view therapy as a practical problem-solving effort.

SUPERVISOR.   Once she's started therapy she sort of has the ball rolling toward solutions. She's not as demanding.

THERAPIST.   Yeah, but I didn't pick up the anger that the previous therapist had mentioned in her and she did seem fairly at ease. I would like to try and record the next session again because I'd like feedback from you on my input.

On to more problem-solving effort; and more reinforcement of the therapist.

SUPERVISOR.   Yeah, she's giving you a lot of information which means you've got lots of materials for the therapy and you're using it well.

   The second supervisory session between the therapist and the supervisor is reproduced below. This second session took place two weeks after the first one cited above; the skipped session was due to the illness of the supervisor. This session is likewise, a 25–30 minute recorded session between therapist and supervisor.

   It will be noted in the second supervisory session that the notes come closer to carrying out the second and third steps among the four steps elucidated above, and that the comments also fit in more clearly with the overall schema proffered in Chapter 3. The novice therapist recorded here had not gone through a desensitization exercise previously with a patient, hence there were a number of halting steps. The impression should not be gained, however, that a desensitization program is usually easy, pat, or highly reliable once it is agreed upon by patient and therapist. There are many idiosyncracies in setting up a desensitization hierarchy and many adjustments that have to be made with the patient and between the patient and the environment as the desensitization program proceeds.

Recapitulation.

SUPERVISOR.   It has been a couple of weeks since we've met on your patient and we left the therapy with three or four questions or three or four areas of possible concern.

THERAPIST. Yes.

SUPERVISOR. Maybe you have some observations on those areas that you can tell me about.

THERAPIST. What has come up since the last time we talked is the fear of driving seems to be the most important area.

SUPERVISOR. The one that gives her the most trouble right now?

Listing some major areas of concern.

THERAPIST. Yeah. Also what has emerged even more, I think, is a general lack of assertiveness and some problems expressing anger.

SUPERVISOR. Those are two problem areas that we talked about before; are they clarifying a little bit as you go along with her?

THERAPIST. Right. Yes, they are. Her problem with tall buildings seems to have subsided or else she'd been able to avoid the buildings that give her trouble.

Further review of presenting complaints.

SUPERVISOR. This driving business was the third point where there was anxiety—first, in crowds; second, when around tall buildings; and third, with driving. You are telling me now that she reports the driving is most important and the other problems are being solved or minimized?

THERAPIST. Right. The patient has also reported that she has not had the headaches that she complained of before.

SUPERVISOR. That's good—has she been relaxing?

THERAPIST. She's been relaxing more easily, has been using the relaxation tape every night, and seems more and more able to benefit from it.

SUPERVISOR. What about headaches and relaxation?

THERAPIST. Today, for example, she reported that she hasn't had a headache since the last session—several days—whereas she used to have them daily. Also she reported that she had driven three times last week without too much trouble.

Asking for specifics.

SUPERVISOR. Where did she drive to and from? Was it necessary, like shopping or driving to work? What was the context in which the driving occurred?

THERAPIST. One time was simply getting in her sister's car and driving up and down 16th street, just to drive the car for her sister, who was out of town for the time.

SUPERVISOR. To keep the car going while her sister was away?

THERAPIST. Right. Another one was to a grocery store, and the third one was here to the clinic today.

SUPERVISOR. But she didn't have much anxiety in any of these cases?

THERAPIST. Not as much as previously. She did have some, and the most anxiety she has had lately is coming to the clinic. She ran into some unusual traffic problems, she said.

Offering another hypothesis regarding patient's behavior.

SUPERVISOR.   Worse traffic than usual?—plus the fact that she was coming to talk to you about herself?

Reviewing another (old) problem.

THERAPIST.   Probably, I am not sure . . . I think that coming here has some influence although I am not sure how much. Another area that we've discussed was hypoglycemia. She has had, besides nervousness and anxiety, a lot of dizziness and exhaustion and was hospitalized last January for fainting and dizziness. The doctor she saw administered the glucose tolerance test and is unclear on the outcome, but it appeared that she probably is hypoglycemic.

SUPERVISOR.   Did they give her any medication?

THERAPIST.   No, they didn't. The physician whom she saw doesn't believe in hypoglycemia and in fact told her to eat sugar which, I have heard, may be the worst possible thing she can do. She borrowed a copy of Abramson's book which has a diet for hypoglycemia, which I think she's been following the last two weeks. She reported she is much improved in the last week. She's checking it with her family physician.

SUPERVISOR.   Good. By watching her diet she's improved?

Reference to specific therapeutic techniques and other related experiences.

THERAPIST.   Yes, but there were several variables—she had watched her diet, she had a week's vacation, she had quit her job which was a problem for her. So she's not sure how much is her own relaxation. What I have done with her is instructed her to begin working on relaxation without the tape so that it is easier to do it in the office, and explained to her the hierarchy and what that entails.

SUPERVISOR.   The hierarchy was related to what? Driving, wasn't it?

THERAPIST.   Yes, related to the driving. We began working on this last week and I gave her instruction sheets which explained the construction of the hierarchy and had her work on it herself at home which she had done.

SUPERVISOR.   You have kept a copy of that instruction sheet?

THERAPIST.   Yes, and we spent the rest of the session this morning filling out the hierarchy. We have probably 20 items and I told her that probably next week we could begin working on it.

Summarizing how therapy is proceeding.

SUPERVISOR.   So you are getting her ready for it by letting her read first about how a hierarchy is established, about how she would apply it to her own driving; then next week she can begin to report to you.

THERAPIST.   Yes, but she did have some questions. One of the questions she asked today was whether it would be helpful for her to practice driving by just driving back and forth to the grocery store. I didn't see that there would be much help in her doing this at this point. I did think that it might be helpful *after* we've gone through some items in the hierarchy to then have her go out and try that.

Differentiating therapeutic tactics and conditions.

SUPERVISOR.   In other words doing the driving under more prescribed conditions now rather than just driving in the face of the anxiety?

THERAPIST. Yes. Today I suggested she begin working on relaxation regarding driving without the tapes so that she's able to do it in the office. I explained, and and as I said, have given her instruction sheets about the hierarchy and what it would entail.

Checking out the particular therapeutic tactic.

SUPERVISOR. Can she afford to wait? I mean are her errands so complicated or necessary that whether she goes on the bus, rides with somebody else, or drives herself, makes a big difference?

THERAPIST. Probably not—not right now anyhow. Later, she should drive herself as she overcomes the anxiety.

SUPERVISOR. That plan is all right with her then?

Some tactics require more active patient participation.

THERAPIST. Yes, what she was suggesting was essentially a practice driving session—not just going to the grocery store in order to get something—but a more specific effort which I tend to agree on.

SUPERVISOR. Fine! She's eager to work on it, which is a good sign. What you may want her to do is work under the best possible auspices in overcoming the anxiety connected with driving after she's learned some relaxation and desensitization techniques.

Preparing for a broad therapeutic strategy.

THERAPIST. Yes, that's right and I would like to go over the hierarchy with you.

SUPERVISOR. Go ahead.

Details of a strategy.

THERAPIST. This is the hierarchy we worked out. And I think that the rules are essentially. . . . Well, we started out doing what has been suggested, getting a zero level, going up to 100, and filling in from there. One question that I have here is there are a lot of variables. I am not sure whether I should put them all in the same hierarchy, or not. Zero level would be riding a bike on the street with little or no traffic. Also with zero level is such a thing as seeing a car parked or seeing a car in motion at a distance. Then level 3 would be seeing a car parked; 4 would be seeing a truck or bus moving; 5 would be getting in as a passenger in a friend's car or getting in a bus without a hassle which means nonrush hour and no crowds. Ten would be anticipating driving—for example, this weekend she needs to drive from her place in S_____ to F_____, and just the anticipation of doing that is anxiety provoking; 15 would be getting in the car to drive herself somewhere; 20 would be being a passenger for 10 blocks; 25 would be driving her own car for ten blocks to the grocery store in a nonrush hour situation—that would take about 5 minutes; 30 is driving her own car to the clinic which takes about 15 minutes; 35, driving for a longer time—say 20 minutes to her mother's, with stoplights; 40, riding on the bus for half an hour—the problems with that are that she feels trapped on the bus with the noise and confusion when she's alone; 45 would be a passenger in a friend's car coming home from somewhere in a light rain—rain for her is much more palatable than the sun—the sun makes things more noticeable and produces visual confusion. Coming home in a friend's car on a freeway.

SUPERVISOR. With the friend driving?

THERAPIST. Yes, with the friend driving. A rating of 50 would be riding in a friend's car, on the freeway during nonrush hour, the weather being sunny; 55 will be driving on _____ Park at night alone. Night is less anxiety provoking than day. A rating of 60 is getting in a bus as a passenger in rush hour after having walked two and a half blocks through noise and confusion; 65 is being in _____ Park during the day in nonrush hour driving alone.

SUPERVISOR. That's because of the twisting and turning?

THERAPIST. It's more because there are no stoplights—there's no break in the speed.

SUPERVISOR. When there's no break in the speed that creates more anxiety because she has to do more things?

THERAPIST. No. Less anxiety because she goes more slowly. A rating of 70 is driving her mother's car alone in _____ Park during the rush hour. In the last session it came out that she was much less anxious in her mother's car than in her own.

SUPERVISOR. But this is a higher rating.

THERAPIST. Right. Let's see. What we put in there was *during rush hour*.

SUPERVISOR. OK.

THERAPIST. We go from a nonrush hour situation in her own car to a rush hour situation but in her mother's car. Then the next is 75, driving her own car in rush hour situation. I wanted to tell you a little bit about the difference between the cars. She mentioned last week that she felt her own car, although she knew this was not true, but there are times she felt her own car had "a mind of its own." She felt it wanted to crash, it wanted to kill her. She didn't want to commit suicide herself but *it* wanted to.

SUPERVISOR. That wasn't true in her mother's car, or in riding in another person's car?

THERAPIST. That's right. We'll pick that up later. A rating of 80 is being a passenger in a bus during the rush hour where there is a lot of traffic. Apparently the bus is anxiety producing for her. An 85 would be driving on _____ Highway in normal traffic in the outside lane with a soft rain; 90 would be on the same highway in pre-rush hour on a sunny afternoon in the middle lane; 95 will be driving on the same major highway in a traffic jam in rush hour and driving alone. In the worst condition, she would be driving on _____ Highway to S _____ making it a long trip, starting in afternoon rush hour, alone, in the middle lane which makes her feel trapped, in sunny weather, driving her own car—that's the most problematic.

SUPERVISOR. So breaking that continuum down and getting that hierarchy would give three, four, or five variables?

THERAPIST. At least.

Temporary evaluation of a strategy.

SUPERVISOR. Whether she's in her car or someone else's car; in a car, in a bus; in heavy traffic, in light traffic; rain or sunshine; middle lane, outside lanes; distance that she's going, etc. But, that's all right, they all package themselves, don't they?

THERAPIST. Well, it seems to me that we are putting enough of them in at different places so that all of them get handled.

SUPERVISOR. Is there enough reliability in this hierarchy? I doubt very much that you can get this hierarchy next time, even for one variable like driving her own car.

THERAPIST. I see.

SUPERVISOR. See if she *can* reproduce her hierarchy for her own car. I suspect there are too many points. She might reproduce 0, 25, 50, 75, 100 but I doubt if she can reproduce all.

THERAPIST. I wouldn't think she could.

SUPERVISOR. And it's not important that she can. It's just important that we don't spend too much time on small differences.

Seeing that patient is ready to work on specifics.

THERAPIST. At the end of the session this morning, I ran over quickly to be sure that things were in fairly proper order. She felt comfortable with the hierarchy and seems to be ready to go on this week.

SUPERVISOR. Even if it were a very reliable hierarchy of 20 points each—5 gradations from 0 to 100—you wouldn't be able to reconstruct all those particular conditions and work on them, all the different combinations that occurred. We are probably just going to have the main 0, 20, 40, etc., up to 100, based on driving in her own car, to really work on with her in real life (this refers to the therapist going along with the patient in her actual driving).

THERAPIST. Right. In fact, not even necessarily those gradations because it will depend on the weather, the time of day, etc.—even when driving her own car—when she comes in for the sessions. One of my questions is whether you think this is all right to "go" with?

SUPERVISOR. Yes, I think so. I think the main thing is it's probably too elaborate and will have to be collapsed at various points. But she'll probably do that anyhow because she's not going to remember and make all the combinations that are being made here with these descriptions.

Applying a given tactic/strategy.

THERAPIST. But should I be the one who reminds her of the combinations, when I present the situation to her?

SUPERVISOR. I would think you are not going to deal with more than 0, 20, maybe 25, 50, 70, or 80, etc., unless you find new points on the hierarchy again, just when she's driving her own car.

Problems in applying a given tactic/strategy.

THERAPIST. You mean you think that I won't use 15 or 20 different hierarchical points? How do I decipher to determine which ones I use and which ones I don't? Go from 5 to 15 and if there's problem there I'll go back to 10?

SUPERVISOR. Right. Because if these circumstances and ratings are not terribly reliable, they can mislead you and the patient. Let's say, hypothetically, the 12th floor of a tall building produces in a patient the worst anxiety; you have to go through other levels before you get to the 12th floor—there's no question. It's a continuum, it's fixed. But the other continua in this patient's hierachy in relation to driving cover various points, may mix with other continua, related to the weather, and other conditions, and so on; they are going to be very hard to duplicate in real life.

THERAPIST. I see.

Further clarification of a procedure.

SUPERVISOR. Every hierarchy that I know about has changed somewhat with the review of the hierarchy and the discussion of it, not to mention the changes that take place when it's tested in real life.

THERAPIST. It's an approximation, not a ladder with fixed steps.

SUPERVISOR. Yes, it's a rough approximation.

THERAPIST. So you would suggest going from 0 to 5 to 15, then to 25 or. . . .

SUPERVISOR. Yes, as a first approximation; the patient is your guide, however, and the fineness of the steps that are useful depends upon her.

More clarification regarding a strategy.

THERAPIST. How many times would you think I should go through this before taking her out?

SUPERVISOR. That's very hard to answer. I think she's got to be ready to go out. She's got to concur in your having done enough vicariously to give her some confidence, and you, in turn, are going to get some feedback from her on how she's handling it. I would say you would probably be pretty far up on the hierarchy before you go out into real life for the actual driving, even on a limited basis.

THERAPIST. Is there some rough rule about how many hierarchical points can usually be covered in one session?

SUPERVISOR. Probably not. It may be impossible to cover all 20 or so points in one session. You may cover only a few the first time you do it; and it would be better to go as slowly as you can during the first few times. You are in no hurry about this desensitization and if you are too hasty you may loose her confidence in the technique. So take it easy. You might need three, four, five, or six vicarious sessions before she's willing to go out and try it. But, of course, "trying out" is not a total effort either; trying out must start with a very simple, mild situation.

Mixing up tactics too much.

THERAPIST. OK. I see it is all pretty open. One thing that I told her today which I am not sure about saying—that she would hopefully include some of her other anxiety problems; they might be subsumed under the relaxation training related to her driving anxiety. Would you have told her that? Do you think . . . ?

SUPERVISOR. I think it's more something you probably just keep in mind right now and you don't need to tell her. You don't want to promise her something you cannot control. Better, later, to observe a possible generalization, rather than state it as a prospect.

THERAPIST. The reason I mentioned these other possible benefits is because she's been getting flagged by her boyfriend who sort of looked at her as if she were crazy when she said she was going to the therapist because of her driving phobia.

SUPERVISOR. But you can't answer her problems with her boyfriend for her in this respect.

THERAPIST. I see.

Further clarification of a tactic/strategy.

SUPERVISOR. Does she relate to him the details of your discussions?

THERAPIST. No. I advised her to just not talk about it with him and she did drop it.

SUPERVISOR. OK. Let it rest there for now.

Discussing other tactics, other issues.

THERAPIST. I am wondering whether for the next few sessions should I or we just concentrate on the hierarchy? Or should I ask her about other things going on in her life? How the week has been or whatever?

Helping the therapist restructure the therapy hour.

SUPERVISOR. Yes, if you and she agree, I suggest a review of the week and how things have been going in a general way, relating to the other problems, the ones we have named as problem areas. And then, secondly, you get into the hierarchy—again, if it meets the approval of both of you. That way you leave 15–20 minutes to deal with the hierarchy and other things you want to talk about as a result of the hierarchy. So I would say the first third of the hour would probably be used to cover the points—the problem areas—we have already mentioned; second, the middle third of the time could be devoted to the hierarchy and the last third would be the reactions to the hierarchy and what's coming up in the next week or so, and anything else she thinks of. That assumes you both feel this to be an efficient and useful alignment of the time.

Some review of patient evaluative behaviors.

THERAPIST. I follow you. Today she reported how much better she felt; she even was able to kid with me about "Now I am cured—ready to go—is there a 90-day guarantee?" and she seemed very hopeful and forward-looking to me.

SUPERVISOR. Yes, she's feeling some good results, which is fine—very reinforcing for her! And you!

THERAPIST. Yes, but also she's taking her problems a little bit less seriously, not as overwhelmed by them, more able to approach them.

Firming up the therapist's role; asking for evidence or data.

SUPERVISOR. Let's find out wherein she's better. Don't take that statement at face value anymore than you are taking a complaint statement at face value. Determine how, under what circumstances, she feels better. She can say, "I went downtown and the tall buildings didn't bother me." Or, "I went to a party and I moved around and talked to people and I didn't feel pressured and anxious." Get documentation of these things.

THERAPIST. For example, the fact that she had no headaches, that she drove three times with little anxiety, that she's not feeling the general anxiety that she usually gets—these are what you mean?

Further identification of patient's positive and negative results, including feelings.

SUPERVISOR.   Yes, they are each good examples if clearly identified and supported. Do you have any evidence that she's asserting herself better in social situations, interpersonally, say with her boyfriend or mother or somebody?

THERAPIST.   Last week she mentioned not being able to assert herself with her mother. We had somewhat role-played on that topic before, but she was not able to carry it through. She was, however, able to assert herself with her boyfriend to a point that she said she really didn't want to watch a particular program on television. At least she was able to make that one small step where the boyfriend was concerned by telling him what she wanted. I also gave her an assignment doing something for herself during the week of vacation.

SUPERVISOR.   Doing something for herself, meaning what?

THERAPIST.   Doing the things that she particularly wanted to do and she did that—she went to see a movie of her own choosing, rather than going along with her guy to wherever he wanted to go.

SUPERVISOR.   So there are several sides to her assertiveness?

THERAPIST.   Right. So should I continue checking on the assertiveness, encouraging that?

Restatement of therapist's behavioral goals vis-à-vis patient.

SUPERVISOR.   Yes, in fact the first part of the next session you might touch base on the problem areas what we have already identified. One of them is assertiveness, as you will recall. Let's see how all these issues appear next time—assertiveness, driving-a-car-anxiety, handling crowds and the like.[1]

SUPERVISORY COMMENTS ON AN INTAKE INTERVIEW

The following intake interview was recorded by a tyro therapist who had had about three months' therapy supervision in a university psychological clinic setting but had only limited experience with intake interviewing. Both therapist and client were females, the former being a clinical psychology graduate student, age 26, the latter being a graduating senior, age 21.

[1] A six-month follow-up of this patient revealed the following: She began to cope more successfully with family members, reducing her anxiety level considerably; she made more clear and explicit vocational/education plans and secured a better job, one offering experience closer to her chosen professional career; she was able to drive her car or another person's car readily about the city and on the highway without appreciable anxiety, and on one occasion drove approximately 1000 miles with her fiance on a round trip to a midwestern city; and although she was able to settle many differences with her fiance, she remained somewhat beholden to his efforts to control her, causing her periodic anxiety as they encountered minor crises in their relationship.

The supervisory comments were not delivered directly, as per this recorded transcription, to the young therapist, but were inserted into the main protocol by way of the italicized comments shown below. Several comments may be made in reference to the interposed supervisor comments: First, there are many more projected comments by the supervisor than are offered by the tyro therapist. This springs partly from experience, partly from a greater tendency to "keep structure," and partly from the style or activity level differences of the young therapist and the supervisor. Second, the supervisor is more inquiring from the beginning than is the therapist. The supervisor evidently has more grasp on the overall nature of the patient's problems than does the as-yet-inexperienced therapist. Third, in attempting to "keep structure" and move the therapy along into significant problems, the supervisor tends to summarize or make comments considerably more often than the therapist. Presumably this greater attention to keeping structure can aid the patient, as well as the therapist, in understanding and dealing in practical ways with the patient's problems. The feeling of "getting into the problems" is much greater with the supervisor's stance than with that of the therapist. However, the therapist is learning and needs time to gain both the tactical skill necessary to interact gainfully with the patient and feel on top of the whole therapy enterprise. Fourth, the supervisor senses that the patient is caught in several conflicts and may require several short interviews on a more immediate basis in order to modify her concern, to get her eating and sleeping and routinizing her life more ably, as well as meeting the upcoming examination schedule, visit home, and other exigencies in her life. The patient is rather deficient at this time in her self-esteem and in her self-management capabilities; active support by the therapist that is both emotionally relevant to the patient and structuring in the sense of getting into the task of changing her behavior is amply called for. In this intake interview, the patient seems to evidence little or no recognition that things she says and does—or does not say or do—have much to do with her anxieties. The more the therapist can first follow the emotional lead of the patient and, while discussing the feelings openly, carry them onward into a *recognition of the circumstances* that underlie the emotional upset and the circumstances that will hopefully change the emotional upset, the more ably will the therapy progress.

THERAPIST. I read about your reasons for coming here—can you tell me a little bit more about how we might be of help?

PATIENT. Yes. I haven't been very active lately and things are getting worse; I got sick about the middle of October with a very severe strep throat, and I was very weak and tired and very sick and had to stay home for about two and a half weeks.

I had to quit my job which wasn't much but it was keeping me busy, because I needed only four courses to graduate at the end of this semester.

Supervisor: You have felt a great letdown from the illness and the loss of momentum, it would seem?

I used to study quite a bit—now I don't. I have too much time on my hands; I didn't previously have the same lethargy. I think I've tried to get back to things too quickly and wasn't recovering fast enough, so the doctor told me to stay home and finally I went home last weekend. I got better, got back to school, and just took the MSAT just for the hell of it; that was the same day I was taken sick and I didn't realize that it had affected me so much. I wasn't really into taking the test. I didn't do very well, but I wasn't really counting on it.

Supervisor: Just one bunch of problems after another have been upsetting you, you seem to be saying. And they adversely affected your qualifying tests?

I lost a tremendous amount of weight as I have stopped eating; that was triggered off last Sunday night—I haven't had an appetite and I was very upset too. I was nauseous and physically fatigued; I wasn't sleeping either; I went back to the doctor on Friday who I've been seeing—she's really nice—we talked for a while and I let things pour out. Part of the problem, she says, is that I have an allergy that has been affected by my illness.

Supervisor: And on top of all the emotional upset there is a physical problem or two?

She gave me a new medicine which has helped a lot (I even feel nauseated saying this), and I've been trying to calm down . . . but I talked to a friend of mine who is in a clinical psychology program and he suggested that I come here and talk about things.

Supervisor: You are saying you felt it was about time you took matters in your own hands instead of just being so upset all the time?

A lot of it just all of a sudden hit me but I am graduating and I have a major that doesn't really give me much hope in looking for a job in January. I have to look for something though.

THERAPIST. What is your major?

Supervisor: This is a fair-to-middling question in one sense but it is a response to a trivial part of the previous monologue of the patient, which included many topics of importance.

PATIENT. It is French Literature and Culture. But I have been pretty much accepted into graduate school here on a part-time basis; it ought to keep me busy.

Supervisor: Keeping busy seems to be an important consideration for you now that you are both anxious and less well occupied in your studies, and uncertain of your future after graduation?

I got afraid that I won't see enough people after graduation, and all my friends will be moving away. I am afraid of getting very lonely. My boyfriend will be studying all the time and I won't see him. This may put a strain on the relationship.

Supervisor: You see your boyfriend pretty regularly now? And other friends, too?

It got me uptight, got me nervous, and I was making myself so much sicker that I was physically sick. The more I thought about it the more I was getting myself mentally sick and right now I'm just a bundle of nerves.

Supervisor: The boyfriend situation, graduation, no clear job prospects all pose serious conflicts for you?

I've pretty much recognized all my problems and it seems to me like they are foolish but I am going to have to cope with them. But the nerves are still there—my stomach is very tight, my emotions tend to get my muscles tight. I am still not eating that well, I have to find ways to relax myself, get rid of this anxiety and I thought that talking to people who are objective will help me more than being a burden on my friends, and especially my boyfriend.

Supervisor: Well, you certainly reveal a number of problems we can together begin to work on. Can you say which one or ones are the most important to start off with?

We are planning to get married in about a year and a half and frankly he says he can't if I turn out to be someone that he can't handle.

Supervisor: He's made you feel uncertain about what you mean to him? Especially if you bring a host of problems to your relationship with him?

My parents are behind me one hundred percent and support me, but I guess I am the one to cope with this nervousness. Like I wake up every morning at 7:00 a.m. with my heart beating so fast. I can't sleep late, I get too exhausted, I can't sleep very good.

Supervisor: Even though others express concern, it is essentially up to you to get to work on your problems.

THERAPIST. Has this kind of thing ever happened to you before?

Supervisor: The loss of sleep, or poor sleep, seems to add appreciably to your problems.

PATIENT. Well, I get uptight too easily. I remember in my freshman year I was unhappy in school but just for a while. Ever since I quit my job I have had so much time on my hands I can't use it well. I used to study so much but this past week I was just watching TV and doing nothing.

THERAPIST. Just no motivation?

Supervisor: A fairly adequate response, but the therapist could respond more to the issue of abundance of time as it conflicts with poor self-management.

PATIENT. I am paralyzed. I just get so upset and scared. I think too much.

THERAPIST. What happens, what's the fear?

Supervisor: You may be afraid that you can't solve the problems, that they may over-burden you—is that correct?

PATIENT. I just let my mind go. It keeps going and going thinking, and doesn't stop thinking. But it is not creative thinking though.

THERAPIST. The feeling of being lost. . . .

PATIENT. Yeah. It's scary stuff.

THERAPIST. Tell me a little bit about your family. Do you have brothers and sisters?

Supervisor: A question not at all called for in this context, and the question suggests the therapist has not "kept structure" or discriminated the several conflicts evident (or inherent) in the patient's remarks. The question is generally misleading, poorly timed, and insensitive.

PATIENT. Yes. I have a brother who is a freshman in college. He is in _____ and he goes home a lot. He goes to _____. We are really close. Our family is really close.

THERAPIST. What do your parents do?

Supervisor: Another diversionary and even misleading question. Continuity with all the patient has said is essentially forfeited.

PATIENT. They are accountants. They work together. They are really good. My mother is often blunt with me. She said I should let my problems out. She doesn't like the idea of my getting nervous because she gets nervous. I grind my teeth and I was even taking some Valium® given me by my dentist. I tried using that last week to calm me down and all it did was made me more sluggish.

Supervisor: Do you not have confidence in trying to get help or relaxation from drugs?

THERAPIST. How do you feel right now in comparison to how you felt in the last few weeks?

Supervisor: A good question relative to other questions asked by the therapist.

PATIENT. I feel better every day, a little bit. I am facing things. Once I get going I am all right. It just hits me—the anxiety. Sometimes in the afternoon I get physically weak from not eating, and from being so nervous.

Supervisor: You're feeling somewhat better I can see, but there is still a lot of work we may have to do to help you get further control of yourself.

THERAPIST. Is it because food is not attractive to you?

Supervisor: Not a really good question, but it may pass.

PATIENT. Well, I want to eat and I sit down and then can't eat anything. I am trying to eat. I did lose a lot of weight but to start with, I wasn't heavy. I needed to lose about five pounds but I think I went over that too fast. The funniest thing was I was perfectly all right when I was home the week before. As soon as I got my law boards results it just triggered off everything.

THERAPIST. You were feeling better again at home?

Supervisor: The board results did upset you—let's hear more about that. The therapist really missed the main point here, but could have come back to how the patient felt at home versus how she felt upon returning to school and then getting to the board (MSAT) results. There's lots to tie together there and it might take some time and effort to do it.

PATIENT. Yes, I rested, I slept, and I ate good meals and all of a sudden. . . .

THERAPIST. Your anxiety got back after getting your results? It's almost as if you were reminded again of where you were in your life right now.

Supervisor: A very good response, tapping the relevant issue in a sensitive and leading way.

PATIENT. Right. But I've been feeling this loneliness. In fact, I was feeling low in my apartment. When I was sick and during that time it was hard to try to make up the midterms—I tried to get back too quickly.

Supervisor: You overworked yourself?

THERAPIST. Did you get all that done?

PATIENT. I got it all done.

THERAPIST. How are your grades?

Supervisor: A fairly good question but it risks losing the relevant issues of falling behind now (versus earlier excellent achievement) and how all this ties in with the patient's other conflicts regarding anxiety about relations with her boyfriend, graduation, job versus graduate school, and so forth.

PATIENT. Very good. My last two semesters I got straight A's. This semester I won't get straight A's but close to it.

THERAPIST. So you have been pretty successful in school.

PATIENT. Yes, I've enjoyed school. I didn't at the beginning until I learned to enjoy it. I talk to my parents when I go home, worked with my mom. This semester I have been very different possibly because of my boyfriend. It's the first time we've been going out during the school year starting this summer. He gets upset when he sees me sick and it affects his work and I can't let that happen to him. He's a very dedicated student.

Supervisor: In spite of good grades you're much more concerned about your relationship with your boyfriend and that conflict overrides many other matters—is that a fair statement?

THERAPIST. So there's pressure if you don't get over this pretty quick?

PATIENT. Before he has another exam, like before Monday. I know I am expecting miracles but I think I made a positive step by coming here.

Supervisor: This tends to corroborate what was inserted above and seems to be saying she wants (hopes) that the relationship with the boyfriend will prove stable and that her own problems won't interfere with that relationship. It is entirely possible that the relationship with her boyfriend is the pivotal issue in her life and that her illness, her psychological problems, and her less-than-expected score on the MSAT all conflict with what her boyfriend expects from her or what she thinks he expects from her. This relationship may, indeed, be our central issue.

THERAPIST. I agree. I think it's a real good idea. Let me tell you a little bit about what we can do. It sounds like, to me at least, this is a pretty situational anxiety attack that has gone over a couple of weeks and it's probably getting more and more scary and harder to get rid of the more pressure you see from outside. Now there's only a couple of weeks left and you are going to be gone for vacation. I would say that it might be helpful to set up a program for you to do some relaxation, to focus on what these anxieties might be about and try to find some other ways of getting it out of your system rather than putting it in your stomach and making yourself sick.

Supervisor: A fairly good summary of some aspects of the patient/therapist relationship. Of possibly more value would be a statement to the point that the patient is experiencing (evidencing) several conflicts between herself and her environment, and also "within" herself (conflicting purposes), and that the therapy can work toward clarifying these issues in several ways.

PATIENT. I always keep it inside. I get tense. When I get tense I get muscle spasms and I can feel that in my stomach and my heart beats too fast.

Supervisor: The patient has given a very good capsule statement of her problems. It can be coupled with what has been suggested above by the supervisor.

THERAPIST. It sounds like it's something we could work out. Since this is close to the end of the semester, we kind of have to work out what your schedule is like and how long you are going to be here (meaning enrolled in the university) and all that stuff.

PATIENT. I'll be going home for vacation. I will be going home for Thanksgiving. Then I'll probably be going home the 15th of December to January 7th.

THERAPIST. What would probably happen would be that someone from our clinic will be in touch with you soon—tomorrow is the day the committee gets together and looks into the intakes and makes assignment of cases.

PATIENT. I really would appreciate it. If my health wasn't affected I wouldn't mind but the doctor at the health center said I was just getting so weak—and like today I felt like I was getting sicker and sicker, and that's not good.

Supervisor: The action you've taken in coming here for help will enable us to get started on your problems. It would be helpful, I think, if you began by making some notes–keeping a log–on how you feel each day, what your "ups" and "downs" are, and started observing the situations that seem to make you feel your best or worst, so we can have some more specifics on what is troubling you and what we can, together, do about these matters. Is that all right with you?

This patient was very full of positive, negative, and confused feelings and rambled excessively—as do many patients—propelled by the consuming anxiety that controlled much of her behavior. This anxiety was fueled by many conflicts: the relationship with her boyfriend, who had apparently thrown some doubt into her feeling about their relationship; an absence of self-management of time in connection with quitting her job and with more leisure at the end of the semester; a confrontation as to what she would do the following semester owing to doubts about entering medical school, graduate school, getting a job, and the way her actions in these matters would apparently affect the way her boyfriend felt about her. On top of all these problems she had developed some physical illness, perhaps arising partly out of poor habits of eating and sleeping, and the constant anxiety of not knowing what to do about her general situation. She came to the clinic for therapy probably on an off-remark by a friend who was a graduate student in clinical psychology, rather than having considered this as a concerted step. She could have come expecting immediate and unqualified relief as a result of following another's suggestion of "what she ought to do" and conceivably have been disappointed and quit therapy before she got a real hold on matters. However, the more the therapist could structure these conflicts, from moment to moment, as they occurred in her "recital," the more she could be given the feeling that the therapist was understanding and supportive and that the problems could be stated in a way that permitted working on them concretely. This action by the therapist could reinforce the patient's feeling that therapy could help. It is very important in the early stages of therapy that the therapist react to the patient's problems in ways that structure, define, and open up possibilities for self-control and change; the patient is provided not with a wholly clear or certain pathway to problem solving, but one that lays down realistic and testable guidelines, one that is meaningful to the patient at the time.

Therapists can err in promising too little or too much. The patient gains a large number of impressions of the therapist and of the work of the therapy itself in the early interviews, and thus it is essential that the structuring of therapy take place in ways that are reassuring and coping rather than being too delaying or, the opposite, too superficial and overly optimistic. The novice therapist can hardly be expected to find this dividing line easily; it comes from experience and from an open reaction to the patient and his or her plight, plus a willingness to call on general principles of behavioral interaction that have to be learned in the exchange between patient and therapist rather than from a list of techniques, per se.

This patient did not need to be "taught" to recognize her feelings—if anything, the feelings and emotional reactions were florid and confused and left her further dependent upon the sheer recital of feelings, in contrast to learning more about the events in her life to which the feelings bore a relationship. Many therapies seem to say that the patient must get in touch with his or her feelings and some therapists center almost the entire therapeutic work on these issues. It seems to be assumed in the more classical, dynamic, and "depth" positions that all or nearly all feelings are repressed, dormant, unrecognized, or unavailable to labeling and discussion. Although feelings may sometimes be poorly discerned and, as behaviors themselves, not related to antecedent and consequent conditions, it is sometimes the case, as it appears to be with this young woman, that feelings are rampant and easily lost from their moorings. If a therapeutic approach takes as its vantage point dealing with feelings abundantly available and also misses the opportunity to begin to tie the feelings in with other behaviors of an antecedent and consequent nature, the therapy may bog down or wander aimlessly.

AN EXAMPLE OF KEEPING STRUCTURE

The following case represents an effort on the part of the therapist to "keep structure" as firmly as possible in an intake interview. This interview was conducted by an experienced therapist with a young, female graduate student who, as the protocol indicates, presented herself for help for several problems. As part of the effort of the supervisor conducting this interview, the therapist-in-training, a young man 26 years of age, sat in on the intake interview and later made comments and asked questions that might be construed as helpful to the tyro therapist.

This patient was a 27-year-old married woman, a graduate student, who worked as a stenographer prior to graduate school. She was seen for a total of eight interviews, each about 30 minutes long, mostly on a once-a-week basis. The interview recorded here was the first one following a brief intake interview in which she filled out a demographic form, indicated her preferred times for consultation, and briefly wrote out what she considered to be her reasons for seeking psychotherapy.

As indicated, a graduate student in clinical psychology sat in on the interview. Later, when the taped interview was transcribed—some details were left out in order to preserve anonymity—some of the student's comments and questions were included, as shown in the italicized portions of the protocol. This procedure—allowing the beginning student to sit in on an interview, with permission from the patient—is felt to be a very helpful one in bringing therapeutic issues to life in subsequent discussion. What was transpiring in therapy, and some rationale supporting the therapist's conduct were often the focal points.

In addition, this patient listened to her own therapy sessions between each pair of sessions (see Chapter 2, technique 53) and often commented on how much she derived from the second listening where, as she put it, "I could listen with *both* ears."

In studying and discussing this protocol, the reader should refer back to the beginning pages of this chapter and note, again, the emphasis on structure, on the rationale proffered, and on how well the interview kept pace with these strictures.

THERAPIST. In your write-up on yourself, you mentioned difficulty concentrating and becoming easily bored; sabotaging yourself. You wanted to find out why, what you can do about it and how to find more efficient procedures for all kinds of things. Is that correct?

PATIENT. Yes, I mean *all kinds of things*. Since I couldn't come in last week, I spent a lot of time thinking and I think even deciding to do this has helped me.

THERAPIST. Started you thinking and looking at things?

PATIENT. Yes, I've been trying to figure out what was basically wrong and why I am oversensitive to criticism.I expect too much of myself, I think. I am unrealistic and I become very frustrated when I don't live up to what I think I should be gainfully doing. As soon as I start doing something well, I become bored with it or whatever—and I stop paying attention.

THERAPIST. You get bored *too* easily?

PATIENT. Well, I don't know whether it's boredom or if it's . . . I'm not quite sure what it is. But I just can't seem to be able to concentrate.

THERAPIST. Concentrate on school work for example, or on anything?

PATIENT. Oh, school work or things like what I want to do when I "grow up." (Laughs nervously). Even hobbies—I find something that I've become very interested in and start doing well, then lose interest—I quit.

THERAPIST. You get bored again, and you give up.

PATIENT. I sure do. I don't know whether it's giving up in the sense of "Gee, this is hard so I am not going to work at it." Or "Well, OK, I can do this I know so I should find something else."

THERAPIST. Or prove to yourself that you can do it and find something that is more challenging? (Pause) But you never find anything that continues to be interesting and challenging, I gather?

PATIENT. Right. Exactly. I am 27 years old and I think I should start settling down. I guess I've come a long way because I think there should be something better before I just have to say "That's the way I was."

THERAPIST. Have you worked on these issues before? Had therapy before?

Beginning therapist: Why did you ask this question at this place in the conversation?

Therapist: Just to determine if her present plight had occurred and had been worked on in a therapeutic way before, and possibly how her present move to therapy came about. It may well help mobilize her present determination.

PATIENT. Not really. In high school I had a guidance teacher who had his Ph.D., I'm not sure in what, but I talked with him quite a bit during my sophomore year. It was sort of like therapy.

THERAPIST. Sounds like it.

PATIENT. It was very good for me.

THERAPIST. And since then?

PATIENT. No. Nothing.

THERAPIST. Then, you've been contemplating it without getting around to doing it?

PATIENT. Yes.

THERAPIST. How long have you been thinking about it?

PATIENT. Golly, for years. I'm not really that bad off though. People who know me think I'm very stable and calm. I guess I just keep it all inside. In fact I went to my physician last spring because I was having trouble with my stomach and he said I was working on an ulcer, which is another thing that I've decided to do something about.

THERAPIST. Have you got an ulcer now?

PATIENT. No. I've quit my job, which was very frustrating. But I begin teaching soon. My husband and I went to W_____ for a month and I've just tried to avoid the situations that bother me so much.

THERAPIST. Are you working now?

PATIENT. I'm teaching part-time and going to graduate school. I'm in the doctorate program here full-time in _____. I guess as I get closer to the degree I start thinking whether this is really what I want to do. Is it worth it? Why don't I go raise puppies? I ask myself.

THERAPIST. Do you have any other interests or hobbies or other skills that you can pursue if you wanted to?

PATIENT. You mean as a career? I don't know—I haven't really developed anything.

THERAPIST. You said raise puppies. Are you just picking that up out of the blue or what?

Beginning therapist: Is this important now or is it a deflection from the main topics in therapy?

Therapist: It is just a side issue, I felt, tapping whether she is, in fact, looking seriously to alternatives to graduate school.

PATIENT. We've got two dogs. I like puppies.

THERAPIST. But you haven't actually considered raising or breeding dogs?

PATIENT. No.

THERAPIST. You don't have any other skills?

PATIENT. Well, I've worked as a secretary. I worked here while I got my master's degree. Once I got my master's degree, I decided not to be a secretary again, and that was 1973.

THERAPIST. What have you done about these problems of boredom and not concentrating and so forth?

BeginningTherapist: You changed back to her earlier stated problems here; why?

Therapist: The immediately previous discussion was mainly a fact-finding one and we appeared ready to return to the real issue of her coming for help.

PATIENT. Well, I put things off until I'm under so much pressure that I have to get them done.

THERAPIST. Procrastinate a lot.

PATIENT. Yes, I practice that a lot.

THERAPIST. Is that how you study for exams?

PATIENT. Generally. I have a very excellent memory. I can get by. That's another thing—I feel that I could do much better than I have and I've done reasonably well, but maybe I'm striving for self-actualization or something. But underneath it all I'm just thinking about why I do these things. I really don't think much of myself. I don't have much self-confidence; I don't have self-esteem. Anything that I'm working on I can put off for somebody else because what I'm doing can't be that important. And I've always given in to other people, and put aside what I've wanted to do, to do what they wanted me to do. I think that's a lot of my procrastination. I just overcommit myself. I honor my commitments to other people before I honor my own commitments to myself. I have good days when everything is all right but when something goes wrong I really get down in the dumps.

THERAPIST. You base your esteem on the approval of others by placing them first and doing things for them rather than for yourself. Can you give me an example or two of that?

PATIENT. Well, for one thing I find it very surprising to think that people find me attractive. My husband has a way of looking at me with this adoring look and some days I find myself . . . the question pops into my mind like "I wonder what he sees in me?" That kind of thing really shakes me up. And I'm constantly surprised that people like me. I'm surprised when people do something nice for me although I do nice things for people.

THERAPIST. Have you had something like that occur recently that bothered you or made you stop and think?

Beginning therapist: I see you are always attempting to nail things down, get specifics, to relate feelings to actual events.

Therapist: Yes, a good observation on your part. Feelings are behavior, too, and must be attended to in that light rather than detached from other behavior.

PATIENT. Well, the thing with my husband Sunday—it just sort of shocked me when . . . I wonder what he sees in me.

THERAPIST. But you think you don't appraise yourself the way others do?

PATIENT. Right.

THERAPIST. But this thing with your husband occurred to you all of a sudden? It's not an old problem that recurred many times?

PATIENT. No, it didn't *just* occur. He looked at me and said I was crazy.

THERAPIST. He was a little astonished that you raised the question at that time and place?

PATIENT. Quite astonished.

THERAPIST. Have you raised that question with anybody else? Friends, for example?

Beginning therapist: Were you looking for a broader basis for her problems rather than self-estimates just with her husband?
Therapist: Yes, quite. I want to know other times and places of the same or similar problems—if they exist—as these, too, have to be handled in their emotional context and related to still other factual conditions.

PATIENT.   No.

THERAPIST.   You said a while ago when you started talking that you are unrealistic and expect too much. Do you think that's connected with these feelings of self-abnegation? Expecting too much *conflicts* with reality.

PATIENT.   Oh, yeah. Since I should do everything perfectly the first time, since I don't—obviously—I'm not very good and I see two sides of the same coin. There *is* a conflict, then.

THERAPIST.   So you're bound to defeat.

PATIENT.   Right.

THERAPIST.   So if you change your expectations, that might give us a handle on that jug. Now, by definition, you can't succeed; you're bound to failure. So if you keep expectations too high, what is going to *hit* you is failure. But what is also subtle and persevering here is that you're so perfectionistic. In other words you should do better all the time; not doing better is, perforce, failure. That's the conflict again.

PATIENT.   Rationally, I know that. That doesn't help me much.

THERAPIST.   But don't you have a *superiority* feeling rather than inferiority one? In other words, superiority comes first, inferiority, failure, later?

PATIENT.   I'm not really sure. I think maybe it does. That's one to ponder.

THERAPIST.   What makes you think it may be true for you?

PATIENT.   Well, just the fact that I haven't given up, that I keep on trying. But really, I know that I'm intelligent, that I can do things, I mean I've seen what I've done.

THERAPIST.   You mean you have evidence that you can do well?

PATIENT.   Yeah, I have all sorts of evidence.

THERAPIST.   But you are not perfect, even though you do well. You want to be *perfect.*

PATIENT.   Right!

THERAPIST.   And when and as you want to be perfect, your denigration comes from imperfection rather than doing a reasonably good job. In other words, you are way up here in your expectations (raising hand high), you may perform here (lowering hand), but since you expect the higher one you may drop way down here (lowering hand still lower) in terms of your feelings of self-appraisal. Later, reasserting your *expected* superiority keeps you in kind of a vicious circle, doesn't it? A conflict that repeats and repeats.

PATIENT.   Yes, I can see that somewhat.

THERAPIST.   What do you think triggered off this self-appraisal Sunday with your husband? What do you think triggered that off?

PATIENT. Well, I've just been doing a lot of thinking more or less the last couple of weeks and I guess probably just the fact that I've been asking myself questions like "What am I doing and why?" I was just sort of in tune for that.

THERAPIST. Did he say or do anything that triggered that off?

PATIENT. He just looked at me adoringly.

THERAPIST. How do you know it was adoringly?

PATIENT. Because he put his arms around me and gave me this soft smile, you know like a puppy with big soft, brown eyes. I just don't feel worth it.

THERAPIST. How do you feel toward him?

PATIENT. I respect him a lot. I think he's very intelligent; he's very well organized; I think he's a pretty superior person. I respect him a lot.

THERAPIST. Do you let him know you feel this way?

PATIENT. Yes.

THERAPIST. Are your likings for each other on a different basis? Do you love him as well as respect him?

PATIENT. Oh, yes. We're best friends. He's a very romantic person. He's an _____; he took a lot of literature and philosophy too. He's a very humanistic type of a person, very intelligent. He's more realistic. He wants to do well but he knows he can't be perfect so he just does the best he can, but he's very competent. He does work on the car, plasters, he does things in the arts, he writes, and so on.

THERAPIST. Very versatile!

PATIENT. Yeah.

THERAPIST. Now, if this feeling that you characteristically display springs from too high or false expectations or perfectionism, wanting too much, which is risky, which is to say you can't get what you want, and then following that you feel down and unworthy—what do you think you can do about this state of affairs?

Beginning therapist: I see you returned again to the issue of expectations versus realizations and seem to be hammering hard at it.

Therapist: Yes, that's true. Not hammering but recalling its apparent significance to her and trying to tie it in to her feelings of degradation, into her occasional and spontaneous negative self-estimates and into her relationship with her husband.

Beginning therapist: This theme is important with her and so needs to be emphasized—but it is also important in some other patients I see.

Therapist: I'm confident you have good points on both counts.

PATIENT. Well, I keep telling myself to be more realistic, to know that I can't do everything perfectly.

THERAPIST. How do you tell yourself that?

PATIENT. I don't know, sit down and lecture myself.

THERAPIST. Did you do that lately?

PATIENT. Yes.

THERAPIST. Give me an example, please.

PATIENT. Well, I am taking _____ lessons, and someday I'll have my first exam or appearance, or recital.

THERAPIST. Are you preparing for this date?

PATIENT. Yes, the other day the instructor was there helping me. I was really tired and not doing well. I can handle things all right until I'm tired. Once I get tired I just fall apart.

THERAPIST. Well, how do these lessons apply to our discussion of perfectionism?

PATIENT. I made a mistake. I didn't do it right the first time through. I should have gone through my part exactly as I aspired to, and since I didn't do it right, there's something wrong. Rationally, after I got over being so tired, I said to myself that that's the reason I did poorly, relatively. The instructor knows better than I that I can make these mistakes; he's not hard on me. Yet, the initial feeling I had afterwards, I sort of crawled home and wanted to crawl in the corner. I just felt like I was bombed out.

THERAPIST. Do you know what you did wrong now, in retrospect?

PATIENT. Yes, and I'll probably never do it again.

THERAPIST. So you learned from it but you are so perfectionistic you couldn't allow yourself—especially in front of the instructor—to make the mistake in the first place?

PATIENT. Right, which is why I've avoided some situations where there was a possibility of failing. I've always been very conservative as far as trying to do things. That's one thing my husband has done and is trying to coach me. And I think just from the fact that I'm doing them, allowing for mistakes and finding out that it's not the end of the world, that I am now beginning to make progress.

THERAPIST. Loosened up a little? How long have you been taking these lessons?

PATIENT. Since July—three months only.

THERAPIST. Are you competing with others for the quickest certificate, a minimum time? You would like to walk off with your certificate after 10 lessons and say, "Look what I did!"

PATIENT. Oh, I'd love to. Yes.

THERAPIST. Are you really striving for that?

PATIENT. No, I've decided that that's unrealistic.

THERAPIST. Do you fantasize about it?

Beginning therapist: You talked here and at other times about fantasy. Is that behavioral?

Therapist: Yes, any verbal report is, perforce, behavior. Any report on feelings, images, et cetera, introduced by the patient is behavior. All we have to deal with is behavior, although this point is often obscured by fuzzy language and unclear conceptualizations. You couldn't say to the patient "We won't talk about images, dreams, fantasy because they are not behavior"—they are just more subtle than many forms of behavior we deal with but nonetheless important.

PATIENT. No, not right now. When I first started the course, I did.

THERAPIST. You did resort more to fantasy earlier in the course, then when you goofed up last Sunday that threatened your fantasy and expectations too much. Maybe other things did too but at least that occasion threatened your global expectations.

PATIENT. Right.

THERAPIST. Were these mistakes you made in your program unusual?

PATIENT. No, they are typical. It is sort of what happens when you get in there trying to do "your thing." You get carried away and you forget to do some things.

THERAPIST. You develop new cues to go by, so as to monitor your performance?

PATIENT. It's a learning experience. Somehow, somewhere, I got this idea that everything should be up here (pointing to her head) already, that I shouldn't *have* to learn anything, that if I go into a new situation I should already know about it. And that's what I'm trying to overcome, I guess.

THERAPIST. Then if you should already know, then you'll be perfect. So there's nothing to learn because you are already supposed to know how to do it.

PATIENT. Right, or be told once and never forget it, never make a mistake.

THERAPIST. Well, that's a pretty high order, isn't it? What else can you do about that? If you think it's correct or valid to observe this about yourself, what else can you do about it?

Beginning therapist: You have asked again what she can concretely do about these high expectations.

Therapist: Yes, I want to reiterate the importance of the expectations–realization dichotomy, but equally important is to get her to begin to think about how she can bring this tendency under control. The formulation of the discrepancy is one thing—a big conceptual leap in understanding her problems—but, consonant with behavior change efforts, it is important that she see and concretely test out how she can begin to challenge and to overcome the problem.

PATIENT. Well, I keep trying to be more realistic when I get into a situation not to expect too much if things don't go perfectly.

THERAPIST. Well, how do you do that? *Specifically.*

PATIENT. Prep myself beforehand. If I'm rehearsing my part in a recital I just tell myself it's not all going to be perfect. I'm not going to do it right all the time. That's why I'm practicing.

THERAPIST. And does that help?

PATIENT. It does. It's just when too many things happen at once that I sort of get off on the wrong foot, or lose track of what to say and do.

THERAPIST. Other than in your rehearsing for the recital, have you tried to scale down your perfectionism?

PATIENT. Well, I took an art course this summer—a drawing class—I think I did all right. I didn't expect to be Picasso first off. But I started doing water colors this spring and everything that I started out to do I expected to finish the picture so that I'd have it framed.

THERAPIST.   Did you frame any of them?

PATIENT.   I've got one that I'm going to, but I've not gotten around to doing so.

THERAPIST.   So anytime you try something, you expect it to be up there—perfect—right off the bat. How did you learn this sort of behavior?

PATIENT.   Well, I've got a couple of theories about that. One is that I was the "boy" in the family. I don't have any brothers. In fact, I was supposed to be a "Joe." That's how it came to be "Joan," because they didn't have a girl's name picked out. I was always my father's helper, and my father, my parents, were older when they got married. My father was just a very competent person, did a lot of mechanical, handicraft, and artistic work around the house, and every time he would measure something he would always be very exact and would measure it a little bit longer so that if it wasn't quite right he would cut it back, which is easier than adding on. But he worked very slowly, very meticulously and everything always came out right, it seems to me. Because I was around there all the time, I guess I never stopped to think that he had to learn how to do it, too, once upon a time. It just seems to me that people I was around all *knew* what to do—were perfect—and that once I grew up I would know too—and be perfect too.

THERAPIST.   They were so success-prone and skilled as models that you didn't learn what they painstakingly had to learn to make for success versus failure.

PATIENT.   Also, I'm a reasonably intelligent person. I had no trouble in school; I never had to work at it; I never learned how to *work* or struggle at anything. I never failed, though—outright failure.

THERAPIST.   But you are not failing now?

PATIENT.   No, but it bothers me that I don't seem to be able to handle things.

THERAPIST.   Well, are you contradicting yourself? You told me you're intelligent, you are able to do a lot of things; now you're telling me you're not. I think you are possibly caught up on this. I think you are not sure which is which. Or, maybe that you don't get them—your notions of success and failures, expectations, realizations—together at the right times and places. What's coming up ahead now where you can exercise some restraint on what you expect?

Beginning therapist: You reformulated again the fundamental paradigm describing her problems and, again, asked her how she can—in upcoming situations—bring this formulation to bear on her problems. You expect her to state now, in advance, how she can do that? Is this asking too much of her this early in therapy?

Therapist: I don't know, of course, but I'm reiterating the point, not just as an abstraction or as an "insight" but as a functional analysis intended to give her something to go by and to test out our work here. The therapy hour should reach out into the patient's environment as much as possible.

PATIENT.   Well, just in my rehearsing for one thing. I know I'm not going to make my preparation complete in 30–40 hours. I know I'm going to make mistakes, I know I'm going to do dumb things every once in a while.

THERAPIST.   When do you go to your rehearsal again?

PATIENT. Sunday.

THERAPIST. What will you be expected to do?

PATIENT. Plan the rehearsal. Coordinate the roles of others and rehearse my own part.

THERAPIST. And where else can you watch the too-high-expectations thing?

PATIENT. Well, with school, I'm not going to get a "100" on every test.

THERAPIST. Have you any test coming up that you're trying to be perfectionistic about?

PATIENT. No tests—I've got papers mostly.

THERAPIST. Give me an example in your school work where you can scale down this perfectionism or be more realistic in some ways.

PATIENT. Well, with teaching, for one thing. I taught for the first time last summer and got students' course evaluations back that I was very nervous about. I wanted to get the information, yet I didn't necessarily want the administration to see it. I got fairly good ratings and there were some low ones; but in that case, after first being upset that anybody would give me "D's" or "E's" I just said to myself that I can't please all the people all the time. There are going to be some people there who don't like me, so I think I handled that. I'm teaching again, so I'll have teacher evaluations again. I think I'm more realistic than I used to be but I still think that I'm unrealistic enough that it is hampering me from doing as well as I could.

THERAPIST. Are your present teaching preparations all right?

PATIENT. Yes. I think so. It's the same course I taught last summer. So I've got the notes pretty well developed and it's material that I already know. But in my *graduate* work I don't seem to have much confidence in my judgments even though I'm getting toward the end of my graduate program. I still don't think I know much. First, it really bothered me, but now I'm starting to think that, of course, I can't know everything. I think maybe I'm on the right track; perhaps if I can get some help generally getting myself straightened out I'll be more efficient.

THERAPIST. Since our time is about up, could I make a couple of suggestions of things for you to do?

PATIENT. Yes.

THERAPIST. One, I'd like to suggest you keep a log, a daily log, very brief one on the "ups" and "downs" you experience, socially, overtly, or in your own subjective appraisal of yourself, things that are both positive and negative. We can then have a kind of "temperature chart" on your emotions and feelings day to day. It helps you to observe yourself better, it gives us grist for the mill when you come in, and it helps you get data on the problem of self-appraisal in these important situations and gives us more to work with. Second, pay particular attention to when you are "down" and also to whether you are up too "high" with your expectations just before you come down. In other words, are you vulnerable, walking into vulnerable areas, with too much perfectionism or too high an expectation that is bound to be dashed? If you cut down on expectations, then you are going to cut down the failure part. Third, see if there are any places where you can sort of beef up your performance, maybe like checking your notes before class lecture or checking out your role more carefully before rehearsal. Plan out what you will do before you go off next Sunday to rehearsal and see if you've got some of the details in mind instead of assuming that you already know all of them. In other words, challenge that assumption that "I am already supposed to know it perfectly." Challenge your expectations of perfectionism and already knowing everything, and try beefing up the performance in specific ways so that you know in fact what you are going to do.

PATIENT.   I guess I've been entrapping myself by thinking that I should already be able to do anything well so I don't do enough preparation, then I don't do well enough; maybe that's why I procrastinate, because I don't think I need to start working on something because . . . because I am supposed to be able to do it already.

THERAPIST.   It's a vicious circle, isn't it?

PATIENT.   Yeah. Why start working on it now, I seem to say, since I can do it tomorrow just as well. (Pause) Then I get under the time pressure, then I can't do it as well, then it doesn't come out well. That makes a lot of sense that I trap myself this way.

THERAPIST.   And it does repeat itself as you've said. It's a vicious circle because after a "down" then you recover later but when you recover you go back to the old pattern rather than say "Look I've got to revise my expectation, my estimation."

PATIENT.   Yeah, it makes a lot of sense.

THERAPIST.   All right, let's see if we can apply this notion to some areas of your experience—teaching, studying, preparing for your recital or performance—whatever kinds of things that you seem to be vulnerable about, in light of this discussion.

Beginning therapist: I see you tied up the whole thing again: high expectations versus performance, her doing this repeatedly in several situations, your trying to get her to observe this tendency in the future—as well as reflect on past practices—and relating how she feels as a result of this tendency. She seems pretty savvy and optimistic about managing this tendency.

Therapist: True, but let's not go too fast, as these are all verbal formulations here; useful as they are, they have to be tried out and tested out repeatedly by her, on her terms, in the weeks to come. She will come back with pros and cons on all of these items. She will see applications and nuances I can't possibly know or predict, and will use the knowledge and the new discriminations as they fit into her own behavioral economy. I'm reinforcing her, not only in her clarification and conceptualization of problems, but in her readiness to put the ideas to the test.

This case illustrates a fundamental observation in psychotherapy or, if one prefers, in psychopathology: That the *problems* people face can be abstracted and stated in terms of a discrepancy between what they expect (wish, desire, need) on the one hand and what actually comes to reality on the other hand. If there is no discrepancy, except that which can be adjusted to readily, there is no pathology, no problem of any moment. Without a discrepancy, the individual goes directly to a solution, more or less adequate; or, in the case of avoiding or escaping aversive conditions, the organism (individual) forthrightly does just that. Unless something "ties" the person to the situation—involvements with other people, one's own aspirations, one's needs—unless there is a compelling push–pull, the person attends to one or the other condition and forthwith "solves" the problem. Earlier protocols in this chapter might have reached greater conceptual clarity, hence a more practical advantage, had the conflict elements been more solidly stated by the tyro therapists. (See, also, Chapter 3.)

In therapy, then, the therapist does some of his most important work in helping the patient to define the conflict situation—the push–pull conditions—that are "holding" the person's feet to the fire, and that are precluding a solution unless a resolution as to direction is faced and followed. This is part of the review of the antecedent and consequent conditions so important in fully describing the patient's plight.

The last patient recorded here was beginning, even in this first interview (only 30 minutes in length), to define the conflict between aspirations or expectations—born as they were presumably under the guidance of a too perfectionistic upbringing (although this is conjecture, and an issue one seldom, if ever, solves in therapy). She was beginning to state in her own words wherein she was too expectant, and how, when unable to achieve the expected, she denigrated and demeaned herself; although when calm and considerate, and not under the reeling influence of an emotional upset, she knew she was capable and had an achievement record to back up that impression.

Conflict resolution, perforce, comes from first recognizing that one is, indeed, putting himself or herself in an impossible bind; recognizing the elements in the conflict and how they are behaviorally displayed; then taking moves to bring down the expectation and beef up the performance, so that the discrepancy is thereby diminished or put at a tolerable and functional level. This sounds like a pat solution to people's difficulties, but carrying out the formulation is often arduous. The many "side problems," this woman displayed—doing things for others before herself, procrastination, doing "hurry-up" jobs at the last minute, feeling she was (or should be!) perfect and not preparing for her performance requirements (scholarship, teaching, painting, preparing for the recital, etc.)—

are offshoots of the conflict situation she was caught in. By definition, the conflict prevented a direct solution to her problems; the efforts she then followed were indirect, full of vacillation, perturbations, low self-esteem, failure to set and follow objectives or goals, and a persistent or redundant failure to come to grips with the discrepancies involved.

CHAPTER 6

The Clinical Situation: I. Diagnostic and Conceptual Considerations

The fundamental question facing the clinician in the clinical situation is how best to approach the problems presented by the patient. Although this question addresses the matter of type of therapy—that is, behavior modification, Gestalt, psychoanalysis, Rogerian therapy, and the like—it overarches this consideration and asks a question that is, in a sense, prior to the type of therapy employed. It asks a question concerning what we are going to make of the patient's presence and of the data we receive from the patient (or about the patient) (Maslow, 1968; Jourard, 1971; May, 1971; Ornstein, 1975a, 1975b; Lincourt and Olezak, 1974; Fischer, 1973).

One traditional solution to this question is that of relying on standard nomenclature, diagnostic entities, and nosologies. One can easily spend a lot of time "diagnosing" the patient and testing out fine details as to whether the person is this or that type. Often diagnostic efforts are time consuming, but they seldom lead to articulate and reliable approaches to changing the patient's behavior. This diagnostic enterprise too easily becomes an end in itself, leading nowhere but to the file cabinet!

A series of questions that the clinician could ask himself or herself would be much more useful, more scientifically valid, more therapeutically heuristic, and of more value in direct communication with the patient at any or all junctures in the therapy. These questions, while not exhaustive, might go along the following lines:

1. Is the patient ready for therapy in the talking-out sense at this time? That is, are there contingencies the patient is advancing that seem to the therapist to aid, or to militate against, therapy?

2. Has the patient had any experience with therapy (or advice receiving) of any type prior to this that would influence positively or negatively the current activation of therapy?

3. Does the patient live in a milieu that would appear to support therapy as now practiced in this setting; or will there need to be a trial period before the patient is ready, willing, and able to go forth? Or are there outright contradictions for therapy?

4. Will the patient be likely to cooperate in specific suggestions, practices, assignments, and the like that might seem to the patient and the therapist to be useful? Is the therapist an effective reinforcer?

5. Does the patient have (articulate) goals he or she wishes to achieve? If not ready with such articulation, does the patient respond reasonably and thoughtfully upon questioning along these lines?

6. Are the patient's presenting complaints such that they can be readily communicated between therapist and patient? Are they initially, potentially convertible into at least implicit, if not explicit, goals?

7. Are there extenuating circumstances in the patient's life in the form of economic or financial pressures, living conditions, health, family, social, or related matters that seem to put a damper on how well the patient can use the present therapeutic opportunity?

8. In general, is the patient's repertoire of behavior, as currently and provisionally judged, one that includes a "readiness" for talking therapy?

9. What positive reinforcement opportunities now exist in the patient's repertoire or in patient's environment for change?

10. What negative or restraining or competing influences exist in the patient's repertoire militating against change at this time? Are these influences amenable to change?

Of some importance, to be sure, is the judgment that the therapist places on the patient, his or her presenting complaints, and the possible answers to these and other questions. No set of answers to these questions can be so objective that all therapists (even behavioral therapists) would agree on them; there is still a lot of room for maneuvering on the basis of timing, how strongly the therapist wishes his or her contingencies met, and the long-range view that the therapist has of the therapeutic enterprise.

If the therapist is reasonably satisfied that positive answers can be fitted to the questions listed above—or, indeed, to most of them—then the enterprise should go forth. If the criterion level of the therapist is much higher, he or she may send the patient to someone else, put the patient off for an agreed-upon period of time to see if changes in "readiness" have been stimulated by this discussion, or try the patient on a very lean therapeutic schedule in order to allow for an outside chance that the therapist was wrong about most answers to the question.

FROM QUESTIONS TO DIAGNOSIS: DEPRESSION

Useful as many questions such as those cited above may be to the clinician, it is important to address here the problems related to diagnostic and conceptual considerations and to relate traditional diagnostic efforts to behavioral analysis. It almost seems that traditional diagnoses are one world and behavioral analyses of these categories a wholly different world. How do we get them together in order to display differences and similarities? We begin this enterprise by referring to depression.

Depression is probably the most commonly used diagnostic category (Beck, 1967; Ferster, 1973). Depression also occurs in common association with other diagnostic categories such as hypochondriasis, hysteria, psychasthenia, and schizophrenia, and in various relationships with manic states. Depression appears clinically clear—the patient is slow, retarded in movement, speech, and affect; displays a loss of interest in social activities; exhibits worry, complaining, low self-esteem and a generally negative outlook on life. If the depression is a "reactive" state, that is, apparently in response to some recent loss of affection, job, security, or the like, the contrast between the depressive state and the pre-depressive state is often marked.

All the above features are behavioral manifestations of depression; they are all signs of behavioral change, even though the person may report also on his or her own feeling states which generally tend to corroborate the overtly observable behaviors. In common-sense ways, the so-called internal feeling states are said to "explain" the observable depression— the person "doesn't feel like getting up," so stays in bed.

It is economical in trying to conceptually clarify depression to put the emphasis on the observable behaviors but to try, also, to relate the subjective states to the observables since they basically are one process, not two separate ("inside" and "outside") processes.

Probably more than any other behavioral psychologist, Ferster (1973, 1967; Ferster, Culbertson, and Boren, 1975) has written about depression as a "loss of behavior." This term refers to several features of the depressed person. One is reduction in frequency of commonly engaged in positively reinforced activities such as social interactions, eating, sleeping, and sexual activity. Another is escape from aversiveness in the sense of asking for help, complaining, and avoiding or postponing effort and responsibility where previously the person handled these obligations satisfactorily. Futhermore, the depressed person shows a loss of behavior in his or her failure to initiate, sustain, and be reinforced by those activities that maintain a high degree of relationship with others and with the work-a-day world necessary for ordinary economic and social intercourse. When the depressive condition is particularly intense, bizarre or unusual behaviors may result (excessive speech unrelated to the behavior of the presumed listener; incoherence in speech or other motor behavior; ritualistic behaviors such as pacing, hand-wringing, and crying). These behaviors generally signal a more severe absence of ordinary social reinforcers derived from interactions with others and further indicate a change from positive social reinforcement to aversiveness in association with others.

Figure 8 suggests how, from a functional, behavioral analysis standpoint, depressive states develop (Ferster, 1973). There is a marked shift, for whatever reason (loss of loved one, loss of financial security, etc.), from gaining positive reinforcement from the environment to a predominance of aversiveness, and ultimately the development of highly preemptive bizarre behaviors that tend to isolate the person from his or her usual social environment and make change less likely. In a behavioral position, one has to be mindful of how the shift in reinforcement occurs, then put the emphasis in therapy on gaining positive reinforcement from the patient's natural environment rather than trying to deal directly with the aversiveness, the complaining, and the bizarre behaviors themselves. Paying attention to the aversiveness beyond a modicum can easily lead to the reinforcement of talking about aversiveness excessively in therapy, to the therapist reinforcing whining and complaining, and to unproductive efforts to "tease out" the labyrinths of bizarre behaviors which are

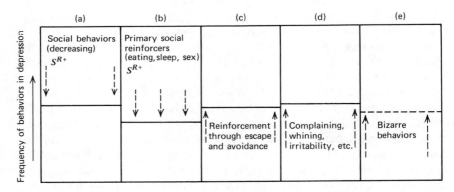

Figure 8. Amending and adapting some of Ferster's discussion (Ferster, 1973) to fit the present context, we see common social behaviors (a) diminishing, along with primary reinforcers (b). As these behaviors diminish in depression, reinforcement through escape and avoidance (c) increase, along with complaining and whining (d), producing in the more disturbed depressive state bizarre behaviors (e) that may tend to dominate the individual's social behavior. The task of counseling/psychotherapy with the depressed person is to increase the reinforcement potential of the first two columns (a and b), to help reeducate the person so that escape behaviors, complaining, and bizarre behaviors (c,d,e) decrease in probability. Depression, then, is not approached as an entity or as a separate problem but as functionally related to the probability of columns (a) and (b) developing and remaining predominant in the person's behavior economy. (The author is indebted to Steven Sowards for some formulation in relation to this figure.)

mostly by-products of the lack of substantive, social reinforcement. If the person in his or her pre-depressed state commanded a wide range of social skills, these can be reactivated under proper contingent control. If the individual possibly never learned a wide repertoire of social skills, these deficits will probably have to be focused on in psychotherapy or counseling and may even necessitate the activation of prosthetic environments of some type (see discussion in Chapter 1 on "rules" in relation to psychopathology, pp. 19–24). Social skill loss, however temporary, or social skill deficit, becomes the focal point therapeutically in overcoming many depressive states. The more profound, or so-called endogenous, depressive states may be differentiated, at least in part, by a recognition of the degree to which previous social skill repertoires were once functioning adequately. Where a competent behavioral economy of social skills never existed, the therapeutic task may be more challenging and difficult and this may well be what we mean by endogenous depression in contrast to reactive depression.

The patient–therapist interactions become important when attempting to overcome depression, as it is easy for the therapist to be drawn into the patient's complaining and aversive withdrawal tendencies. In responding to the patient's feeling states—hopelessness, despair, complaining, crying—it is difficult for the therapist to avoid reinforcing these aspects of the patient's behavior. At the same time, the therapist may experience difficulty in getting the patient to "try out" old (or new) social behaviors since contingent control of these efforts is not often available to the therapist. Verbal techniques are the most likely sources of therapist-to-patient reinforcement attempts, and these may appear weak when the out-of-therapy environment of the patient is hard to manage. Emphasis on in-therapy transactions, while important, may not yield enough data to encourage the patient to attempt to build social skills of the order needed; hence the support of others (spouses, other family members, the work environment) may be required.

There are three frames of reference about the patient's behavior when the patient and therapist are talking, this being true of depressive as well as other types of difficulties: First is the immediate interaction between patient and therapist, that which is actually transpiring verbally and nonverbally between the two during the therapy period. Second, there are the references the patient uses to describe his or her out-of-therapy behavior ("I didn't get up to go to work this morning, I felt so badly.") which may become an important part of understanding both the repertoire of the patient and the value of the connection between the in-therapy and out-of-therapy reference points in the patient–therapist interactions. There is a constant play, back and forth, between what is currently transpiring in therapy and what is referred to in the out-of-therapy environment of the patient. One value that behavioral techniques have is to bridge the gap between in-therapy and out-of-therapy considerations, and to prevent both therapist and patient from losing sight of the integral relationship between these two interconnected sets of events. The more the therapy interaction itself can pay attention to both the immediacy of the situation and its wider implications in the behavioral economy of the patient, the more leverage or contingent control can be established to benefit the patient. If the therapist pays attention (responds) only to what the patient says about his or her outside experiences, then the nuances of the interactions of the moment are lost and the therapist passes by opportunities to bring into focus those facets that allow for the development of self-control first through the immediate patient–therapist interaction and, later, on the patient's part in his or her own self-interest.

On the other hand, one can focus therapeutically too stringently on the immediacy of the situation (this is what many of the newer therapies appear to do in stressing the here and now emotional experiences of the patient) and thereby isolate the patient from his surroundings, many of which may actually give rise to the emotional attitudes and opinions expressed verbally (or nonverbally) during the therapy interaction itself. One can become isolated in the present as well as superficial in dealing only with the out-of-therapy events. A comfortable balance between the two is sorely needed.

A third reference base of importance between patient and therapist in the depressive case (it occurs with other sets of complaints as well) is where the patient refers to nonobservable (presumably causal) events located elsewhere. Ferster (1967, p. 35) put the matter cogently when he said: "The way a depressive patient talks about himself is an important class of factual information and it becomes non-behavioral and unobjective only when it is taken as symptomatic of events elsewhere rather than as an activity of importance in itself." When the patient says something like, "I think I am trying to cause myself to fail in school and this depresses me . . . ," the data here are not only the spoken words, which are of immediate value in the therapist–patient transaction, but it is equally important to avoid being caught up in some esoteric and unassessable "explanation" the patient may offer as to why he is not doing well in school. The therapist might reply something like "Failing might result from not studying, poor study efforts, not going to class, not getting in your work, and so on—does your reference to failure pivot on any of these types of behaviors on your part?" This way, the immediate interaction is called upon to clarify the out-of-therapy activity of the patient and also to disabuse the patient of any nonobjective or nonfunctional way of looking at his alleged failure. Sometimes, too, patients who make sweeping statements such as the above are really academically successful but are pointing to a general discrepancy between their aspirations on the one hand and their actual achievement on the other hand, where the achievement picture is not actually one of failure but one of not living up to expectations. This clarification as part of the in-therapy interaction can go a long way toward defining the presumptive cause of the reported depression, toward discovering the importance of the patient's own "theory" about himself (what he "ought" to do), and toward remedial efforts that can aid in correcting the expectations–realization dichotomy, but at the same time build better work methods in the scholastic setting. Attention to such prosaic matters as how and when the patient studies, the development of schedules of work and play, the setting of personal contingencies whereby he rewards himself with a movie after he has gotten his work done, and so on, represents an amalgamation of in-therapy interactions that pivot on out-of-therapy activities and, in turn, get referred back to the therapy hour where the therapist can contingently reinforce the patient for having made gains in self-control. This self-control, correspondingly, gets turned over to the patient himself in time, and the therapy advances as a result of this integration. In this gainful set of activities in regard to the patient's reported depression and alleged cause of same, we obtain an integration of all three frames of reference: We use the in-therapy interaction to identify the problem verbally; the out-of-therapy activity is coordinated with the therapeutic discussion; and the patient sees more practical ways of conceptualizing his problems and of overcoming his deficit (which is presumably responsible, in part, for his reported depression).

Some important generalizations when viewing depression in a functional way are the following:

1. Depression, as such, does not need to be the focus of therapeutic attention; the therapy should focus on developing positive alternatives (some of which may be in the patient's behavioral economy) and to playing down (avoid reinforcing) aversive reactions.

2. Bizarre behaviors will tend to drop out as positive behaviors become more problem solving.

3. Withdrawal behaviors supportive of depression that are learned under intermittent schedules are harder to overcome than behaviors learned under nonintermittent schedules. Since we do not know the exact conditions under which persons learn given behaviors, we *infer*, if change is difficult, that the depressive (or unwanted) behaviors were probably learned under intermittent conditions.

4. It is difficult in the case of the depressed patient not to unwittingly reinforce (through attention) the withdrawn complaining or aversion-avoiding behavior of the patient. Learning what maintains this behavior is important in therapy; then, moving to alter these maintaining consequences is of utmost importance.

5. The application of the various techniques (see Chapter 2) serves not only the process of behavior change but links the in-therapy observations and formulation with the out-of-therapy ones. It is essential that in-therapy and out-of-therapy formulations of the patient's behavior be synchronized and conceptually clear, and, through the selection of behavioral technique, show the way to behavior change.

DEPRESSIVE REACTIONS AS A VICIOUS CIRCLE

One can look at the phenomena of depression as a cybernetic loop (see Chapter 9). In the clinical description of depressive reactions and feelings patients often refer to the cyclic or recurrent nature of their experience. They are not depressed all of the time; some depressive reactions are more noticeable than others; some depressive reactions seem to stem from certain classes of experiences. Moreover, all these phenomena tend to recur in a somewhat orderly manner, even though it is difficult to say at first just what the ordering is.

In offering a cybernetic loop type of description, we might select "avoidance behavior" as the pivotal consideration for purposes of illustration. Figure 9 shows how this loop might be constructed on the basis of what the patient reports about himself. The patient states that he goes to parties, "But I get off to myself, don't talk to anyone, sit alone in a corner, and leave after a short while. Then when I go home, I feel guilty for having left, hate myself, resolve to do better next time, but just do the same thing again—it seems like I get caught in a vicious circle and while I know it, I cannot change it. All this makes me very depressed and feeling out of control." Later this patient added: "Even if someone tries to talk with me, I tend to be short with them, or too witty, or try to make some other impression that is nonsense—I don't just talk simply and easily with anyone."

The kinds of depressive reactions discussed in the clinical literature are at least epitomized in this description, although individual cases may differ in content and detail. Breaking into the vicious circle might include a number of therapeutic maneuvers with patient and therapist concurring: by having the patient agree to attempt to talk for a few minutes to at least one person at the party; by avoiding sitting in one place but, rather,

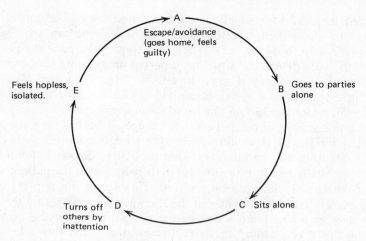

Figure 9. A description of one patient's "typical party behavior" ending in his going home prematurely and feeling guilt thereafter. This was a highly repetitive pattern. If the pattern continued unabated the patient might develop more isolated and even bizarre behaviors. As this "vicious circle" continues, it tends to narrow in the sense of taking less time to reactivate and complete (the patient spends less and less time at parties, goes more infrequently); some junctures in the loop might drop out (e.g., skipping "D" by sitting alone a while then getting up and going home).

circulating around the room (or house) a few times during the evening; by agreeing not to leave the party until the contingent social behaviors have been engaged in; and so forth. If possible, the patient in question might attempt to go to the party with another person (this can often be difficult to arrange, as the prerequisite behaviors may be lacking at the outset); or might attempt to "hitch a ride home with someone," and so forth. Breaking into the vicious circle at one or more junctures ("A," "B," "C," in Figure 9) would be a tactical position taken by the therapist and patient together with the patient at least verbally understanding (and concurring) in a how-to-do-it plan. Apropos of the above discussion, the in-therapy "plan" would make explicit the conditions under which the present depressive behavior takes place and would, further, attempt to change some of these behaviors by an out-of-therapy assignment which, when attempted, would be reported on for further discussion during the next therapy session, and so on through gradual steps wherein some social skills and efforts became more manifest.

One advantage to the "vicious circle" type of analysis is that it pivots all the descriptive junctures on what the patient tells about himself and relates his or her feelings of depression to the type of activity (or lack of it)

engaged in at various times. Esoteric or nonobservable causal explanations by the patient are less likely if the patient can see, with the
therapist's help, how the very series of activities the patient shows may
end in the very distressful situation reported on as being unacceptable to
the patient. The therapist says, in effect: "Here you are, Mr. or Ms.
Patient, engaging in a series of activities you describe and knowingly
engage in, which lead to an untoward consequence; our task, now, is to
cut into this vicious circle and effect a change—where is the easiest place
to begin for you?" It would appear that this procedure can become a
highly effective way to integrate what transpires between therapist and
patient (verbally and/or nonverbally) in therapy and in the patient's world
out-of-therapy. Picking up on and conceptualizing the depressive "vicious cycle" aids the patient and the therapist in anticipating the conditions that may reactivate a depressive period, gives advice on how to
prevent this reactivation "the next time around," and shows how intervention at various junctures in the cycle may be appropriately managed.
The cyclic junctures of a depressive reaction are, themselves, ways of
maintaining depression; the vicious circle is, in a sense, the depression, as
it describes and supports all aspects of what we call depression. (Refer
here, also, to Chapter 9 on cybernetics.)

LEARNED HELPLESSNESS AND DEPRESSIVE REACTIONS

This model of depression stems from both laboratory (animal) studies
and from human studies (Seligman, 1974; Seligman and Maier, 1967;
Thornton and Jacobs, 1971; Page, 1971; Brush, 1969). The main thrust of
the argument is that people and animals may learn passivity and inactivity
in the face of frustration, hence not escape or perform other acts instrumental to avoidance or to the reduction of stress. The basic theoretical/
experimental paradigm is put in the following way by Seligman and Maier
1967, pp. 8–9):

"Learning theory has stressed that two operations, explicit continuity
between events (acquisition) and explicit non-continuity (extinction) produce learning. A third operation that is proposed, independence between
events, also produces learning, and such learning may have effects upon
behavior that differ from the effects of explicit pairing and explicit non-
pairing. Such learning may produce a S who does not attempt to escape
electric shock; an S who, even if he does respond, may not benefit from
instrumental contingencies."

If we think of escape and/or avoidance as a near-inevitable response to aversiveness, we have now, according to Seligman and Maier, to consider the possibility that the organism (animal or man) may learn simply not to respond, to be utterly passive, helpless. This condition of passivity, extended in time, would probably be tantamount to depression, as there are many similarities between both human and animal subjects and depressed human clinical cases in this helplessness paradigm.

Studying human subjects in the "helplessness" paradigm, Thornton and Jacobs (1971, p. 371) assert:

"In reality, the whole basis of helplessness is transfer of a learned state from one task to a second. Whereas animals transferred a self-learned helplessness state, humans transferred an instructional set, internally verified, learned helplessness state. The point is that they did transfer 'helplessness' to a second task which, in fact, offered control."

The experimental situations depicted in these quotations from Seligman and Maier and from Thornton and Jacobs are extrapolated to clinical situations and offer an explanation of depression that results from a different learning paradigm (different from acquisition and from extinction), and that seems to result in such a deficit on the subject's part that no way of learning escape or avoidance appears possible; depressive helplessness is the outcome. Learned helplessness can, however, be viewed as an avoidance reaction itself, not in terms of fleeing but in terms of avoidance through minimal effort. The environment in the sense of the experimental manipulations in these studies has resulted in a null class of response possibilities. This state of "learned helplessness," with respect to the possibilities of responding in the experimental situation, derives from an "instructional set" (as if to say to the organism, "You're better off *not* responding at all"), and contrasts with the notions of depression where there has been an otherwise adequate repertoire (in reactive depression states) but currently a "loss of behavior" that depletes the repertoire.

In a sense, then, the two models—the one discussed earlier based on Ferster's work and the currently discussed one based on the work of Seligman and others—are *opposites* in some respects as they discuss the origins of the depressive state. As indicated above, the Ferster proposal suggests that, among other things, aversive stimulation be avoided (this might be part of the therapeutic task), that low-response rates toward social situations be increased through reinforcement contingencies, and the like. The person is not rendered "helpless," but simply slower to respond, characterized by weaker response as well. Seligman's model seems to create an impasse without offering much recourse to the organism. Elsewhere (Seligman, 1974) discusses the proposition again that responding and reinforcement are independent. How, then, one may ask, does anyone ever get out of a depression? What occurs in the responding–reinforcement interdependence that allows the person to begin to respond, however tentatively? Is some responding–reinforcement kept intact, some lost? In this discussion, Seligman (1974, p. 100) says:

"There is no contradiction between the learned helplessness and extinction views [of Ferster] of depression; helplessness, however, is more general. . . . Extinction commonly denotes a set of contingencies in which reinforcement is withdrawn from the situation, so that the subjects' responses (as well as lack of responding) no longer produce reinforcement. . . . Reinforcement, however, may also be presented with a probability greater than zero, and still be presented independent of responding. This is the typical helplessness paradigm, and such procedures cause responding to decrease in probability."

As to overcoming the helplessness of experimental animals—dogs, in Seligman's report (Seligman, 1974, p. 191)—the animals had to be forcibly pulled from one side of the shuttle box, thus allowing for a compartment change (in the shuttle box) which terminated shock. Seligman says, "The experimenters pulled three chronically helpless dogs back and forth across the shuttle box with long leashes" (Seligman, 1974, p. 101); this was done up to 50 times before the dogs began to respond initially to escaping from the aversiveness of the experimental procedures (overcoming their "helplessness"). Thus, a kind of "total push" effort had to be made, a statement reminiscent of very early work by Adolph Meyer. In some earlier experimental work by Anderson and Parmenter (1936, 1941); Gantt (1936, 1944); Masserman (1946); and others, there is discussion of the various types of impasses experimental animals were put in and the resultant incapacity of the organism to respond (while still in the experimental condition), resulting in a response deficit similar to Seligman's "helplessness" paradigm.

As noted in Chapter 1, one difficulty with extrapolating from the experimental laboratory to the clinic is in recognizing that while an experimental arrangement may typify *some* response characterisitics of the human clinical/social situation (as in depression, for example), the fact that the animals are kept in, or returned to, the experimental conditions suggests, itself, a stimulus complex possibly too aversive to allow for the animal's learning new behavior. If such experimental animals were put into "remedial" or "rehabilitative" settings which systematically manipulate certain features (variables) in the original experimental situation, one might discover that the "helplessness" was, indeed, a function of the situation which, when changed even in modest ways, might allow the organism to learn to respond more functionally. In the human case, the individual in therapy is encouraged to "make new friends," "to find a new job," "move to a new setting," and the like, in order to break up the stimulus complex that is so aversive for the patient and so likely to cause (or allow) the patient to maintain his or her nonresponding ("helplessness").

It is entirely possible that the experimental paradigms producing depression or depressive-like responding, comparable to the human case, have not gone far enough in their inquiries. What these studies have shown—as did the earlier work of Parmenter et al. (1939), Gantt (1936, 1942), and Masserman (1946)—is that experimental animals can be made "neurotic" (depressed, inactive, helpless); but little has been shown as yet how these paradigms match the human case when it comes to *overcoming* the results of depressive/helpless/nonresponding behaviors.

Then, too, the cyclic nature of the depressive reaction is not properly accounted for in these formulations (see pp. 175–179 above), a viewpoint which allows for more change to occur in the patient–environment interactions than is accounted for in either Ferster's or Seligman's model. It is this constant change between the patient and his or her environment that allows for, gives rise to, or may even encourage, a diminution of the response deficits characterizing depression, whether these deficits are due to a loss of reinforcement in Ferster's sense or to learned helplessness in Seligman's sense. Although both these formulations go a long way in providing clarity and understanding about depression and how experimental paradigms can render more specific the underlying variables, they both appear to fall short of accounting for some aspects of the human case of depression, namely, the cyclic nature of the complex itself.

LOSS OF BEHAVIOR, HELPLESSNESS, CYCLIC PROCESSES, AND CONFLICT/DISCREPANCY IN THE DEPRESSIVE CASE

It is not possible for a general theory of depression to be proffered at this time. Too little is known about depression from both clinical and experimental studies. However, it is possible to offer a *tentative* set of notions hopfully integrating some prominent existing hypotheses about depression and to apply these notions to the clinical context, specifically to psychotherapy in the verbal, face-to-face setting.

Factually it seems evident that behavioral loss, helplessness, cyclic processes and conflicts abound in depressive reactions (not to mention other deviance reactions). One problem is that of getting some aspects of these proposed views together in order to assist the clinician in his or her work. Some propositions such as the following might contribute to this enterprise.

1. In order for behavior to be described as "a problem," as "unwanted," as a "deficit," there must be some *discrepancy* between what is anticipated (predicted, expected, previously observed, typical, etc.) on the one hand and what is currently observed, on the other hand. If there is no discrepancy there is no problem; this appears axiomatic.

2. The existence of this descrepancy further indicates a *conflict* between what the organism might do (has previously been able to do, the behavior that has previously characterized the repertoire or behavioral economy) and what the organism is now actually doing (present functional characteristics). The conflict signals, or becomes, an active *working on* the descrepancy; the discrepancy is not a static matter like the overly filled file drawer or the too-long trousers a man wears. As soon as there is some active working on the discrepancy, the conflict can be said to be a dynamic (i.e., changing) state of affairs in which the underlying variables interrelate with each other as a function of their quantitative (strength) relationships.

3. How binding or constricting the conflict is depends upon how active the organism is in attempting to overcome the conflict–discrepancy that prevails. As the organism (person) moves toward one or another end of the conflict continuum the values of the conflict in a quantitative sense change; movement toward one kind of solution to the conflict may be reinforcing and encourage a "success begets success" reaction. On the other hand, retreating from the conflict into minimal activity may be reinforcing in that no activity (or minimal activity) is better than punishment. The skilled clinician watches for small signs of approach or avoidance (retreat) from the conflict arena, behaviors that even momentarily reduce the discrepancy between what is "desired" and what is "reality." These small and short threads, allowing the therapist to catch hold of the patient, may often result in a turning point toward more problem solving success by the patient and should be closely watched by the therapist.

4. In addition to the perturbations characterizing the dynamic approach–avoidance exchange in the conflict situation there is, cybernetically speaking (see Chapter 9), a set of cyclic process going on between the patient and his or her environment. These cyclic processes—eating,

sleeping, interacting with others during certain times of the day, working, and so on—tend to reactivate certain aspects of the conflict and the depressive state. For example, the mornings may be the most difficult for the patient such that if he or she can once "get going" the day may be salvaged, but if the patient stays in bed beyond a critical time, all is lost for that day. Seeing these cyclic process as they are reactivated daily, or on other discernible schedules, allows the therapist and patient to get ready for them by minimizing their effects, by altering some part of the "vicious circle," by changing the consequences of a given juncture in the cybernetic loop, or the like. A number of behavioral interventions might be suggested in the instance of a patient reluctant to get out of bed: set an attractive breakfast tray (if the patient enjoys eating) some distance away from the patient's bed so he or she has to get out of bed to eat; help the patient shape the behavior of getting out of bed by first-one-leg-out-then-another, and so on; manage or arrange other contingencies that influence highly reinforcing aspects of the patient's daily routine (once out of bed, many such patients are then reinforced by elements in the daily routine and loose their depressive countenance quickly); and so on. Other junctures in the loop may be interrupted: The patient may go to bed earlier so that arising at a given, critical time increases in probability; the patient may avoid eating in the late evening thereby lessening the likelihood of a turgid, unrestful sleep; the patient may increase physical activity during the day so that sleep is more required, more physically restorative and not simply the end point of an inactive day. Of course, the therapist should not neglect talking with patients about how they can rearrange their lives' contingencies in ways leading to more satisfaction.

5. The prevailing therapeutic task is to be primarily concerned with the *behaviors* of the so-called depressed person and to look with all possible acumen for instances where even the slightest modification in the direction of greater problem solving can be encouraged. One would really do best to forget about "depression" as a label and pose this therapeutic question: "In what ways can the behavior of this person be increased with respect to given goals?" If a salient, simple, and direct question of this type can be held to in the therapeutic exchange, chances are increased that the patient's behavior can be improved with respect to mutually shared, objective goals.

6. Consonant with the above stricture, plus being a central issue in all behavior change, is the following: Behavior change of an observable nature comes before feelings change; the depressive feelings will relent to the overt behavior change once the latter is correctly targeted and effectively interrupts the previous vicious circles of unwanted behavior. With

this reinforcement possibility, new behaviors can come into the behavioral repertoire, or the behavioral economy can shift in important ways, and the patient is on the way to improvement.

OTHER DIAGNOSTIC CATEGORIES

Although depression has been the focus thus far in this chapter, other diagnostic groupings can be looked at in behavioral terms. The main thrust in attempting a behavioral account of such other diagnostic groupings as hypochondriasis, hysteria, and psychasthenia, is that these complex conditions represent essentially avoidance or escape behaviors. One can say that all psychopathology is engendered by discrepancies or conflict and maintained by avoidance or escape behaviors. The role of symptomatology in the diagnostic sense of hypochondriasis, and the like is to reduce tension (from conflict and from descrepancies) by way of escaping or avoiding the worst aspects of the uncomfortableness the person experiences.

Hypochondriasis

Hypochondriasis is characterized by excessive complaining, bodily aches and pains (not substantiated on medical grounds), and concern over bodily functioning or malfunctioning. People showing signs of hypochondriasis are often unduly negative in their outlook on life and may have the effect of making others feel badly or dislike them. Many consult physicians excessively, have shifting or varying complaints, and tend to be defeatist, cynical, and depressed in outlook about themselves and about life generally.

Conventional clinical descriptions of hypochondriacal patients often report them to show "displacement" of symptomatology; that is, displacing psychological complaints onto somatic areas, while at the same time trying to appear reasonable, rational, and socially acceptable in their psychological makeup.

Upon reflection about these kinds of complaints and upon interacting with individuals whom one might describe as showing a hypochondriacal symptomatology (as on the Minnesota Multiphasic Personality Inventory), the clinician is impressed with how much social reinforcement such complaints yield the patient. People feel sorry for the complaining one, do not look upon such a person as able to hold his or her own socially and responsibly, and yield to the complainer. The hypochondriacal person seems to be saying, "See how miserable I am and yet I still keep going

. . . give me credit for all this." The person behaves in ways that do, indeed, obtain reinforcement from a sympathetic interpersonal environment, although others may often become exasperated while giving in to the complainer.

The person with hypochodriacal complaints is good at getting others to offer help and to show concern over the self-centered complaints that are common. This kind of attention reinforces the complaining person's behavior, first by showing concern for the reported ills and second by allowing the complainer to avoid unpleasant or unwelcome responsibilities. The self-centeredness acts as a powerful set of contingencies which say, in effect: "If I am to do what you want, I'll have to feel a lot better than I do now." Or "If I do this, you must understand it is under great pain and suffering for your sake." And the like. The verbal behavior of the complaining/hypochondriacal person is self-reinforcing: "I am a great person for going on despite these hardships and others must appreciate my effort."

Since complaining is so common among "neurotic" difficulties, it might be useful to summarize some of the types of complaints the clinician is likely to meet. There are often seen with hypochondriasis.

1. Complaining intended to ask for help (often on an unrealistic basis). "I'm unable to mow my lawn due to my sore arm—can you mow it for me?" Or, "I don't know when I can ever get my grocery shopping done—can I give you my list, since I can't get my car started?"

2. Complaining owing to one's own guilt and to perhaps intending to make another feel guilty in the same connection, that is, making another responsible for one's plight. "If you had written down the time and place for me, both of us would have avoided the unnecessary wait in the rain."

3. Complaining intended to get another person to change his or her behavior—in effect to get the other person to assume a responsibility. "If you would change your mind and go with me, I would not feel so scared or lonesome—you owe me that."

4. Complaining that intends to absolve the complainer of his or her already existing responsibility, (i.e., an excuse): "I couldn't make it to your party with the dessert because you didn't tell me what to bring or how to get to your place."

5. Some complaints are intended to arouse sympathy: "You should know how much I do . . . how hard I try even though I fail."

6. Complaints arising out of wanting another person to admire the complaining one; wanting the other person to say, "I don't know how you do so much and put up with it all; it must burden you terribly that others are so insensitive to you and your needs."

A behavioral therapy position vis-à-vis a hypochondriacal patient would attempt to treat the person in several ways: First, by putting more emphasis on the positive aspects of the patient's behavior—"You really did go to the play and you said you enjoyed it in spite of your splitting headache which you say you get each time you have to go out." This type of reply might emphasize also getting the patient (not wanting to "go out") to make small excursions "out," so that the effort is less, the rewards greater, and the chances of making an issue are reduced. This would be, in effect, a shaping effort in social and interpersonal situations. This might be accomplished in part by agreed-upon assignments and agendas between therapy sessions.

A second behavioral emphasis with hypochondriacal patients would be to teach them relaxation techniques in ways that help them discern early in their vicious circle of complaints (feel badly, don't go out, feel guilty—momentarily disappointing others—in not going out socially, retreat more into complaints, feel self-justified by actions taken, prepared all the more for the next time to decline the social opportunity), just what it is that they are complaining about (bodily, or in terms of the social situation they are avoiding) and to build relaxation and desensitization measures specifically around these complaints.

Third, the therapist might be prepared to ignore entirely the complaints of the patient that appear to be hypochondriacal and systematically socially reinforce only positive efforts, while at the same time perhaps engaging the efforts of family members or others to arrange opportunities for social exchange or other activities that challenge the hypochondriacal and complaining withdrawal the patient usually displays. The enlisting of help among family members is usually easier if the patient is a child or adolescent, but it may work successfully with older persons depending upon particulars in a given family constellation.

A fourth point revolves around the fact that even hypochondriacal patients are not complaining 100% of the time; they select issues which meet subtle, but discernible, purposes. The therapist can point out these discrepancies and confront the patient with them, suggesting at the same time how the inconsistencies can, through certain efforts, become compatible for the patient in terms of his or her prevailing goals, values, and preferences. The positive, noncomplaining, and socially reinforced efforts of the patient in some aspects of his or her behavioral economy can serve as a model, hopefully in considerable detail, for changing those behaviors that are typified by complaining and ineffectual efforts.

As a fifth point, some behavioral therapists would add to the above approaches aversive or punishing efforts to bring the patient's complaints under control: "Every time you have a complaining thought (of a given type, as well defined as possible) snap this rubber band on your wrist," or similar approaches. Although mild forms of hypochondriacal complaining might submit to such direct aversive tactics, more refractory cases might find the complaining behavior reinforced on grounds that too much attention is being called to the complaining behavior and additional "suffering" is reinforcingly added to the patient's already too apparent suffering. Even if aversive methods are used in milder cases, it is always prudent to attempt to set up and reinforce alternative, noncomplaining, nonhypochondriacal behaviors to replace the unwelcome ones.

A therapeutic technique that attempted to map out the vicious circles of complaining and avoiding, in the cybernetic sense, should be welcome as a sixth approach to overcoming this problem. Illustrating and verbalizing how vicious circles are formed which have a predictable outcome of bodily aches and pains, complaints, and social avoidance can be communicated to the patient with considerable clarity; the patient can then often invent ways of interceding in his or her own behalf (see Chapter 9).

Hysteria:

Extreme cases of hysteria may involve sudden, impulsive acting out that lacks wisdom and foresight and that may end causing more problems for the individual. A sudden impulse to quit a job, without available recourse, upon the advent of a misunderstanding with the boss might be an example. Hysteria cases are also slow to admit or confront interpersonal or emotional difficulties: It is as if all the problem was in the immediate provocation by an agent or condition "outside" or unrelated to the person so reacting—"It was all because of something that happened that caused me to react as I did," might be the theme here. On the other hand, approach behaviors toward people tend to fall into categories that can be called demanding, manipulative, and uninhibited, and are often found on superficial, immature, and unreliable levels, where the hysterical-like person is often engaging and assertive socially in provocative ways. These people tend to have very little "insight" into how their behavior affects others.

Behaviorally, hysterical ractions tend to bring immediate social reinforcement, but in the long run the hysterical person's immaturity may diminish greatly his or her social reinforcement power. People catch on to the hysteric as "all talk," or "all pretense," or as "blowing hot, then cold," and so forth. The engaging and manipulative aspects of the hysteric's approach to others seems at first socially productive but as these relationships prove unreliable and even create difficulties, the hysteric's reactions are superficial, and non-insightful (that is, such a person does not see or confront his or her own contribution to the difficulty), and the hysteric moves on to the next conquest, making "great starts but poor endings," as one person put it about himself as therapy progressed and got into the details of his life and relationships.

Therapy may often take a confrontive stance with people who are actively hysterical, attempting to minimize the immediate impulsive, manipulative aspects of their behavior which is, at first, so rewarding but later may pale considerably. Hysterical "falling in love" with instances of manipulating the other person are not uncommon among adolescents and young adults; as these instances of falling in and out of love accumulate in the therapy context, it becomes evident that there is much manipulation, that the "falling in love" is mostly impulse with little substantive basis and that the manipulator often leaves the love scene as summarily as he or she entered; but later bemoans the fact that he or she "cannot form a lasting relationship."

Some verbal directiveness in therapy may hit the mark: The therapist may ask, "What is there in this new relationship that is so gripping, how is it like previous ones?" And, "Looking ahead now, how do you think this relationship may turn out if we use your recent history as a basis for generalization?" These are verbally confrontive therapeutic tacks that attempt to play down the immediate reinforcement value of the interaction and call attention to the longer-range manipulation and loss of reinforcement consequences that often befall one acting in this more immature manner.

The therapist being available on immediate notice to the hysterical-acting person may have some value. The therapist is "on call" presumably to counteract the impulsive actions of the patient, to intercede with some "wisdom" that may act in a cautionary way and allow the patient time to think over the potential action. Asking the patient, again, to weigh the pros and cons of the likely impulsive action may be a deterrent to prematurely behaving in a destructive way, that is, being reinforced for again engaging in escape or avoidance behaviors.

Among those hysteria cases that are more subtly superficial, and manipulative, and less impulsive, similar therapeutic tacks may be taken except that there is more time for the therapist and patient to work out solutions. Confrontive questions to the patient such as, "What do you think that kind of behavior on your part means to another person?" "How is what you are now doing related to other problems we have recently discussed such as _____?" "Is what you're contemplating not a superficial response—in the light of the last problem of this type we discussed—and are you not heading down the same dead end as before?" And the like.

The standard techniques related to keeping logs of activities, setting agendas for work on problems between therapy sessions, carrying out specific assignments—all essentially out-of-therapy activities—may also be found to be fruitful. One constructive thing about these measures is that they put the patient on the spot to act deliberately in the presumed interest of solving the problems presented. As it is sometimes the case, and part of the standard knowledge of therapists, that "hysterics do not respond well to psychotherapy," this assumption is continually put to test in a behavioral mode.

Psychasthenia

Obsessive–compulsive (or psychasthenic) complaints are also challenging for the behavioral therapist, sometimes seemingly as refractory to change as depressive cases and, because of their often fleeting nature, harder to bring under control than lingering depressive states. The obsessive part of the O–C syndrome refers most often to covert or subjective aspects of the person—ruminating, worrying, repeating thoughts in ritualistic ways, being unable to concentrate on ordinary stimuli and being preoccupied with essentially nonsensical and nonfunctional thought, often falling into sleeplessness, and being inattentive in social situations owing to the subjective preoccupations.

Included in this set of subjective signs of obsessiveness are inability to make decisions, worry over past decisions, reliving events that represent "unfinished business" for the person, trying to "take back and relive" events where the person feels he or she erred or left bad impressions, failing to differentiate between relevant and irrelevant considerations in making decisions, and so forth.

Overtly observable manneristic behaviors accompany the above-cited covert processes—engaging in rituals (touching things, avoiding stepping or going different places, saying ritualistic things to one's self and also aloud), engaging in "superstitious" behaviors, placing behavioral sequences in unusual or nonfunctional order, and so on. A patient who typified many of these covert and overt signs had the following complaints: Before she would retire each evening, she would have to turn the lights on and off several times, examining and reexamining the room to be sure nothing was present that was unwelcome (this was not restricted to people but might include a loose button on the floor, some dirt, or a door left ajar instead of being closed); she would leave the house only under the condition of the clock being 12 ½ minutes after the hour; she used her fingers to rim out any last remains from coffee or other drinks in a glass before placing the glass aside or replenishing the drink; she would stop on the roadside every mile or two when on her way into a nearby town to shop, get out of the car and walk up and down the road surveying each side of the road to see what was present, perhaps doing this several times before proceeding on into town; she touched each door in the house at a certain place as she passed from one room to another for whatever purpose throughout the day and evening; she would sit on a chair as exact a distance from the back of the chair as possible before going on with eating, talking, or whatever; and many other remarkably restrictive behaviors. This person spent considerably more time in carrying out these ritualistic behaviors, both covert and overt, than she did in pursuing the ordinary intercourse of life. All of the drug treatments and "depth" therapies she had received succeeded only in temporarily suppressing some of her unwanted behaviors or in mollifying her momentarily as to the "meaning" of these behaviors.

Clinical descriptions of psychasthenic or obsessive–compulsive persons may also include considerable anxiety manifest in certain situations, irrational fears, being generally tense and "high strung," displaying inability to concentrate or follow through on presumably wanted and agreed-upon behavior, and pronounced lacks in self-confidence. Sometimes these persons appear wretched, helpless, agitated, and sorely in need of help, but correspondingly unable to engage in discussing themselves without interferences from the anxiety and obsessive–compulsive complaints that typify their plights.

Behavioral intervention, or any intervention for that matter, is difficult. The therapist has to be extremely careful not to try to help the "whole person all at once," else he or she will be overwhelmed by the patient. Settling on one or two *very specific behaviors* is the essential way to begin therapy. Picking a behavior that the patient feels he or she can bring under control most easily is the best early tack, having data kept by the patient on this item, with frequent feedback to the therapist as to how matters are progressing. In the case of the patient cited above, it was considered most fruitful to try to avoid touching doors at certain places as she passed from room to room (alternative behavior: using only the door knob or door handle for opening doors and not closing any of them between rooms within the house but only the outside doors using the handle, and to avoid using her finger to "clean" the empty glass or cup after drinking a liquid (but to rinse out the cup before reusing it if she preferred). Frequency charts were kept for each behavioral objective and the patient reported daily over the phone as to how each behavioral objective was progressing, with strong reinforcement from the therapist for even the slightest progress at first. She agreed that a good self-reward at the end of the day was to watch the evening news on TV for no more than a half hour contingent on her call to the therapist, her having kept data on herself and, at first, on her having "progressed" some toward her objectives (longer TV viewing allowed her to become distracted, to ruminate about other things, and to dampen the value of concentrating on TV as a source of reward for self-control efforts).

From among the behavioral techniques possible (see Chapter 2), one might think of aversive controls of various types (snapping a rubber band when certain thoughts occurred or when certain rituals were performed), but some patients are not able, at first anyhow, to systematize their self-control this much and to select out a given behavior (for rewarding or punishing) that requires a high degree of concentration itself and close correlation with the unwanted behavior. Also, the tactic with this patient—and it is believed to be the better approach generally with obsessive and compulsive behaviors—is to *emphasize increasing the amount of time between obsessive–compulsive events* rather than on the immediate consequence of the event itself in the form of punishment. The latter tactic reinforces the patient for paying attention to the act that is unwelcome rather than on the act's alternative, namely, nonperformance (and increasingly so over time) of the obsessive–compulsive act. In fact, from the vantage point of the present writing on behavioral intervention where obsessive–compulsive cases are concerned, the main reason most approaches to controlling these often highly intractable behaviors are less successful than they might be, is that too much attention therapeutically is drawn to the unwanted behavior and this attention is reinforcing, thereby helping to maintain the very behavior we want to extinguish.

The role of obsessive and compulsive behaviors needs some attention. If we hold to the general proposition that psychopathology is produced by discrepancy and conflict, and that reinforcement occurs through escape or avoidance of the "problems" created by the conflict, then any measures which prohibit, reduce, change the consequences of these escape/avoidance behaviors will, presumably, reduce the probability and strength of the unwanted behavior. This is not to say that obsessive–compulsive patients do not have problems other than the specific unwanted behaviors; they do. They are characterized by a myriad of anxiety-provoking sensitivities, almost always at odds with their environment and devoid of satisfying social interactions. The therapeutic issue is that of finding a foothold, some real leverage, at the point of the execution of the easiest-to-control O–C behavior, freeing the person from the "need" to escape and avoid, thereby reducing vigilance and tension, resulting in the person's better self-observation and more reinforcing reactions to the environment generally. With some amount of control of the O–C behaviors, the person then becomes more reflective about his or her life generally, sees more clearly how demands are made on one's self and others which cannot be fulfilled, maintaining a more or less chronic state of tension that is escaped from, or handled by, the O–C ritualistic complex. The O–C behavior is a set of more or less fortuitous contingencies that fail to solve large problems but that are maintained by the immediate consequences of bringing under control limited behavioral segments—escape and avoidance of tension—that are easy to execute and that preserve the fiction of "doing something" about one's tension (the "doing something" being the opposite to the "doing nothing" characteristic of depression cum "learned helplessness").

To try first in therapy to break up the vicious circle nature of the O–C complex is to enable the patient soon to consider larger problems. On the other hand to focus first on the larger issues of life is to risk failing to get a grip on any behavior, thereby inadvertently assuring that lots of attention therapeutically is given to the distress, which reinforces it and bypasses the focal points of needed self-control in small but pivotal ways. Rather than regarding O–C behaviors as "defense against anxiety," the behavioral view is that these behaviors service the purpose of escape and avoidance and as long as this activity continues there is little chance of solving either the larger issues of life or of bringing under control the nettling obsessions and compulsions. Rather than trying to find out what the patient is "defending himself against," it is far more heuristic to try to interrupt the O–C behaviors themselves, thus freeing the patient and the therapeutic enterprise itself to tackle any other issues one may wish to encounter. What one is presumably "defending himself against" invokes notions of depth theory, implies a medical disease model of psychopathology, and sends the therapy off on relatively unproductive byroads.

What of the "expectancies" of obsessive–compulsive and psychasthenic personal complaint systems? These expectancies are surely present; the O–C person is highly aspirant, perfectionistic, and intolerant of imperfections (in theory), while facing the fact that performance itself is far below "standard." Holding on to these high expectations keeps the person trying desperately to fulfill them, but also entertaining some doubts about the outcome, perhaps then actually trying less appropriately than would otherwise be the case (with less tension), but ending with a considerable degree of expectation–realization discrepancy and evolving conflict. If the patient then avers that he "hasn't really tried hard enough to reach those goals," he reissues, as it were, the expectancy, redoubles effort, and again faces the expectance–performance discrepancy. Thus the vicious circle continues.

INTEGRATING THE DIAGNOSTIC PICTURE

As has been amply stated, diagnostic categories, except for loose, administrative purposes, are not very heuristic. Diagnosis, as such, does not tell us how the behavior came about, what maintains it, nor how to overcome it. The role of diagnosis should be more than simple, topological classification if it is to serve general scientific and therapeutic ends. One way of looking at diagnosis, which has been proffered here, is to regard the behavioral circumstances under which any so-called pathological behavior is generated and to then move on to considering how the unwanted behavior is both maintained and overcome. The matter might be put in the brief conceptual schema in Figure 10. In this figure, we see how, first, the discrepancy occurs between expectations and realizations. This might come about in a number of ways, and many theories of pathology are centered on this problem (Ferster, 1973; Seligman, 1974; Beck, 1967). It may occur through "loss of behavior," through "learned helplessness," through the reactivation of previous conflicts in one's life that remain "sensitive" and unresolved, and so on. As long as any presumed reason for psychopathology can be put under the discrepancy

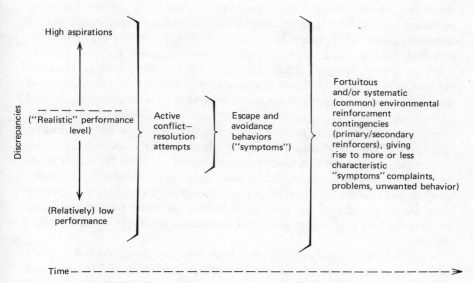

Figure 10.   This schema begins with an aspiration versus performance discrepancy, moves into conflict, then symptom formation—unwanted behaviors that may have a number of characteristics such as being systematic or fortuitous, primary or secondary.

paradigm, it is of secondary importance whether the exact causal condition is of one or another type (insofar as present knowledge takes us and insofar as the present schema is concerned). One may "lose behavior" by losing job, spouse, or health. One may "learn helplessness" by being so confronted with life's exigencies that effective escape and avoidance, not to mention resolution, become virtually impossible. Or one may find upon the dissolution of his or her third or fourth marriage or dismissal from the tenth job in five years, that the "same old issues abound" and real problem resolution has not yet taken place. These are all profound discrepancies in one's life, and they may also be experimentally demonstrated with animals in a large variety of ways.

Not only does facing discrepancies seem axiomatic in understanding psychopathology, but also one engages in attempts to resolve the discrepancy and this engagement takes the characteristics of active conflict (Dollard and Miller, 1950; Brown, 1948), where the discrepancy does not remain a static matter but is responded to in terms of approaching or avoiding the various conditions and contingencies one is faced with. Thus, if one is dismissed from a job, this is not only a sizable discrepancy but a conflict: Should one fight the dismissal? Should one try for a different field of work? Can interim jobs be found to sustain life? How about one's self-appraisals during all this conflict? And so on. The most profound and moving experiences human beings have come in the way of head-on clashes with discrepancies and conflict, whether they arise from personal, family, vocational, ethical, or other arenas.

If one can resolve the conflict forthwith—get a new job as good as the old one, conclude that the discrepancy and conflicts are minimal and transitory, not experience any assault on one's general competence and values—then the matter ends there. We all deal daily with minor discrepancies and conflict, from fixing unwanted flat tires to exonerating one's self with a friend whose luncheon engagement has momentarily and embarrassingly escaped us, and we are probably none the worse for it all. But, given profound and difficult-to-resolve discrepancies, especially those thrust summarily upon us, we are often bereft of solutions, and the more we are faced with the need for solutions the more we are caught up in the pros and cons (approach and avoidance conflict) of this or that solution.

In the throes of these conflict situations are born the myriad of "symptoms," a variety of ways to avoid and escape the conflict. Escaping and avoiding are phylogenetically serviceable and likely to ensure momentary survival. However, in complex society and in dealing with one's own behavioral economy, escape and avoidance may cause more problems than they are worth and not solve the basic issue (the discrepancy) either. However, "doing something" (and "doing nothing" is not really "nothing" but still "doing something") is called for and is reinforcing, because it may address itself to two issues: solving the real problem and assuaging tension (conflict). One experiences tension; one is caught in a conflict. The conflict is the conceptualization of the matter; the subjectively felt condition is that of tension and that is what one grapples with for the most part. It is only when people can use their conceptual potential to develop a functional account of their plight that they can rise above the details of the tension itself (bodily distress, anxiety, self-deprecation, and so on) and see the properties of conflict as they are activated daily. Knowing about the conflict and discrepancies involved in one's distress is a step in the direction of posing the problem properly, asking the right questions, and then pursuing change. The task of therapy is, of course, not only to pose the right questions—organizing the abstract discrepancy/conflict aspects of the paradigm along with the subjectively felt tension/distress/anxiety—but to elicit new or more adequate behaviors, help select, direct, and reinforce them, and aid the patient in moving toward self-control and self-reinforcement in these matters. When the patient can do all this conflict resolution for himself—as most people do most of the time—then there is no need for "outside help." But therapy must meet the test of life—it must pursue problem solving in a way similar to that used by people who do the right things for themselves. If this criterion is met, as is presumed in the present schema, then esoteric theories of pathology and therapy are uncalled for; what is needed is a straightforward account of what happens in nature.

The study of escape and avoidance behaviors in the face of, and wake of, conflict is indeed an absorbing and complex enterprise. We are only touching base with the problem here. Presumably the selection of avoidance and escape routes and the assuaging of tension, however momentarily, are the bases for the symptom complexes that we so arduously examine in interviews, in therapy, and in diagnostic efforts (psychological testing, for example). These complaints, these unwanted behaviors, these "symptoms"—however we speak about them—are learned in the complex interaction between the patient and his or her environment.

Some reason may exist to think of these symptom complexes in four ways. First are those that assuage primary needs related to eating, drinking, sleeping, eliminating, sex, and the behaviors that represent primary reinforcers. Second are those unwanted behaviors (or symptoms) that relate to secondary reinforcing conditions—social behaviors, values, self-appraisal behaviors, social skills, and so forth. These conditions of primary and secondary reinforcement in relation to depressive symptomatology are amply covered in Ferster's work (Ferster, 1973).

Two other environment conditions that need recognition in regard to the selection and maintenance of symptomatology—and these are seldom treated systematically—are those related to highly structured aspects of our social environments, giving rise to fairly predictable symptom complexes, such as those related to suicide, alchoholism, and excessive drug use; and also those found on the various scales of personality questionnaires such as the MMPI (those items on, say, the depression scale that are answered in the significant direction contrasted with the more rarely answered items which, while they occur with some frequency, may still be somewhat idiosyncratic). The standard culture, subdivided somewhat for ethnic, social class, age, and sex characteristics, would provide, so to say, a grab-bag of symptoms that one "selects" in his or her avoidance/escape behaviors, in grappling with tension/anxiety/distress feelings. Thus, given some parameters of a disturbed population (age, sex, etc.), one could predict a large number of the symptoms that would occur commonly (say, more than 50% of the time) among this population.

On the other hand, complaints (unwanted behaviors, symptoms) may be idiosyncratic to some degree, rare or very rare; these would presumably be fortuitous events in the tension-reduction or escape–avoidance efforts of the person that would be reinforced and thus learned and maintained. One might think here of the patient reported on above who cleaned out the inside of a drinking vessel (using her fingers) with utmost compulsive care before either putting down the vessel or obtaining more liquid. Or, consider the patient who would return to his apartment five to ten times each morning, after once leaving and locking the door behind him, to ascertain if he did, indeed, turn off the gas stove in his kitchen. One could hardly imagine items relating to such idiosyncratic behavior occurring on any standard personality or diagnostic instrument; yet this general kind of thing—the obsessive–compulsive care—occurs frequently, covering a wide range of commonly experienced rituals (hand washing, for example).

The more bizarre and idiosyncratic symptoms do not, per se, spell greater pathology; their rarity, it would seem, is part of the fortuitous reinforcement afforded the person in his interaction with the environment. Such rare symptomatology may be interesting in its own right but its "meaning" therapeutically or conceptually would appear to be no different from the way other symptoms are formed and maintained in the interest of escape from and avoidance of tension. However, rare symptomatology may occasionally challenge the therapist to provide suitable

Primary reinforcers (food, drink, sex, sleep) giving rise to "symptoms" or complaints.	Secondary reinforcers (social activities, social skills, other learned behaviors) giving rise to "symptoms" or complaints.
"Systematic" reinforcing conditions provided by the culture or subculture (e.g., common items on personality inventories) giving rise to "symptoms" or complaints.	Fortuitous or idiosyncratic reinforcing conditions in the patient's environment giving rise to rare or bizarre "symptoms" or complaints.

Figure 11.   A schema showing how one might conceptualize the patient's array of "symptoms," complaints, unwanted behaviors. This is one alternative to conventional diagnostic classifications, and one functionally related to the patient's behavioral economy.

contingency control of the complaint and to fathom how it fits in the vicious circle routine characterizing the patient's behavioral economy.

Summarizing this discussion, we have Figure 11, which indicates that, looking at a patient's set of complaints, the therapist might describe or conceptualize this aggregate as representing two sets of reinforcement contingencies: primary or secondary on one continuum, and the behavioral content, derived as it is from fortuitous or systematic (common, cultural) reinforcement, on the other continuum. Such a conceptualization would provide some economy for the therapist: He or she would have a leg up on discovering the possible reinforcement contingencies maintaining much of the patient's behavior and, upon clarifying this phenomenon with the patient, be able to enlist further help from the patient as to the manner and means in which the unwanted behaviors are maintained, their functional value to the patient, and so forth.

CHAPTER 7

The Clinical Situation: II. Therapeutic Theory and Procedures

The clinical situation is based on what may be called a "a fundamental dichotomy," namely, a dichotomy or difference between the clinician and the patient as to where the comments and perspective of each is originating, and a difference in the way each relates to the other person. This dichotomy obtains, of course, in any dyadic exchange (and more so, to be sure, when several people communicate), but it is of crucial importance in the clinical situation because of the nature of the "contract" between the two participants: to change the behavior of one of the participants (the patient). This is not to say that the clinician's behavior does not change, because it does as a result of interacting with the patient, but the clinician's or therapist's change is presumably in response to achieving greater efficiency or effectiveness in the relationship to the patient, and not for the therapist's own sake (he or she does not need a change in behavior in the same way the patient presumably does).

The therapist seeks ways of understanding the problems, the viewpoint, the feelings, and the style of communication offered by the patient. The patient does not come fully ready to communicate optimally about his or her problems, but comes, as has been said before, out of suffering, malcontent, fear, or the wish to realize a better and fuller living potential. It is the therapist's job to understand the patient, not vice versa; at least at first, this is the case. Since the patient is dominated by primarily emotional, as contrasted with objective or factual considerations— although both patient and therapist are forever intertwined (see Chapter 1, pp. 3–6)—the therapist is hopefully relatively more objective and has more factual knowledge and orientation. The communication matrix between patient and therapist is no easy matter and cannot be taken for granted, to wit:

A 25-year-old, married woman appears for therapy. She reports she works successfully daily, keeps a small family going, together with her husband, and has friends and a social life. Ostensibly, her life is full and enriched. She talks, however, about problems in making friends, in sexual union with her husband, and in feeling sufficiently tender toward her children some of the time. As she talks about these problems, she smiles all the time; and even chuckles or laughs in a muffled way as the therapist comments, questions, makes observations in response to her revelations. Are her smiles related to deliberately showing pleasure at portraying a seemingly contradictory stance, that is, the difference between the ways she appears and what she is talking about? Is she so "split" that she cannot get emotion and fact together? Is she merely being pleasant and agreeable and wishing to leave the impression that she is generous in talking about her problems and anxious to get help by inviting the interest of the therapist through her pleasantness? Is she musing about some covert incident in relation to the events and feelings she relates that remains, as yet, unspoken? Or is she lying about her life and telling us more by her smiles—what she does not say in words—than what she actually says?

In simple dyadic communication, a direct statement such as "Pass the sugar, please" encounters little or no difficulty. A slightly more complex communication might raise a host of questions: "The coffee is too bitter." It may refer to displeasures of a repeated nature aimed at one's spouse who has again incorrectly brewed the coffee; it may indicate to the wife (or husband) that the coffee must be replaced; it may indicate to the host that he had better revise his concoction before the guests arrive; and so on almost interminably.

Natural language constitutes the easiest, most effective way to communicate with others about most problems (the more technical the problems of communication become, the more precise languages—mathematics, graphs, charts, and the like—are needed). Natural language formulations, supplemented by technical terms and principles, will probably be the chief medium of communication in psychotherapy for some time to come; for, even as body language and other nonverbal communications are better understood and utilized, one measure of their utilization will probably be translating nonverbal formulations into words and into technical meaning!

One way of looking at verbal communication is to marvel that it works at all! The young child has trouble making language work and resorts considerably to nonverbal expression for several years. Even as adults, few, if any, of us are skilled in converting all the feelings and ideas we have into communicable and easily understood language. Semantics is often such a hodgepodge that, lacking ways to clear up meaning, we simply stop with the statement: "Oh, that's a semantic issue and not a *real* one." Semantic issues are just as real and, from the standpoint of psychotherapy, often more formidable than "real" problems; they are so much the crux of the communication issue that success or failure in treatment can rise or fall at this level.

When a therapist, then, sits down to speak with a patient, they are both about to engage in one of the most complex of human enterprises. It is no wonder, then, that they often misunderstand each other; that very complex theories are spun about this exchange process and what it "means"; that the verbal interaction between patient and therapist gives rise to many theories and interpretations about what the patient's life and behavior are all about; and that often the exchange itself between patient and therapist is extrapolated backward and forward in time to include a host of generalizations that should make us blanch even to think about them.

Natural language communication in psychotherapy—not to mention other human enterprises—may be at once simple and direct, then again bafflingly complex. To enter into this enterprise without sufficient warning is tantamount to diving into a distant pool of water about which one has not the slightest notion of depth.

Each person, therapist and patient, comes to the psychotherapy communication setting with a repertoire and a behavioral economy that is then put into service. This service continually requires knowledge about where the other person is "coming from." Since this communication pivots first on the therapist and secondarily on the patient, a heavy burden rests on the therapist to know, to find out, and to work effectively with, the verbal repertoire of the patient and what this spoken repertoire represents in the therapy as well as in out-of-therapy settings.

PUSHING COMMUNICATIONS IN PSYCHOTHERAPY TO NEW LIMITS

Communication difficulties in psychotherapy could be illustrated—and, indeed, even studied systematically—if some or all of the following situations were contrived for this purpose.

1. Have therapist and patient from two different, nonoverlapping natural language backgrounds, in order to see how they might invent communication about the patient's problem and how to remedy it by pantomime, gestures, paintings, drawings, and the like. Such a procedure might not bring therapy to a successful conclusion—after a few tries at this procedure, the patient might well be transferred to a therapist speaking his or her language—but it would highlight the urgent importance of the communication, suggest how natural language communication can be

substituted for through other means, and how empathic the participants might prove to be. (It goes without saying that both participants would have to enter this communication with an experimental attitude and be willing to suspend the usual "rules" of therapy and to terminate the contract if matters bogged down too much.)

2. Have the patient act out as in the game of "charades" the problems he or she wishes to present, with the therapist groping for words and other communication in response, keeping the verbal communications one-way (i.e., from therapist to patient). (This arrangement, also, would have to be provisional, experimental, ready to be dropped when a real impasse was reached, and entered upon with a wholly open and flexible set of attitudes on the part of the two participants.) The more successful the procedures, as with the one above, the more we would learn about communication in psychotherapy.

3. Have both therapist and patient use only drawing or painting as a medium of communication, with no implication of artistic or other prior communication skills needed. One might add "construction materials" (that is, toys, plastics, sand, water, or the whole armamentarium of elementary school supplies) to this setting. No words would be spoken, or, by prior arrangement, words could be spoken only at previously agreed-upon junctures such as halfway through a given series of meetings, or at the end.

4. Use writing therapy, as already covered in Chapter 4, but extend its usage by having the patient write throughout an entire series of agreed-upon sessions—say, ten, on an experimental basis—with no therapist replies at all; or allow the therapist's replies only at the end of the patient's writing. Using writing, the therapist and patient could also proceed generally as has been illustrated in Chapter 4, but have the therapist respond *only* to positive statements by the patient, and compare such protocols for content and other features with "regular" writing therapy efforts. (A study is now under way at the George Washington University Counseling Center to begin a writing therapy program with a three-session baseline, where the patient writes for three sessions before the therapist responds.)

5. Have a given number of patients and writing therapy therapists form a matrix arranged by chance, such that each therapist responded randomly to each patient in a limited series of, say, 10 sessions. Each therapist's reply would contain the information from previous writings of patient and therapist, and the emphasis would be on the utilization of the principle of behavior change as explicitly as possible. At the end, all patients would, of course, have the right to confront any or all therapists in open, verbal exchange.

6. Have patients simply talk into tape recorders about their concerns, listen each time to the previous recording (or to still earlier ones, if one wished, which would remain on file and available), and receive no communication at all from a therapist except at the end of such a series. Protocols could be studied for a variety of effects.

Possibly other altered communications purporting to be psychotherapeutic—or even those not so purporting, but simply carried on for their own intrinsic scientific interest—could be derived once one is willing to suspend the usual verbal, talk-it-out kind of therapeutic stance. The point is that the alteration of the usual procedures might prove to be serendipitous and feed back information of use in all forms of therapeutic communication.

A built-in safeguard would be included in all these "experimental nonverbal communication formats" that would allow the patient to opt out at any time and to elect access to verbal psychotherapy upon request. The immediate point that is important here is that, having considered these altered states of communication as possible worlds to study, we are now better prepared to look again at the clinical situation, at the communication between patient and therapist, and to analyze some possibly important features of this common arrangement. These altered states of possible therapeutic communication would be interesting behaviorally in the sense that probably not even allusions to subtle phenomena (images, etc.) would be encountered except in obviously overt ways (e.g., a patient pointing to his or her head with a pounding motion suggesting a throbbing headache, or the like); and this constraint might tell us more about the role of subjective factors in therapeutic communication.

Descriptive Junctures in Patient-Therapist Interactions

Turning attention now more directly to the patient–therapist interaction in the usual verbal manner, we can discern several junctures that are of descriptive importance in understanding psychotherapy. The reader should review the strictures offered in Chapter 1 referring to a flexible behavioral approach so as to be mindful of the scientific as well as the communication problems inherent in this process. These junctures are as follows:

1. *Where the therapist first enters the patient's verbal repertoire or behavioral economy.* This refers to what the patient says about himself, how the problems are presented verbally (or nonverbally) by the patient, and how the therapist then reacts. The behaviorally oriented therapist more or less takes the presenting complaints as behavioral data to be

further observed, described, placed in context. More conventional therapists tend to wait longer to react to the patient, tend to regard the presenting complaints as "symptoms of a deeper problem" owing to repression of the basic problem because of its anxiety-producing potential. The conventional depth therapist tends to view the presenting complaints as more or less "defensive" rather than as data in their own right. Put another way, the presenting complaints are referred to a kind of diagnostic catalog system by the depth therapist, depending upon the particular persuasion represented in the therapist's orientation. An example here would be a patient of a behavioral therapist who reported on his earlier conventional therapy in regard to the patient's problem of frequenting prostitutes, a problem he avowedly wished to overcome. In the former, depth-type therapy setting, the actions of the patient surrounding his hesitations and final decision to visit a prostitute were referred to a kind of categorization system which labeled the vacillating behavior in several ways, but among these labels he found references such as "adult," "parental," or "childlike." The patient observed that in his behaviorally oriented therapy, the vacillations he reported—walking back and forth in front of the massage parlor entrance for several minutes—were treated in terms of what he was then thinking about; what pros and cons he dealt with; what stimuli (subjective and objective) were currently impinging upon him; what alternatives he could have followed at the time; how he could have prevented putting himself in the locale of the massage parlor in the first place; how much he considered during his vacillation how he would feel after he spent what was for him a large amount of money; and how much he could consider the more acceptable alternative of social and perhaps sexual contacts with females in his natural social orbit. In the depth-type therapy, formerly encountered by the patient, he reported that he never was encouraged to give consideration to these "very practical issues of how I was actually behaving at the time" and was referred instead to labels, speculation about historical causes, and judgments about his "maturity." He averred, "I could talk forever about these various descriptions of my actions and never deal directly with the actions themselves."

First impressions of the behaviorist are probably no better than those of any other observer. The first impressions, the presenting complaints, the patient's initial descriptions (which often, also, include guesses at causality which have to be sifted out from the rest of the verbalizations) have to be taken above all as concrete instances of how the patient behaved—or how he *reports* on his behavior. These behaviors cannot be set aside as "symptomatic" only. If the behavior of the patient in the interview itself matches or gives reasonable clues to outside-of-therapy behavior, all the better; but the patient's in-therapy behavior, including his or her words, have to be taken at first as the best guide to what's what with the patient.

Too much emphasis, however, on "interpreting" the patient's in-therapy behavior—the reticence, arrogance, confusion, and the like, often tachistoscopally and kaleidoscopically presented—may halt the patient's revelations about himself and further confuse his impressions of himself and of the therapy. Although most therapists cannot fully suppress their proclivities to "assign" categories, meanings, diagnostic opinions, and so on, to the patient's behavior—(it is better to stick with silent hunches about triggering stimuli, possible reinforcers, and what's generally present in the patient's behavioral economy)—this interesting and often fruitful process should not intrude in the factual, data gathering about the patient's life and demeanor in therapy.

There is always plenty of time for possible "interpretations" of what the patient's behavior means, and one should pursue this route with great reluctance, since there are so many sources of data, especially as therapy continues, on the patient that can be tested out in very concrete ways. If we take seriously our admonition that communication is, itself, a kind of miraculous enterprise that should be judiciously handled, we will not want to further complicate and obfuscate what otherwise are delicately achieved, but abundantly present, exchanges between patient and therapist!

2. *What the therapist makes of the data presented by the patient.* Here we have not only entered into the stream of behavior, but wish now, as therapists, to stimulate changes in the way the patient regards himself; study how this change in the patient's self-regard can lead to the observation of more positive data about himself; see how the positive, problem-solving aspects can be spoken of first by the therapist and then understood verbally and tried out overtly by the patient; and observe how the patient can begin to "take over" from the therapist the way he or she approaches problem solving, therapeutic task setting, and observing generally. These efforts do not need to wait for some especially ripe time in the course of therapy; they may be begun at once, or soon after the therapist and patient can concur on some solid basis of information from which can be projected specific and concrete change efforts. One patient put it thusly: "You know, when you said you thought I was not so much depressed as I was clumsy and thoughtless about interacting with Margaret, I began to change how I approached her and how I reacted to her negativism, and then I was more successful in dealing with her and not at all depressed." The patient went on later in the hour to say that, although

he was not as skilled as he wanted to be in interacting with his wife (Margaret), he now understood that he could do a lot of different things to improve their relationship and to thereby avoid always blaming himself and feeling depressed. He said, "I had thought of depression as some hole I was already in and always desperately trying to climb out of—but now I see I just simply dropped myself into this hole by what I did or didn't do with her." This "insight," basically a change in actual overt behavior vis-à-vis his wife, was brought about by first actually observing better and discussing in therapy his wife's critical behaviors toward him, then by changing his impressions of these criticisms, and finally by developing new responses thereto. *After* he made these changes, he verbalized his "insight," because it had become a valid generalization only following the desired behavior change. The patient's proclivities for dwelling on felt hurt, confusion and depression can, so to say, "lead the therapist astray," and deter the movement of therapy from considering as primary the context in which the feelings arise, rather than redundantly addressing the feelings themselves.

3. *How the therapist admits nonverbal data into the therapeutic interaction.* This item has been referred to somewhat above, but must be considered in its own right. Many of the "newer" therapists of recent years (Harper, 1975) have pivoted much of their novelty on taking in new data in the clinical situation; which is to say, mainly, that more nonverbal data are accepted and woven into the therapeutic context (Harper, 1975; Wachtel, 1967). For whatever reasons, psychotherapy has been essentially verbal over the decades, although no one legislated against including other data. Correspondingly, behavioral therapists have admitted subjective data (see Chapter 1 in this respect) more willingly in recent years (Mahoney, 1974; Mahoney and Thoresen, 1974) all to the enlargement of the psychotherapeutic context. Admitting these kinds of data does not go against a behavioral framework. Neither science generally nor behaviorism specifically (Skinner, 1974) claims that data of any particular type are inadmissible—they only set criteria for the definition, inclusion, and use of data. All students of child psychology have, however, included any and all kinds of nonverbal data even in psychotherapy. It is, then, primarily the *adult* psychotherapy scene that has been modified in this respect in recent years. Most of the nonverbal data are observationally derived in psychotherapy; seldom does precise measurement, other than simple counting, occur. Admitting that nonverbal data are sometimes difficult to handle, one can nonetheless learn to weave them into the psychotherapeutic context to the enlargement of the entire enterprise. One interesting observation occurs when nonverbal data are included in psychotherapy: Seldom is the motor activity, body stance, expressive

behavior, and so on attributed to deep psychological causation; it is mostly accepted on simple, observational grounds. The more behaviorists have employed nonverbal data, the more the context of behavior change has shifted from psychotherapy to settings like classrooms (Haring and Phillips, 1972); token economies (Ayllon and Azrin, 1968); and the therapist as a reinforcer of given nonverbal behaviors such as anger expressiveness (Wagner, 1968). Seldom has nonverbal social behavior, such as might be observed in, or have an effect on, psychotherapy, been systematically studied (Rosenthal et al., 1974). Much of the recent emphasis on nonverbal therapy is, then, a rediscovery of the wheel, rather than an architectural addition or restructuring of verbal psychotherapy. However, that doesn't mean that nonverbal data and issues in psychotherapy are unimportant; they are vastly important but this importance has not been matched by the acquisition of data of a substantive nature about these nonverbal issues. Some nonverbal issues in psychotherapy that merit systematic study might include the following: Very long periods of silence in therapy, especially after verbally "productive" periods; a whole therapy session with no verbal response whatsoever from the patient; anger episodes on the patient's part (breaking objects, pounding the table, walking out, slamming doors, tearing up objects, etc.). Expressive behaviors might also be studied: amount of movement of hands, arms, and legs; the way one sits in a chair; facial expression presumably contingent on or related to verbal exchanges; tics and other "nervous" habits (see Chapter 2, p. 42); and so forth. Psychotherapists might try to formulate general rules or guidelines regarding how to respond to nonverbal cues such as: Relate the nonverbal cue to a verbal context; ask the patient if the particular nonverbal behavior has been observed to occur in other settings; ask the patient what the nonverbal behavior seems to be expressing (e.g., "Pulling at your face seems to signal tension?" "Wringing your hands suggests you are showing anguish or impatience?" "Swinging your head from left to right suggests you are silently saying 'no' to the idea?"). These leading "interpretations" are suggestive only in that the therapist needs to enter more precisely into the patient's behavioral economy and acquire access to more data that might bear on the problems at hand. Nonverbal data would presumably fall under the usual behavioral rubrics: reinforcement, signs of aversiveness, expressions of tension, and the like. One would expect, also, that the various signs of nonverbal behavior, especially if they signal tension, would diminish as therapy progresses successfully and increase when therapy was not going well. Correspondingly, there might be expected a high level of nonverbal signs of tension at the beginning of therapy, with a diminution observed as problems were solved and a mutual termination reached.

Attention is now turned to the last item distinguishing important facets of the therapist–patient communication matrix. This item refers to how the therapist capitalizes on the first three descriptive dimensions cited above in order to equip the patient with the means of changing his or her behavior and with the means for maintaining these changes. Changing behavior within the therapy context is important but of still greater importance is the maintenance of these changes, which, in turn, are contingent on some—but we do not know how much—environmental constancy and on the opportunity in the environment to gain the self-control needed as a hedge against unexpected exigencies.

4. *How the therapist facilitates change*. There are many ways that one may react to this descriptive category: First, the patient, not the therapist brings about the change; second, no one "brings about change" if forcing or coercing is implied; third, change is not the focus in the older, classical or "depth" therapies but is assumed to occur as and when the patient is ready for change. The meaning of "bringing about change" in a behavioral context springs from the fact that the therapy exchange itself is an environmental arrangement of some degree of intention and specificity calculated to induce change. The therapist acts as a stimulus to change in a variety of ways: By his or her listening to the patient (a minimal condition in face-to-face verbal therapy); by interacting selectively to what the patient says or does so as to increase the flow of information acting to increase the relevance of in-therapy data for out-of-therapy life of the patient; by acting to reinforce those behaviors which appear to be relevant to problem solving on the patient's part; by taking care to actually reinforce observable or valid behavior change; and, finally, by attempting to conceptualize the whole process as the therapy progresses from beginning to end. It is this "keeping structure," staying-on-top-of-the-interaction, being entirely open and interactive with an emphasis on positively reinforcing the patient's desired change efforts that characterizes the verbal, face-to-face behavioral psychotherapy. Behavioral psychotherapy or counseling does not assume that the patient–therapist interaction will uncover the causes of the disturbed behavior. Rather, the therapist *participates in making* (bringing about, inducing, inviting) behavior change in the patient's environment context rather than in finding the reasons for the problem. When the former has been done effectively, the latter—that is, finding probable reasons for the problem, although this is not an important issue in the behavioral context—falls into place. It is often difficult for many to understand that inducing behavior change then loosens up, so to say, the cognitive, emotional, and feeling aspects of behavior; and that better progress comes from treating observable be-

havior first with the benefits then successfully accruing to the "higher mental processes." In a common-sense way, our behavior changes almost daily without our conscious awareness or control. We often "notice" such changes after they have come about, changes that we may or may not have deliberately sought or consciously desired. At the disposal of the therapist and the patient are, of course, all the techniques cited in Chapter 2, which makes for a genuinely versatile perspective on changing behavior. On the other hand, waiting, first, for some kind of emotional, cognitive, or attitude change to precede the other behavioral changes (usually overt ones, usually ones that signal self-control and greater self-confidence and composure) is not only an unproven matter but one that risks great waste of therapist's and patient's time.

MELDING THEORY AND PRACTICE IN THE CLINIC

This section will first examine several important theoretical issues relating to the practice of counseling and psychotherapy, and then take up some related practical issues that are commonly met in the psychotherapy literature which is viewed in the behavioral framework in a particular way. Sometimes the demarcation lines between theoretical and practical matters may be a bit equivocal, but the final implications in either case for the practice of a behavioral psychotherapy should be useful and instructive.

The theoretical issues, taken up in the following order, are: the laboratory as the prototype of knowledge for the clinic and the clinic as the prototype of the *use* of laboratory knowledge; the role of *expectancy* in behavioral psychotherapy; the importance of *discrepancy* and *conflict* in the patient's behavior; *expectations of others* (who sets the patient's goals?); *semantic* issues (global terms and their usefulness); *fortuitous* reinforcement; behavior and its *consequences*.

1. The laboratory as the prototype of knowledge for the clinic and the clinic as the prototype of *how to apply* laboratory knowledge. This topic is a large one, easily requiring a book in its own right; but will be treated here mainly on an introductory basis as a vital topic meriting much more discussion and consideration.

Until the advent of the operant movement, beginning some 40 to 45 years ago, and the application of its principles to the clinic, now some 20 years ago, there was little systematic laboratory knowledge of value to the clinician. Some exceptions to this generalization can be made in reference to classical conditioning, in reference to the application of statistics and measurement to the study of human abilities, and in reference to the whole area of human growth and development. However, it can be successfully argued that these three areas—important as they are to psychology as a whole science—were applied loosely and unconvincingly to "problems of psychological clinic," or to problems related to counseling and psychotherapy.

The advent of operant conditioning, studied and applied to a wide variety of clinical problems (Krasner, 1971), began to change the role of the psychotherapist in several ways: First, it required the therapist to know about operant principles, disallowing appeal to rule-of-thumb notions or easily acquired precedences in dealing with patients. Second, operant principles began to be applied so widely that any practitioner in the behavioral sciences could not help knowing what was going on right next door, so to speak, and being influenced by the influx of new knowledge. Third, the cogency of the operant principles (reinforcement, contingency management, stimulus control, etc.) was immediately apparent, if not obvious, to the psychotherapeutic practitioner, and so it behooved him or her to try to utilize these concepts with patients. Fourth, the appearance of encouraging direct applications to patients by early explorers in the behavioral field (Ullmann and Krasner, 1965), set the style of behavioral intervention in psychotherapy, indirectly if not directly. Fifth, and finally, parallel movements arising out of the more classical conditioning model, in the work of Wolpe (1958), Eysenck (1960), and associates, further corroborated the behavioral stance, although this group operated at first from a somewhat different conceptual and empirical base.

In spite of the fact that extrapolation from the laboratory to the clinic is arduous, tenuous, and sometimes ill-conceived (see Chapter 1), it is the only way we have to go! Experimentally derived knowledge, under rigorously controlled conditions, appears to be the chief modality of science; and there is no compelling reason why this is not true for the study of human behavior as well as for other natural phenomena. However arguable this may be to some, two major outcomes for the clinic are derivable from the extrapolation of laboratory knowledge to the clinic: First, it provides a stock of variables, principles, procedures, techniques, laws— even though the paradigmatic nature of psychology as a science must be recognized (Suppe, 1974)—which are, under proper guidance and care, applicable to the clinic setting. Second, this very application is, itself, a model for extrapolating to society, to segments of society, and to settings other than the laboratory itself.

One could state that the practice of medicine is another example of applying basic science information to a practical domain. And, furthermore, that using laboratory knowledge via the practice of medicine, does, in turn, apply to public health medicine, preventive medicine, and to health maintenance generally. Possibly somewhere in the literature of epidemiology there are propositions taking up this viewpoint; if not, there should be!

Engineering could be cited as another similar case. Engineering is derived essentially from physics; the applications of engineering principles aid in the solution of common problems—even social problems, as we view the roles of the various sciences coming closer together in the interest of the *environment* and its protection for man—and somewhere there must be people thinking about "human social engineering" in terms of melding physics, engineering, and social concerns.

In thinking about human social problems such as crime, delinquency, the state of morale about governmental functions, education, employment, and so forth, one has to ask basic questions derived from the psychological laboratory and applied in the psychological clinic: Who holds the reinforcers? What contingencies are now controlling our behavior and how might they be altered? Do we now have in our vast repertoires of behaviors (i.e., technical knowledge) the means to even begin to solve these urgent problems? If we can answer these questions in the affirmative and, by accompaniment, find economical and problem-solving ways of applying our knowledge—similar, it is hypothesized, to the way we are now learning to apply laboratory knowledge to the clinic—we may be on our way to a new era in the history of applying science more directly and cogently to man's concerns. If so, this would be a most rewarding undertaking.

Clinical and experimental psychology scholars working together (Ferster, 1975) are beginning to resonate to the problem of using laboratory knowledge ever more precisely to frame, work on, and solve pressing clinical and social problems. This is a new area of expertise that is only beginning to be felt in some quarters, but the more students are encouraged to think about how knowledge can be extrapolated from one setting to another, the more we will experience fruitful applications and learn of the strengths and limitations of this exciting undertaking (Campbell, 1975; Phillips and Wiener, 1966).

The reason the behavioral approach is apparently so useful in this extrapolation enterprise is that behavioral psychology is not only a set of highly useful techniques, but is also a broad philosophy, a way of looking at human behavior, a language for describing human behavior, and a convincing body of empirical findings (Skinner, 1974). Even with the enlargement of the clinical situation referred to above, especially in relation to psychotherapy and counseling, one should recognize that a behavioral psychology does not purport to have all the answers, to know about all data that may be gleaned by experiment and observation; nor does it set any preemptory rules that forestall investigation. New data, at the clinical level, or at the social level, can be easily admitted; all the new clinical/psychotherapy/counseling theories can be looked at in terms of a behavioral framework (to the benefit of all concerned); and so can the data that are yet to come in the social arenas which represent the further extrapolation of knowledge from the clinic to society.

2. The role of *expectancy* in behavioral psychology. A student in a seminar on behavior change noted that behavioral psychology not only has feelings but is also "expectant." The notion of expectancy is so prominent in all of clinical psychology (not to mention other facets of psychology, as well) that it cannot be ignored. However, it may be better understood in reference to behavioral principles.

Earlier in this book (Chapter 1, pp. 29–31 and Figures 2, 3, and 4), a discussion covered one way in which expectancy in reference to a child's behavior might be conceptualized. Some extrapolation was suggested for application to psychotherapy. The same point calls for some elaboration here.

One important feature of human behavior is that it is forward referenced: We make plans, project trends in the future, take many actions on the assumption that there will be a time line of some reliability that we can follow. Without this ability to expect the future, man would not be man. Too often in psychology, in nonbehavioral as well as in behavioral approaches, this important fact has been ignored (Bandura, 1974). Although it is easy to deal in everyday language with expectancy, it is more difficult to try to be precise about it and to incorporate it into a systematic framework.

The conceptual role of expectancy is that a person adds, in effect, his or her own reinforcement in a verbal or symbolic way to the reinforcement consequences received in the environment. Presumably in the simpler case—for example, the child learning appropriate social behaviors—the reinforcement comes from the environment directly. However, as classes of behaviors and classes of reinforcers are built up, classes of expectancy can likewise be generated. The more the child experiences reinforcement from the environment, the more a generalized positive "attitude" is displayed by the child. When the environment harbors negative consequences (lack of reinforcement or active punishment), then the "self-images" or generalized verbal/symbolic classes of responding become negative or at least equivocal ("I am no good" or "I stay away from that situation because I am so uncertain of the outcome."). In counseling and psychotherapy one meets patients with a plethora of negative references about themselves or about life. The therapist observes that these negative expectancies are often self-reinforcing; that is, the person's repeating his negative views of things brings notice from others, "justifies" his or her own behavior, acts to ward off (avoid) similar unpleasant experiences; and thus a fairly stable condition of self-reinforcement-negative-expectance-maintenance is observed. When this condition is repeatedly observed, one says of the patient that he or she has "a negative outlook on life."

Appropriate to this way of looking at expectancy as it is met in the clinic is to consider ways of approaching behavior change so as to be helpful to the patient. The therapist could, of course, directly disagree with the patient, but this would risk jacking up the patient's tendency to even greater self-reinforcement verbally of his or her negative opinions. The patient would try harder to convince the other person that he or she, the patient, is correct. (See the discussion on "Complaining," Chapter 6, pp. 167–168.)

Alternatively, the therapist can take the tack that the patient is indeed caught up in a redundant process of self-confirmation of negative self-impressions and attempt to enter the "vicious circle" more appropriately than through direct confrontation. Figure 12 shows how this self-

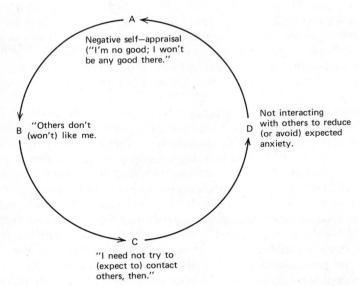

Figure 12. A schema showing how a "vicious circle" or loop process may be used to describe not only the patient's behavior as he or she reports upon experience, but how "expectancies" may also be conceptualized and thus act as a large-scale, orbital constellation of events that allows the patient to avoid learning the new behaviors needed to overcome a variety of problems (depression, negative self-reports, negative "images" of one's self, inept social behaviors, etc.)

perpetuating, circular process may be described. Presumably at each juncture—A, B, C, D—there is verbal self-reinforcement; thus the "system" is maintained. In time, a person becomes very agile in running through this circular process—it is done with a kind of summary statement: "I'm no good." This verbal summary, then, becomes portable in its own right; and shows up as an elevated depression scale score on the MMPI or on some similar measure, or suggests a covert way of "explaining" the depressed person's demeanor.

The therapist's tack here is to find ways of entering the vicious circle or loop nature of this process, such that the self-reinforcement is counteracted by new environmental experiences, or the reasonableness of the patient's expectancy position is undermined through verbal techniques used by the therapist (Ellis, 1970; Phillips and Wiener, 1966), which pave the way for overt behavior change. Such change may, of course, be accomplished by use of shaping procedures, by mild confrontation, by first verbally rearranging the social stimuli, then testing out this rearrangement, by "letting off steam" which is to say extinguishing in the therapist's presence some of the verbal avoidance reinforcers self-manipulated by the patient, and so forth. Eventually, however, any technique has to stand the test of everyday life for the patient.

Other than offering a nonmentalistic way of looking at expectancies, this manner of describing the phenomena also recommends that the therapeutic approach must be versatile, suggestive, provisional, and strongly reinforcing of any positive returns for the patient. As these positive returns accumulate for the patient, one can then say the patient has developed a positive loop of self-regard that is reinforced at many or all junctures in the process.

3. The importance of *discrepancy* and *conflict* as a feature of the patient's behavior (see, also, Chapter 6, pp. 163–179). Conflict underlies all psychopathology (Phillips, 1956; Dollard and Miller, 1950). If the person wishes to approach a goal area (an object, another person, etc.) and can do so forthwith, he or she does so. If, however, the goal area is complicated with negative features (from experience, the negative features are now anticipated or expected), the approach is reduced and avoidance features may predominate. Matters about which one has "two-way feelings" are basically conflict situations. Any problem that a patient introduces as such is fundamentally a conflict situation. The conflict may be between opposing tendencies characteristic of the person (e.g., really wanting to be with his girlfriend when attempting to study); between overt tendencies easily observable (wanting to dance with a given girl but lacking confidence in approaching her forthrightly); between environmental pressures or expectancies and one's own preferred way of behaving (e.g., rushing to catch a plane leading to "nervousness" from fast driving

and risk taking on the way to the airport); and so on for any given set of conditions relating the person to the environment.

Conflict is so important in understanding what we loosely refer to as psychopathology that it is probably safe to say that therapists must always ask themselves this question: "What conflict(s) is this person caught in that helps to account for his or her behavior?" Also, tactically, as the therapist interacts with the patient, references are made to the patient's behavior, such as, "You felt in conflict about that?" or "What do you think your conflict is in this instance?" or "If we characterized your problem(s) in part as involving conflict, what would you say the conflicting elements were?"

Viewing conflict in these terms is entirely compatible with other behavioral observations. Going on from conflict-detection to scrutiny about the reinforcers present, the aversive elements, the availability of alternative behaviors in the repertoire or behavioral economy of the person, constitute effective use of the conflict paradigm. Conflicts are present in everyone's life, if even on a momentary basis; hence everyone is familiar with this conceptualization and can apply it readily to his or her own life. Reference to conflict helps the patient bridge the dichotomous gap between private experiences of felt confusion, anxiety, or inadequacy, on the one hand and the behavioral techniques/conceptions/recommendations on the other hand. The reader is invited to reread the protocols found in earlier chapters in order to further apply the conflict description to the present discussion.

4. *Others' expectations of the patient.* Perhaps one of the commonest areas of complaint offered by patients is that they are not being "themselves," not acting out of or in their own best interest, but are, contrariwise, being persuaded, controlled, advised by others—even if by innuendo—on what is suitable conduct. This is, of course, a common example of conflict between the patient and others of importance to him or her, and conflict between what the patient might do and what he or she sees as constraints—often implied—offered by society, by family, or by unwritten codes of behavior supplied by important reference groups (peers, how the well-behaved person will act, what you do when you are in a given place or position in life, and so on). Social life, peer life, models to go by are abundant in our lives, and it is impossible to escape them. The significant thing is not that these social structures exist but that people are unable to deal effectively with them.

Much of the content of the new therapies consists in ways of dealing with aversiveness—or less openly aversive, but nonetheless subtle and powerful, pressures—in society. Transcendental meditation offers a set of techniques for dealing with everyday pressures, tensions, and anxieties, primarily by suggesting and teaching temporary avoidance or escape measures. (Reinforcement stems primarily from the avoidance or amelioration of excessive or unrelenting pressures, although these "refreshing" meditative periods may also give rise to new, positive thrusts, to reconsideration of the pace one is following, or to other longer-range adjustive and ameliorative actions.) Relaxation measures are similar except that they combine reassertive efforts in the same package. Transactional analysis techniques attempt to reduce aversiveness through calling attention, in part, to the pressures inherent in the socially stereotypic roles ("games") one unthinkingly plays with others which are captioned by denotive titles such as "parent," "child," and "adult." Pointing the clinical finger at these presumptive roles, then, helps the patient to understand what he's actually doing and how he's following the prescriptions of others, and thereby enlarges over time the selection and diversity potentially available in his own repertoire or behavioral economy. Highly confrontive techniques, such as implosion (see Chapter 2), attempt to reduce summarily the tensions one experiences by "uncovering" or confronting a presumptive cause, thereby providing for sudden release (a kind of "sudden extinction" if we can stretch the terms somewhat). The often-heard clinic phrases "getting in touch with your feelings," or "learning to do your own thing" are common-sense examples of teaching the patient—by whatever means, by whatever psychotherapeutic theory—to ask himself questions about how he is acting, whether he is too much under the control of others' influences, whether his problems are based on trying to be somebody or something to the detriment of his own well-being.

The confusion in this area of clinical practice and counseling/ psychotherapy efforts is that there are, indeed, many things in life that *are* prescribed by others—rightly or wrongly—of seeming necessity (job requirements, educational qualifications, minimal social interactional skills, etc.); and so the average person is obliged to "go along with" these strictures. Other matters, however, such as private opinions one might hold, preferences of a personal/social nature, and so on—infinite as they may be—are often subsumed under the "necessary" socialization practices and so are hard to discriminate and differentiate. Almost nobody knows himself so thoroughly and clearly that he doesn't meet many problems in daily life that are confusing and cause him to ask himself: "Am I doing my own things here?" It is an altogether ubiquitous problem and calls for all the skills and acumen and discriminative capacity one can muster to keep a balance between efficacious adherence to "outside" norms and loyal opposition to oppression of one's own proclivities. Most new therapies rest on claims that they have novel and effective means of recognizing, overcoming, and ultimately defeating such blurred discriminations; whether they do or not is, of course, a moot issue.

One danger inherent in blindly accepting the clever verbalizations of many therapy/counseling theories is that of reification of the terms and concepts and theories used—the same problem, indeed, that the theories address themselves to in our own stereotypic behavior! This problem of reifying "good" things is forever with us; many fundamentally useful concepts and practices in the broad field of counseling and psychotherapy diminish their potential value by exhalting their presence and their remedial effort (Back, 1972).

5. *Semantic issues and global terms.* This topic logically follows the previous one. Most of the global terms we commonly use in clinical reference (e.g., self, psyche, persona) contain some useful information. We all know in a general way what they refer to; but, still, we have no really precise way of using the terms to bring about change. To change the "self-concept," for example, we do not manipulate the *self* in any way; we change behavior that makes for increased self-confidence, for increased assertiveness, and the like. In such cases, the self that is presumably modified is a complex of generalizations like those treated above (see section 2, above, referring to "expectancies"), that is, a set of *dependent* variables. If we treat these global terms as dependent conditions, avoid reifying them, avoid treating them as if they were nouns, then we might speak more intelligently and gainfully about them. In short, if we use these terms *advisedly,* we can communicate some information; but if we convert the modest "as if . . ." descriptions to hard, objective fact, by verbal fiat, we lose their value, obfuscate their meaning, and fail to move therapy forward.

6. *Fortuitous reinforcement* (or "superstitious" behavior). A reference to this phenomena from Ullmann and Krasner (1975, p. 47) will serve here:

". . . some stimuli are responded to with regard to their contexts. A related paradigm is that of *superstitious* behavior. Behavior that is immediately followed by a positively reinforcing event is likely to be repeated under similar circumstances. Since living organisms continually emit ongoing activities, some activities will by chance be followed by changes in the environment which had nothing to do with the behavior the organism emitted. Further, to the extent that they are reinforced every once in a while on the basis of sheer chance, these activities may be perpetuated on a partial reinforcement schedule. Students may use a favorite pen or wear a certain piece of clothing for examinations. This particular behavior may have been associated with great success at one time; it is continued even though it has no direct effect on exams. The fact that a long time may pass between studying (which does help exam performance) or the exam itself and the reinforcing stimulus of grades also increases the chances of the development of superstitious behavior.''

This passage suggests that many "peculiar" or "bizarre" behaviors we note clinically may, indeed, be the result of fortuitous reinforcement conditions (see Chapter 6, pp. 306–307, in this connection). If this is true, it suggests further that all "symptoms"—especially the more unusual ones—need not be taken at "face value," examined in their own right, but well may be considered as offshoots of other, more important behaviors that are reinforced (Haughton and Ayllon, 1965). In fact, one might even take as a clinical rule that the more bizarre the "symptom," the less likely that behavioral correction is needed to replace it, and the more the general behavioral economy is upgraded, the less likely the peculiar behavior will continue to exist. In clinical practice, it would not be too difficult to keep track of unusual behavior of the type described and keep a frequency account of the behavior's presence in the patient. Observations of this type by some clinicians suggest that this is, indeed, the case; but the record has to be quantified and researched in a manner similar to Haughton and Ayllon (1965).

7. *Behavior and its consequences.* Everyone knows that the behaviorist considers behavior a function of its consequences. Antecedent conditions and the context surrounding the behavior itself are of great importance, but the consequences of behavior in and on the environment show whether the behavior will recur under similar circumstances. It is interesting, too, that consequences are of central importance in cybernetics (see Chapter 9). Sciences that study the functional relationship between events and their environment tend to develop consequential theories.

Once one discerns the importance of consequences, it becomes important to observe where the consequences lie. Consequences in the observable outside-the-skin environment are more easily measured and assessed than those inside the skin, and some behavioral theorists (Bandura, 1974) have tended to stress a dichotomy here, suggesting even that consequences may not regulate behavior; furthermore, they give more emphasis to the individual's own self-appraisal of consequences than many other behaviorists have done. This is an important matter and one that certainly concerns the clinician. If much of psychotherapy and counseling are devoted to helping the individual broaden his repertoire and improve his behavioral economy, then self-development with an emphasis on the existing repertoire may be of considerable importance. However, this is a "local" or temporary emphasis (in therapy) on the individual's own values and preferences because these very values are, themselves, being upgraded, defined, and clarified as a function of the therapeutic interaction and what that interaction spells out for the larger environment of the patient. Except for physiological and life-maintenance events inside the organism, all reactions to stimuli are presumably learned; that is, the events of consequence for the person in social, self-development, and growth senses, all come first from the "outside" and become related through various behavioral phenomena to the repertoire and behavioral economy of the person.

As we have already seen (Chapter 1), distinctions between "outside" and "inside," "covert" and "overt," are quite relative and of only slight semantic value in nonrigorous communication about behavior. The more precise we try to be, even in describing counseling and therapeutic endeavors, the more ready we should be to drop these artificial dichotomies and resort to the study of the *conditions* under which we find a given description or explanation useful or conceptually clear. The conditional nature of all knowledge must always be kept in mind (Popper, 1959).

The behaviorist, then, should really encounter no serious theoretical confrontation by allowing for more self-reinforcement potential with the patient without losing the value of considering behavior a function of its consequences. It is just harder to know in the case of therapeutic activities what exactly is reinforcing for the patient; often he or she does not know, and part of the therapeutic enterprise is, itself, devoted to clarification of this issue. This is where values for some theorists come into the picture (Patterson, 1966, 1974). However, values, like expectancies, are rather large constellations of reinforced events and consequences in the social environment of the person, and not a separate issue requiring separate lawfulness or conceptualization.

RELATED PRACTICAL ISSUES

The practical issues, selected from among many that might be considered, are: the relevance of *short-term* psychotherapy and counseling in the behavioral context; the role of *recognizing feelings* in a behavioral counseling or psychotherapy position; the importance of *self-appraisal* by the patient and the pitfalls one encounters in evaluating self-abnegation statements by the patient; and how the therapist might deal effectively with some "difficult" problems presented by the patient.

1. *The relevance of short-term psychotherapy and counseling* (Phillips and Wiener, 1966). Although most behavioral therapists do not set out specifically to produce short-term therapeutic effects, the outcome of

more economical, objective, and heuristic practices has this characteristic. The behavioral therapist is more likely to be willing to set short-term goals (e.g., in the context of semesters in scholastic settings and in other life-structuring settings), and is more likely to work through agendas and logs in ways that optimize change and produce shorter-range therapeutic outcomes. One might characterize the behavioral positions regarding short-term psychotherapy as twofold: short-term effects accruing naturally from heuristic and leading practices, and the setting of short-term goals in advance helping, then, to mobilize effort on the part of both therapist and patient, leading to shorter therapeutic practices.

Behavioral counseling and psychotherapy come to the aid of short-term therapy more generally through an interest in community mental health. Here, large-scale environmental conditions are the focus of change. For example, improving the general mental health condition of schools, offices, factories; or carrying out activities in the community at large that are calculated to reduce crime, vandalism, and destructiveness on the streets. One could help a community consider a number of behavioral objectives as "therapeutic" goals: overcoming traffic congestion on the streets; making the streets, parks, and other public places free from trash, disorder, and destructiveness; increasing respect for property in public settings (public libraries, public schools, public governmental buildings, etc.). Working through these kinds of interesting and mundane issues could demonstrate to the community how effective behavioral methods might be, and could pave the way for greater application of behavioral principles to community and social problems without threatening the "integrity" and "self-concepts" of communities the way some behavioral publications sometimes do (Torrey, 1974; Loew, Grayson, and Loew, 1975; Skinner, 1948, 1974; Kinkade, 1973).

2. *The practical value of "recognizing feelings."* As we have seen previously, the recognition of feelings is a sine qua non in psychotherapy, an emphasis found more among nonbehavioral therapists than among the behavioral therapists. However, there has never been any legislation against recognizing feelings, or "dealing" with them, although it is seldom of high notice among behavioral therapists. Feelings are behavior, also; or at least they are an integral part of behavioral acts (behavioral sequences such as the antecedent and consequent conditions of given behavior include many *feelings* dimensions). Many behaviorists are prone to thinking about the change process (that is, getting new or improved behaviors under way) and may ride herd over feelings too often. Of course, "rationality" or "realism" in therapy (Ellis, 1970; Glasser, 1975; Phillips and Wiener, 1966)—as well as other highly emphasized concepts and practices—may also override an interest in the feelings of patients.

There is often current in many therapeutic theories a kind of undertow of impatience with too much reference to feelings, particularly if the patient is considered to be too complaining, petulant, or hostile. However, we have to take the patient first where he or she is, and go from there. The feelings states, as we have seen (see Figure 1, Chapter 1, p. 19), are always present, abundantly so in the beginning of therapy, and never excluded no matter what therapy is used or with what success.

Erring in the other direction, as many "depth" therapists may be prone to do, and as seems to be characteristic of some of the "new therapies" (Harper, 1975), is also a liability. Therapies that seek out ever more and more "meanings" to be attached to feelings and emotional states and reports on one's self by the patient, often get lost in this morass without a way to extricate themselves; hence therapy goes on and on in pursuit of goals that might be spurious from a behavioral standpoint.

In summary, one might safely say that recognizing feelings has an important role in counseling and psychotherapy from any theoretical standpoint, but from a behavioral standpoint, its importance may be stated as follows:

a. Recognizing feelings is part of understanding the behavior of the patient.

b. Feelings are, themselves, behavioral events (or parts of behavioral complexes).

c. Recognizing feelings is a communicative bridge between patient and therapist.

d. Feelings may often be pivotal in identifying discriminative stimuli of importance in changing behavior.

e. Feelings and their recognition may also be important in understanding, in arranging, and in further reinforcing the consequences of behavior change efforts.

f. Feelings are sometimes by-products of more fundamental behavioral conditions and "not the real problem" themselves.

g. Feelings and their recognition tend to play a much larger role early in therapy, less so—but never fully diminished—as therapy becomes successful and is no longer required.

3. *Self-appraisal and the role of inferiority/superiority "complexes."* That the patient enters therapy with an abundance of complaints and problems is typical. Most complaints pivot on criticisms of self and others. When the therapist is confronted with a plethora of self-abnegating feelings and opinions on the part of the patient, it is difficult if not impossible to avoid recognizing this condition as axiomatic, for therapy to proceed. Consonant with the statements issued above, one has at first to take the

patient at "face value" in regard to his or her complaints, feelings, and the like, but then go on to establish the conditions under which these feelings apparently arise.

One way of looking at the negative feelings is to view them as disappointments at not having achieved more, or as not having a better relationship with another person, or at not having "stuck by one's guns." There is inherent in this formulation an "expectation," a prediction, an extrapolation from some given data to some other condition of satisfaction or experience that is supposed to arise out of the former. "What did you expect?" one often asks the patient. "If your expectations were not so high," we often aver as clinicians, "then you would not be so crestfallen when this kind of thing happens." "You feel badly because you never realize what you wish, desire, or expect," the therapist may say to the patient.

The problem, then, is what one *expects*. Self-abnegation follows from not having one's desires or expectations met; it does not follow from an "inferiority complex." Such a complex is viewed here as the outcome, the consequence, of perhaps ill-guided behavior on the patient's part. This is all the more important when the patient repeats the same pattern and evolves a generalized attitude that is self-negating and inferiority-dominated, and which leads to loss of affect, loss of motivation, and a reduction in a normal daily zest for living.

This distinction—whether one views the patient's negative "complex" as a product of "inferiority" or "superiority" feelings—appears to many to be inconsequential. However, the opposite is the case, both theoretically and practically. If the theoretical issue is one of a strong tendency to expect too much, this then suggests the patient is under the control of (possibly) verbal reinforcers which lead him or her to set too high goals, to be unwise or superficial in predicting what is needed to meet a given situation, and the like. Similar to other complaints, this pattern of high expectations/low results–poor-self-esteem tends to be redundant, and the outcome, the negative feelings, are what impinge most on the patient and on the therapist who hears (and observes) these consequences. The clinical/therapeutic issue becomes one of seeing how, under what conditions, the patient is under the control of (possible spurious) verbal, attitudinal, social reinforcers that have a misleading effect, which can, when identified and seen in context, then be altered. This effort then reduces the stated discrepancy, which reduces tension.

Similarly, if the therapy takes as its task the historical origins or the more detailed examination of the negative complaints, it then tends to overlook (or regard as secondary) the high expectations/low outcome discrepancy, and hence focuses on a spurious element in the situation and more easily becomes bogged down in chasing after elusive or nonexistent causes (Phillips, 1956; Phillips and Wiener, 1966). Therapy is difficult enough under all the optimal conditions we can devise; it need not take on spurious problems!

The reinforcing elements in considering the negative reports as *the* issue might include the impression that one is, in fact, "doing something about one's condition" (getting therapy), which "is supposed to lead to betterment," and which "requires that I say all I think and feel." There is nothing basically wrong with these slogans; they just cannot be pushed so far as to preclude the alternative notion that they are the by-products of the high expectation/low results discrepancy rather than the independent causal condition itself (see in this connection the final case in the discussion on supervision, Chapter 5).

When the therapist says to the patient that these low self-esteem items are essentially by-products of other conditions, it leads to the examination, understanding, and control of the discrepancies in two ways: First, by examining and challenging the high expectations ("You want everything to come your way," "You overestimate yourself and underestimate others, or the circumstances," "You are possibly too perfectionistic in this respect, too expectant, won't roll-with-the-punches," "You are acting selfishly, vainly, arrogantly"); a second way in which the discrepancy might be approached therapeutically is to see that in the self-abnegation picture the patient is, often, de-motivated, tries less well (because along with the too high expectation is also a disclaimer of sorts, in conflict with the aspiration). If this is the case, then more realistic efforts and more cautious approaches to one's goal are strongly indicated. Together, the two—reducing expectations and beefing up realistic performance—have a highly remedial effect, can be put into operation very early in therapy, can lead to self-reinforcing, self-clarification results for the patient, and energize the whole therapy effort. The patient typically says, "I think I see how I got into that trouble so often by being too expectant—I think now I'm getting some place!"

Corroborative of this general notion of the importance of expectancies—it would be better to call them "extrapolations," as this is a more neutral term (less mentalistic) and more similar to what all science does where it bases predictions on accumulated experience or data—is the fact that many suicides are people who "have everything." What the suicide lacks is not objective signs of achievement, material objects, or even love relations, but the ability to bring aspirations and accomplishments better in line. The despair that is reported to be typical of many great men and women of history [see Clark's book on Bertrand Russell (Clark, 1975)] springs, it would seem, from the ever-greater anticipation of more accomplishment and the depressing after effects of reality in comparison to unreal expectations. What distinguishes many adolescent suicides is that they are not infrequently high achieving, popular, capable, even exceptionally gifted persons, who apparently never harmonized their realities with their expectations. Humans are separated from lower animals, it would appear, not only on the basis of finger–thumb opposition, an upright gait, a larger brain, and the like, but also in terms of their enormous extrapolation capacities which may get them in trouble as often as they are enhancing. One cannot help here reinvoking the truism: Our greatest strength is also our greatest weakness!

In a more technical vein, verbal, ideational, and representational concepts and images—those symbols in words and "pictures" of deeds we all embrace so lovingly—are under the control of social reinforcers and may well get out of hand. It is as if two somewhat overlapping, yet largely distinctive, reinforcement systems ran parallel in time with a person, the one saying, "ahead, onward, upward, there is no limit to your aspirations and achievement," thus setting the stage for enormous expectations to be self-reinforced as well as eliciting social, interpersonal reinforcement; over against which one observes the slower, more plodding, less yielding pace of reality which says, "target your behavior more modestly" and "don't expect the world to be your oyster so readily." Reality is forever harsh and demanding and severely limiting; those of us who do not learn this efficaciously are likely to be dashed on the rocks of despair, blown again and again by the winds of overly high aspirations and expectations. Therein is our most severe, unrelenting and crucifying problem!

4. *Dealing therapeutically with "difficult" problems.* A therapist's list of "difficult" problems would probably extend far beyond those described here. The present excursion into this problem is not meant to cover all difficult problems but to set up a conceptual model for dealing with them. Applications to ever wider issues of difficult communications between therapist and patient may be encouraged on the basis of the present attempt at clarification.

Among the most difficult problems between therapist and patient one might include the following: *Anger* expressions by the patient against the therapist; *aggressive threats* directed at the therapist (occasionally others) by the patient; preoccupations with *self-blame* on the patient's part; and a total or near-total *lack of verbal communication* in therapy by the patient.

Anger. The *anger* responses by the patient toward the therapist represent most likely a feeling of frustration in the therapy enterprise itself and an oblique way of saying that the patient has no trust or confidence in the therapist. If this is the case, the issue should, of course, be fully aired, with the therapist accepting the anger at face value ("You feel I am not doing my duty toward you, or not helping you enough"). This can then lead to a restatement of the therapy contract conditions—a "contract" of sorts should be attempted at this juncture if one has not emerged before—and to a review of the roles of therapist and patient. The therapist should avoid trying too hard to "explain" his or her position; this will probably lead only to the patient being even more angry because it may be just this attitude of the therapist that is at issue. The therapist should, as he or she is prone to do with other complaints offered by the patient, try to get the fuller picture.

Two other therapist reactions might be considered. One is that the therapist, depending on how he or she feels in general about the patient, might offer to transfer the patient to another therapist (this is easiest when the therapist is in some kind of clinical or group practice setting), and give the patient time to absorb and react at leisure to the suggestion. A second tack the therapist may take in the face of such criticism is that the therapy might be halted for an agreed-upon period of time (say a month, for a trial period) with the patient making notes on himself during the interim, possibly mailing these notes to the therapist, then meeting again with a view to revising, continuing, or stopping the therapy. These kinds of reactions and suggestions imply a full-scale involvement on the therapist's part to reconcile the differences. The matter may turn out in the end to be more profitable for the therapist than for the patient, as the therapist may learn that some "kinds" of patients and/or some kinds of patient–therapist interactions are not the therapist's "cup of tea."

Avoided in these strictures in describing the therapist's reaction is one that says that the patient is simply "displacing" his or her anger onto the therapist, and continuing therapy as it has been thus far is the way to "get to the root of the problem." Unfortunately, this places the burden almost entirely on the patient to make the necessary modifications in the patient–therapist relationship, ends up calling the patient "defensive," and probably teaches the therapist nothing about his or her endeavor. It may well be that loggerheads encountered by therapists with "difficult" patients are often due to similar intransigence on the therapist's part.

Aggressive threats. Aggressive threats or actions directed at the therapist by the patient are examples of further extremes along the anger continuum. Threats here refer to actual threats ("Some time I'm going to bring in a gun and shoot you" the patient remarks to the therapist; or "I've got a hunting knife in my pocket and I just might get mad enough to use it on you . . . or on somebody"). Here, too, the reasons for the threat must be examined more fully in context, with full reference to the patient's feelings toward the therapist as a person and to how the therapy is conducted. The same tacks that are intended to handle angry verbal abuse constructively might apply to the threatening situation. However, the therapist may have to go a step or two further—ask the patient to turn over the gun or the knife, or whatever, to the therapist for "safe keeping" until the therapy is concluded, or for some agreed-upon period of time. This allows the therapist to protect his or her own interests, gives the patient comfort in feeling that the therapist is able to help the patient in this crucial situation of self-control, and reintegrates the threats back into the stream of therapeutic activities. Of course, one has to decide as a therapist if he or she wants to work with these kinds of difficult patients, but in institutional and school settings the therapist may not have a choice. There is a considerable challenge here for the therapist who is moved by these kinds of problems! Other tactics or strategies may, of course, be considered: refusing to see the patient, transferring the patient to another therapist, turning the patient over to the police or to legal action of some kind, but these are hardly instances where the therapist himself or herself rises to the challenge.

Self-blame. Self-blame on the patient's part is also difficult to handle, especially if the therapist feels the self-abnegation is genuine or very intense. Self-blame has probably netted the patient some positive reinforcement in the past, minimally in drawing attention to the patient, more likely in soliciting and getting overt help from others and/or in developing a strong dependency role. The self-blame reflects a status that says, in effect, "I am unable to do things for myself but also feel the absence of reliable dependence upon others." The therapist has to be careful not to reinforce the repetitive verbal statements of self-blame either by paying too much positive attention to them or by minimizing them through verbal suasion techniques. Some structuring of the patient's complaints in verbal ways (Ellis, 1962, 1970; Phillips and Wiener, 1966) is worth trying out, but if it does not succeed, the therapist's continued reliance on verbal suasion directed to the complaints and self-blame themselves should be dropped. What then? Building positive reinforcing circumstances in the patient's life is the preferred manner of treatment, once the self-blame and complaint "system" of the patient is reasonably well understood. By shaping socially acceptable and gratifying behaviors, the basis of self-blame will begin to be eliminated; and the patient will start to set goals, display initiative, and thereby obviate the need to focus on self-blame. Assertive training, social skill development, and the use of positive imagery (depicting situations to himself where the patient has been successful; see Chapter 2, techniques 2 and 26) are techniques of value in this setting. In short, any methods useful in upgrading positive and assertive behaviors is by far superior to examining the self-blame and complaint system of the patient.

Suicide threats. Handling suicide threats is also a tender and important problem in therapy (Shneidman, 1968; Shneidman, Farberow, and Litman, 1970). Although the literature is considerably divided on how to therapeutically handle apparent or real threats about suicide (ranging all the way from severe confrontation as to how idiotic it is, to deep compassion expressed in words to the patient and elaborated upon as fully as possible), not much has been said about not discussing suicide threats or suicide-related feelings expressed by the patient. In one sense of the interaction, the more one discusses a topic the more it risks being reinforced in the verbal exchange. To note that the patient is, to some extent, "toying" with the idea of suicide is, of course, necessary; but to react to the verbal threat as if it were real or as if it were a predictable event is not only risky but wholly unnecessary. The therapist can himself or herself confront the possibility of suicide on the patient's part by referring to the discouraged, angry, and revengeful way in which the patient views his life or a significant part of it. The therapeutic issue should hinge on the circumstances, the self-defeating interactions, and how these may be remedied, rather than on the suicide itself. Even if the patient says, "You don't seem to think I really might commit suicide, do you?" the therapist can reply, "To be sure, I know it is well within your capability to do it," then go on to the reasons, the examination of the patient's experiences that lead him or her to make the threat. Many patients want the therapist, or someone (and the therapist is often the best person around to receive these possibility aggressive onslaughts), to be hurt, deprived, strongly affected by the patient's threats of suicide. One does need to know the patient, to be sure, but the more the possibly intended meaning of the suicide threat is directly reinforced through attention and even lengthy discussion, the more the *additional* risk of unduly or unwittingly reinforcing the prospect is incurred. It is altogether less complicating to discuss the reasons for the abnegation on the patient's part—which is fundamentally the issue at hand—than it is to discuss the possible consequences of the abnegation in the form of suicide threats, since the discussion can too easily contribute to a self-fulfilling prophesy.

Short-range reinforcement versus long-range aversive consequences. If there is a second important distinction in the context of this chapter between humans and other animals, in addition to the expectancy phenomena (see pp. 193–195, above), it is the wise or unwise use of expectancy in the battle between immediate reinforcement of a positive nature versus the longer-range aversive consequences of that reinforcement. The large number of so-called "habit disorders" is a relevant referent here. We engage in many behaviors largely on this basis of a complicated set of personal and social reinforcers which have long-term aversiveness connected therewith. One thinks immediately of overeating, smoking, drinking, gambling, undue risk-taking in driving a car, or in a variety of seemingly more harmless "letting go" phenomena, such as making easy promises that cannot be kept, contracting for performances that cannot be delivered, signing bogus checks, issuing any kind of "promissory note" that is impossible to "cash," and so forth. We take the immediate ". . . cash and let the credit go, nor heed the rumble of a distant drum," as Omar Khayyam so ably put it.

There are really two sets of issues in the immediate reinforcement versus long-range aversive consequences problem. The first is the more obvious one, that of deliberate taking gain and heedlessly avoiding concern for the future. We see this phenomena, of course, in the practice of smoking, overeating, or squandering one's personal, financial, and other resources. These constitute many of the problems one sees in the clinic; much of the behavioral effort is not only invested in developing control systems to overcome these "habit disorders," but in verbally juxtaposing the long-range aversiveness ever closer in time to the act of "taking the cash and letting the credit go" so that verbal support of control systems is in hand.

We can extrapolate this condition to society, too. We squander our natural resources in order to provide unnecessary and wasteful pleasures of the moment, heedlessly ignoring the day when energy resource and distribution may become so critical a problem as to challenge the existence of the very set of civilized "comforts" we have so unthinkingly built and destroyed, like a child playfully building castles with blocks then joyously destroying them. (The child can build his castle again immediately and destroy it many times, thereby learning something from the process, but mankind may well be provoking irreversible changes in nature and in society by this wastefulness.) We often remark clinically that "part of a person" wants to do something and "another part of the person doesn't." We characterize the person as split, we conceptualize the problem this way. No such split exists. What does exist is the operation of different sets of contingencies that, themselves, have not been coordinated. If one is going on a trip and has a limited amount of money to spend, he or she cannot afford to squander it all the first day or two. One has to spend now, contingent on the longer-range plan. The economics of a trip, whether referring to money, arrangements, promises to others, or the expenditure of physical energy, are a miniature example of a person apportioning short-range reinforcements in the light of longer-range consequences. One must do this for one's life not only on a daily basis, but on as long-range a basis as is feasible and calculable. Many people have not learned to do this kind of self-management; hence they erode their pleasure, their self-control, their reinforceableness, and thereby suffer the pangs of the damned. One can not ignore the need for a modicum of orderliness and continue to exist as an integrated person. Pathology is disorder; and much disorder comes from the problem of juxtaposing the short-range and long-range consequences of our behavior.

A second and more subtle aspect of this same problem is that of simply not knowing what the long-range consequence of an action may be. We try, we conjure, but we cannot be sure. We take "normal risks," as we say, and hope for the best. Often society blushes at its own risk-taking: we have built too many roads and cars and have thereby greatly complicated not only our daily lives but have correspondingly built an enormous pollution problem that may take decades to remedy. We built these cars and roads because they "contributed to the growth of the country, gave people jobs, provided needed services," and the like. Only recently have we fully realized as a society that we not only did the "good" things, but we created a horrible monster in the wake of these seeming benefits. One may, in his personal life, invest time, money, and effort in apparently good prospects, only to have his plans go awry, have the market or the economic situation militate against his personal success, or suffer other negative exigencies in life. The plans we have as individuals harbor the risks we can and must take; no venture capital is without risk, whether on a financial or personal, emotional level.

In the later stages of counseling and psychotherapy there is much risk-taking of the more calculable sort. "Should I now return to school and upgrade my skills?" a woman asks who has solved her personal and family problems and now has energy to devote to longer-range goals. "I can go this route or that route in school, but I do not honestly know which is the better one, which one I will relish more in the years to come—it is a difficult choice," a college junior avers after overcoming interpersonal difficulties, study problems, and issues with his parents that vitiated all his previous efforts at getting an education and being successful in daily life. After we put out the "brush fires," we have to clear the land, till the soil, plant the seeds, and make plans for the future. Much of psychotherapy and counseling—a much larger share than is generally credited to the profession—concerns not only the minutia of realistic problem solving of pressing issues here and now, but also lifting up the head to look out and over the immediate to the vistas beyond. This is the kind of calculation, this is the kind of extrapolation from immediate gains to longer-term gains of an even greater value that "grab" the integrated person, the one who is self-fulfilling on a *continuing* basis.

WHY DOES TALKING TO SOMEONE HELP IN THE SOLUTION OF PERSONAL PROBLEMS?

The first answer to this query is that talking does not always help; but it does help some of the time. It is incumbent on the therapist–theorist to develop some notions as to why talking is or is not beneficial. Let us take up first the instances in which talking is helpful.

When one talks about his or her problems there is a verbal presentation of facts, feelings, and interactions characterizing the patient's life. Insofar as these are reasonably accurately represented by words, there may be expected a correspondence between the "solutions" worked out via words and applications to the real world. Thus if one gives direction to a visitor on how to get to a given monument in Washington, there can be expected some high degree of correspondence between the directions, the verbal representations, and the facts of geography. If one speaks fairly accurately about a given relationship with one's spouse, then the discussion of this relationship via words—suggesting how to change this or that interaction, calling up the differences between the behavior in question and how one evaluates his or her own and the other person's behavior, and so forth—can lead to the manipulation of the behavioral elements present and suggest new tactics that can then be tested in the real relationship at another time. Words are the easiest and most convenient way in which we can represent our feelings and the many facts about our own behavior, assuming, of course, there is fair accuracy in the communication.

But words do go awry. We use them carelessly, inconsistently, incompletely to convey our meaning. The other person, the therapist, may not understand what the patient is saying accurately, and vice versa. Sometimes there is a struggle with the problem of conveying meaning and accuracy that has to be worked out over a strenuous period of time. Both parties—therapist and patient—are not always trained or interested in highly accurate communication; they are most often content with a modicum of meaning being transmitted.

Then, too, people use words to play with meaning; they want to paint as many word hues as possible, neglecting the boundaries and overlapping areas, so that verbal communication comes to serve more the purpose of artistic expression than precise communication bent on solving problems. Words are perhaps not the very best friends of therapists but certainly they are a good friend; however, it would be naive to trust the friendship so completely as never to reexamine what is being said.

The use of words in an oral exchange may also present a number of problems. Although the words used in face-to-face verbal therapy are supported by "body language," inflections and the like, there is not uncommonly a discrepancy between what is being said by words and what is being said otherwise. People smile while speaking hostile and angry words; people cry when "feeling happy," and so forth. We all use contrasting differences between words selected and intended meaning: "It certainly was *nice* of you not to tell me you weren't going, thus leaving me standing on the street corner for an hour!"

Perhaps the verbal exchanges in therapy represent a common ground of patient-expression-of-problem/therapist-reply-in-words, such that we all know more or less well that a problem is present and we, as therapist, can ferret out enough meaning to proceed with some degree of validity. We settle for less than we might ideally want.

Writing about one's problems, on the other hand (see Chapter 4), may prove to be very economical and less subject to the usual semantic vicissitudes, for reasons already cited in the earlier chapter. One takes writing rather more seriously than the spoken word, there is less "static" in writing, it is far more economical (hence harbors less opportunity for obfuscation), and is more easily adjusted to therapist–patient time arrangements. One of the best ways to study the *semantics* of counseling and psychotherapy would be via written protocols, but this remains, thus far, a neglected topic. Further testing of the value of spoken communication in therapy might be studied in the manner suggested above (see the first few pages of this chapter discussing the problem of wholly nonverbal communications in therapy). The major point here is that altering the nature of the verbal communication between therapist and patient may not only lead to more knowledge and the enhancement of verbal communications themselves, but may also lead heuristically to improved means of patient–therapist communication. We can no longer afford to accept verbal–oral exchange as the uncontested model of therapeutic communication as it is now commonly practiced. Probably the explanation of some of the "unusual" effects of unorthodox psychotherapies noted by Wolberg (Loew, Grayson, and Loew, 1975) can be found in the semantics of behavior and personality change through verbal suasion techniques.

CHAPTER 8

Great Ideas in Behavior Therapy

It is always difficult to state exactly what are the great ideas in any field of human endeavor; there are bound to be many differing opinions. However, it is still useful to make an attempt at organizing sets of ideas so that one's thoughts are mobilized and, even though differing, the controversies and arguments ensuing will be enlightening rather than simply polemic.

The projections from this chapter intend to concentrate on behavior therapy practices rather than on behavior theory more broadly conceived. However, there are many overlapping areas between behavior theory in a general sense and behavior therapy as a set of practical efforts in the smaller and more specific sense. As always in science, general theoretical ideas tend to set predispositions and directions for practical applications; in turn, practical applications feed back into the scientific body of knowledge and often correct, redirect, and embellish the theoretical posture of a field of knowledge. Perhaps concentrating now on one version of the great ideas in behavior therapy will induce the student of behavioral practices to think both more broadly and more clearly about what he or she is doing.

Stimulus control. Understanding and comprehending the stimulating environment is obviously of great importance in behavior therapy. We want to understand the behavior and its consequences, to be sure, but we need also to know as clearly as possible what antecedent or stimulating conditions bear a functional relationship to the behavior in question. In the clinical situation this is sometimes an arduous task. Most therapists have broken their backs on the rocks of trying to discriminate the remote historical conditions that are presumably accountable for the resultant behavior. One problem here is that the "total" environment is not relevant; psychologists have always worked hard at trying to specify which stimuli may be held accountable for the observed behavior and to bridge a functional relationship between them. Skinner uses the term S^D (discriminative stimuli) to denote stimuli that does bear a functional relationship to observed behavior. To denote nondiscriminative stimuli the term S^Δ (S-delta) is used. In the teaching of new responses, we select from among the stimuli present only certain stimuli (S^D); the organism or the individual is reinforced *only* in the presence of these discriminative stimuli; thus, in this way there is established a functional relationship between the stimuli and the responses of the organism. This is the way behavior change occurs; this is the kind of business the behavior therapist is engaged in and, indeed, the kind of activity all therapists are engaged in whether they recognize it or not.

In the laboratory, controlling the S^D is usually a simpler and more direct matter than trying to specify a similar set of conditions in the clinical environment. Many clinicians have spoken of "structuring" the environment (Phillips, 1956; Phillips and Wiener, 1966; Haring and Phillips, 1962, 1972) which is a somewhat loose way of calling attention to the importance of controlling the stimulating environment when one is interested in behavior change; and in this book the same terminology has been applied. The clinical counselor or psychotherapist must learn as much as he can about the antecedent conditions, attempt to control these conditions where possible, and try to relate them to the behavioral consequences under study. One should be quick to point out, however, that understanding the stimulating conditions, structuring the environment, and the like are not the same as attempting a long-range, backward review of one's life. The relevant stimuli are not the sum total (whatever that means) of one's life but more nuclear events that tend to have similar characteristics whenever or wherever they occur in one's biography.

The internal environment is also part of the stimulus control problem. Contrary to what some think, the behavioral counselor or therapist is interested in the patient's internal environment (including thoughts, images, dreams, etc.) as well as being interested in internal and often very subtle physiological processes within the skin. In fact, one could predict that much of the progress and success of behavior therapy in the future will consist in the effort to make these more subtle processes clearer and to bring them under more open, deliberate, and discriminative control by the individual, sometimes via the aid of instrumentation and sometimes simply by teaching better self-control. The problem often encountered with subtle, internal processes is that they are dealt with too hypothetically (too much loose "theory" is based on conjectures about internal processes) and used as repositories allowing the theorist–therapist to avoid the task of empirical study of subtle processes. What clinicians loosely refer to as the "unconscious mind" or "unconscious processes" are simply as-yet-not-clearly-discriminated stimuli in the current matrix of the person's interaction with his environment (Phillips, 1956).

What, then, does the clinician do about stimulus control? In the sense of arranging the environment, the clinician can do many things. He or she

can influence other significant people in the patient's environment, help
the patient arrange or rearrange his or her own environment, call attention
to the fact that many other environments are possible; help identify the
more relevant stimuli by disabusing the patient of "superstitious" beliefs
in the importance of some environmental conditions, and help the patient
develop a more functional relationship between his or her environment
and the sought-after behavioral consequences that become the goals of
therapy. The more the therapist helps the patient move toward self-
control, the more the stimulating environment and its consequences are
brought under control, and vice versa.

One might view the conceptual problem of understanding the "newer"
therapies in the light of their ability to identify new or heretofore overlooked environmental conditions (Harper, 1975). The behavioral study of
the problems related to stimulus control should give the innovative
therapist–theorist a vantage point for inventing or discovering or reem-
phasizing previously unnoticed stimulating conditions. This does not
make the new therapies nonbehavioral—it may simply enlarge the behavioral matrix and enrich the means for offering counseling and
psychotherapy.

The behavior itself. The first chapter discusses the problem of what
behavior is. The definition of behavior is very inclusive when we are
willing to encompass internal physiological process and self-report data
on dreams, images, feelings, and the like. We infer, and sometimes can
demonstrate, the physiological and behavioral significance of these internal processes; and we count them of some importance in establishing
self-control. Older theorists–therapists tend to set behavior off as a kind
of reflex study, or limit it to motor activity. Correspondingly, the more
traditional thinkers and therapists tend to separate all the internal and
self-report processes from behavior study. In so doing, they beg many
more questions than they answer; for it is much easier and more heuristic,
scientifically, to include these subtler processes under the behavioral
rubric—and thereby bring a methodology for studying them to bear on the
problem—than it is to separate them and be faced with the necessity of
defining differences, discovering a new or different lawfulness, and meeting a myriad of philosophical problems (Skinner, 1974).

Even if one took an extremely narrow view of the study of the living
organism and reduced all function to structure; even if one asserted that
all so-called behavior was epiphenomena and that neurophysiological and
biochemical conditions determined all behavior, one would still have to
describe the relationships between the structural conditions and their
functioning. In effect, one would still have to derive a functional analysis

and description of behavior. As knowledge progresses ever more profoundly into the substrata of neurophysiological functioning, undoubtedly many aspects of presently observed behavior will be made clearer and brought under better control, but we still have behavior to study and describe; we shall always have to study behavior.

Controlling the consequences of behavior. Although some scholars dispute the generalization that behavior is a function of its consequences (Bandura, 1974), there seems to be no serious challenge to this proposition insofar as clinical phenomena are concerned. One problem of studying the consequences is defining how long one might be willing to wait to observe consequences. If consequences are defined as requiring immediate feedback, then this is too narrow and stringent and too quickly rules out the advent of longer-range consequences. One eats too many calories at a given meal; the immediate consequences might be a turgid feeling and a desire for inactivity, whereas the longer-range outcome may be substantial weight increase (if the practice is continued), health problems, and the like. An interesting phenomena found abundantly among human beings is the longer-range consequences of behavior, how these consequences might be "mediated" by intervening events (perhaps behavioral loops of a very complex sort), and how control can be established to prevent or reduce the untoward consequences such as unwanted weight or health problems.

An important part of the practice of psychotherapy is to set up for the patient the proposition that some antecedent behaviors and stimulating conditions *are* related to certain discernible outcomes and that when the latter are untoward it is all the more important to test out connections and to bring some kind of control to bear on the issue. In a behavioral framework, the testing out of these connections is a forward-looking enterprise, not a backward, searching one. In the behavioral framework, one goes with the patient from the present to the recent past—to discovering and describing the likely stimuli connections with the environment—then to the future as a way of testing out the present–past connection. If we know behavior by its consequences, then the testing-out becomes the crucial issue, not whether the present–past connections fit some theory or particular notion of historical causality, even further in the past (as if validity were established by describing a longer and longer history for some behavioral event).

Figure 13 shows how various ways of controlling the consequence of behavior might be juxtaposed. On the right side of the circle in Figure 13 are the more confrontive, direct measures one might take to overcome unwanted behavior; on the left side of the circle are displayed the less confrontive, more gradual measures for overcoming the unwanted be-

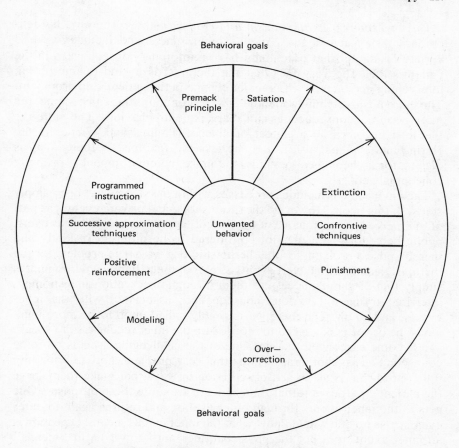

Figure 13. How various methods for controlling the consequences of behavior might be juxtaposed, moving from "unwanted behavior" (symptoms) toward behavioral goals.

havior and leading the patient to more acceptable behavior. The smaller interior circle represents the more limited, constricted, redundant nature of unwanted behavior, while the outside, peripheral circle suggests greater adaptability that ensues when behavioral impasses are solved, but also suggests that the adaptiveness of solving problems might be highly varied—there is no one solution to the unwanted behavioral impasse. Some areas of the circle in the figure are left blank to suggest that other techniques may yet fit into this conceptualization; there has been no attempt to include all known tchniques (the list of techniques included in Figure 13 are only a few of those listed in Chapter 2).

The environment as the causal and control matrix. Therapy, by definition, takes place in the patient's environment and includes a large variety of stimuli that potentially have reinforcing consequences in the patient's life. The very fact that the therapist is a kind of interfering, intervening person is, itself, a major change in the patient's environment. The more positively influential the therapist or counselor can become, the more potential consequences can shape patient behaviors. The more the therapist becomes an architect of change (Phillips and Wiener, 1966; Haring and Phillips, 1972), and the less the therapist is thought of as digging for archeological remains, the more the environment is properly conceptualized.

The environment includes processes within the skin as has been amply stated in this book. However, the more subtle and private events, as part of "perceived environment" of the patient, are not as accessible as overt, public behaviors—but are not considered to be different in kind—and thereby pose a problem for the therapist in one way. The problem for the therapist dealing with covert events as part of the patient's environment is simply that of gaining access to them through observation, questioning, inferring, trying out various consequences associated with the inner events, and so on. The therapist is simply called upon to be more ingenious; he or she is not asked to recede into the inner reaches, so to speak, and become ensconced therein. One of the challenging aspects of doing counseling or psychotherapy is just this very problem: how to bring into full control the issues of self-observation in ways that make them serve the patient's purposes rather than elude or frustrate these purposes. One gets to the inner events through outer events, and returns again to outer events, else no one would know what the inner events meant. Digestion is an inner event, too, but the physician does not know what it "means" until he can observe it and bring it under some kind of control (Skinner, 1971, 1974).

The role of relationships reexamined. Reference to "relationship" in counseling and psychotherapy (Patterson, 1969, 1974; Phillips, 1969) have been an area of dispute and controversy for many years. From a behavioral standpoint, reference to relationship is lacking in specificity and also fails to recognize sufficiently that many negative or nontherapeutic events may transpire under this rubric. When relationship efforts house reinforcing and problem-solving outcomes, we are more able to talk then about reinforcement and problem solving which are the foci of change. We know, also, that most of us change our behaviors all the time without *specific* relationship considerations, although like the environment, the relationship matter is always present in some way. The behavioral therapist has gone a long way toward specifying what is of importance in the environment, but too often the relationship emphasis in cognitive, interpersonal, nondirective, and related therapies is left vague and unconvincing. In a sense, relationships "carry" variables related to reinforcement contingencies; but when we can specify these variables we no longer need the global term except in a loose way.

One way to look more searchingly at the relationship set of notions is to vary relationship as a global condition in therapy. The use of writing therapy (see Chapter 4) is one way; other ways have been suggested in Chapter 7. Surely relationships are minimized in writing therapy, yet to no known disadvantage in terms of therapeutic outcome, insofar as the problem has been researched thus far (Phillips and Wiener, 1966). More studies are needed and abundantly welcome, but few therapists have shown any interest in examining the role of relationships by varying this very condition widely over a spectrum of possibilities.

Reinforcement. One can hardly do justice to this vastly important notion and set of empirical relationships in the brief space provided here. The lesson for the counselor or psychotherapist is that the concept of reinforcement and its supporting empirical bases (Ferster and Skinner, 1957) is so important that one cannot proceed intelligently without it. If the therapist does not pay attention to reinforcement in as refined a sense as possible, then opportunities for improving therapy are lost, and everyone suffers as a consequence.

In writing therapy the therapist's replies can be based entirely on reinforcing (noticing, replying to . . .) only positive (or negative) writings on the patient's part. In face-to-face therapy the therapist could attempt the same discriminations and thereby collect data to show how influential, in terms of certain dependent conditions, the reinforcement practices of the therapist are (Greenspoon, 1961; Greenspoon and Brownstein, 1968). There are many ways in which the reinforcement potential of the counselor or therapist can enter incisively into the therapeutic matrix. The writer, as therapist, has systematically adopted the policy of never reinforcing patient references to suicide, violence, and guns or other weapons possibly usable for destructive purposes, insofar as paying attention to, discussing, "analyzing" these topics is concerned, on grounds that paying attention to them upgrades their value and potential usefulness to the patient. Whether this is a "good" practice remains for research to show, but applying this therapeutic tactic in a reinforcement context appears reasonable and thus far has been constructive.

One can confront one's self as therapist with the importance of reinforcement by asking for evidence that the concept (and related practices) are not needed. Where is the null class referring to reinforcement? If one can be specific, well and good; knowledge and therapeutic practices will have been enhanced (reinforced!), but if a null class cannot be specified, the therapist/counselor will be well advised to make optimal use of reinforcement.

Reinforcement contingencies. Reinforcement implies a contingency, hence it is somewhat redundant to make the separation except for emphasis. The counselor/therapist may think he or she is reinforcing the patient in some way by not allowing for the contingent nature of the reinforcement; that is by giving reinforcement noncontingently (or randomly). However, this is a problem in the sense that the therapist may be misusing knowledge that could otherwise be applied productively, and is thereby allowed to put incorrect interpretations on patient–therapist behaviors. Applying reinforcement noncontingently is of course a widespread practice—teachers and parents do it frequently—but when the contingent nature of reinforcement is understood and used, most of the objections to the concept melt away and the user is reinforced by and through observing the potency of the practice.

There are many ways to apply reinforcement contingently in the hands of the therapist (consulting Chapter 2 again in this context is useful). A therapist or counselor might write down the ways in which a given patient can be reacted to in terms of reinforcement contingencies. One example was that of a supervisee who was seeing a patient in therapy; the supervisee-therapist handled the contingent use of reinforcement in the following ways:

"Well, I just said to her that we were possibly spending too much time on her complaints and not enough on things she could *do* about the complaints. I said I would listen to her complaints—she could write them down briefly—*after* she had reported in some detail on our agreed-upon out-of-therapy agenda for her, and after she had logged some positive things that had happened to her in the interim."

"We agreed that J_____ would play cards with his roommates *after* he had done his math assignment each evening."

"I said to him that he brought up important topics too late in the therapy hour for useful discussion; and that after this he could bring in a written list of the most important topics of the week for him and we would *start* the session with them."

"We agreed that the patient could call me between sessions over the phone *after* she had made the other arrangements on a day-to-day basis that were necessary for her job."

The use of reinforcement contingencies in this manner, agreed upon by patient and therapist and properly woven into the context of the therapy, are not aversive to the patient; they are, in fact, the opposite in that they help to call off otherwise aversive consequences for the patient who feels guilty in not doing the things he or she wants to do or considers germane to progress. It is part of the role of the behavioral counselor to offer these kinds of contingent arrangements to help the patient gain self-control, not simply to wait for the patient "to do it when he or she is ready."

Circularity of complaints. Another important idea in the behavioral movement is recognizing the circularity of complaints. They occur again and again and it is this loop nature of behavior that spells out the enormity of a problem, describes its probable course, and suggests leads for gainful intervention. The emphasis on loops and circularity comes, as has been shown, from cybernetics (see Chapter 9).

The therapist's approach to breaking up the "vicious circle" rests on several propositions: First, to suggest the circular nature of the problem to the patient (he or she may already know this in a vague sort of way); to suggest that these circular processes, by definition, will probably continue to occur unless some "new" information gets into the process; to suggest how and where the patient can enter into efforts to break up the circular process and to help the patient detail intervention efforts; and to test out these interventions, correcting and extending them as indicated by feed-back. Often people can appreciate the circularity of their behaviors more readily than they can grasp the idea that they are indeed being reinforced through the performance of unwanted behavior, ostensibly of a negative cast.

It is important, as well, for the therapist to conceptualize openly the circular processes. This allows the therapist to anticipate a return of the patient's problem without inferring that change efforts have been ineffective and to build ever more effective intervention efforts. Consonant with the discussion of expectancies in other chapters (see Chapters 1, 6, and 9), the patient and therapist attempt to gain earlier and earlier access to the repetitive features of the problem, first to reduce the problem intensity, later to hopefully preclude the problem's occurrence. A linear view of problem recurrence does not help as much here as a circular view. Integral to all life-maintenance efforts is the notion of loops; they apply as cogently to behavioral maintenance processes whether these processes are "wanted" or "unwanted" by the behaving person.

Conflict. Conflict has been referred to extensively in this book (see Chapters 3, 5, and 6 especially) but the pervasive nature of its relevance to psychotherapy and counseling must be reemphasized. From the beginning of Freud's work to the present, it has been obvious to psychologists that the formal notion of conflict was indispensable. Recognition of the importance of conflict in human affairs has been widespread; one thinks here of novels, plays, operas, indeed almost any artistic account of human suffering, travail, or concern. The hundreds of euphemistic ways we characterize the most intensely divisive instances of human suffering are fundamentally indirect references to conflict. Any "problem situation" that a living organism encounters is an example of conflict, however fleeting or easily overcome. There is no way to avoid conflict in human affairs.

The contributions of behavioral psychology to the study of conflict are well known and need not be reviewed here. One thinks first of the work of Dollard and Miller (1950), and Brown (1948); where the conflict paradigm was analyzed in terms of approach and avoidance gradients. When one listens carefully to patients speaking (or writing) about their concerns it is everywhere abundantly clear that they are "caught" in approach and avoidance behaviors with respect to other persons, with respect to their own goals, self-evaluations, and aspirations. Ubiquitous is the name for conflict. Speaking therapeutically with the patient and highlighting the presence and importance of conflict are essential to effective counseling. The therapist should not be content with a passing reference to conflict but should lift up to open therapeutic scrutiny the conceptual importance of conflict and help make the patient's concerns come to life in this way. Patients wander around aimlessly in the quest for clarity, purpose, and direction. The reason they don't readily find these objectives is that they are too divided in their overt behavioral efforts (lack self-discipline, order, self-management) and have, as yet, not arranged their thinking about themselves, nor have they learned to observe themselves clearly or systematically. Good therapy teaches them to do these things.

In reference to therapeutic tactics, the therapist/counselor may say to the patient some such statements as the following: "These problems with your boss might be thought of as conflicts, where you want to approach him with some ideas or feelings you have, but where you are at the same time restrained, hesitant, doubtful—what, in detail, is the nature of this conflict?" Or, "The child seems to want to please you, but you have made it difficult for her to know how to do this, how to get support without criticism, how to gain confidence in doing what you (and she) agree is important." Or, "You want to study and do well and feel good about your achievement, but when it comes to doing the actual work, you give in to whimsical distracting urges or easily postpone your efforts." And so on through almost any imaginable human concern.

Conflict is readily seen as the basis for the aspiration–reality disparity, the expectation–performance split. We all aspire for more than we can achieve. We do not need opium to encourage the spinning of dreams; in expectation, we are always far ahead of our achievement and loftier in its evaluation than is realistic. This is the "human case," this is the human situation. Our great symbolic, conceptual, and abstract capabilities ever guide us into more wonderous achievements, but they also lead us into fog and obfuscation; the patient usually presents more of the latter than of the former.

Dissolution of "depth" notions. Behavioral psychology as it is applied to counseling and psychotherapy is quite adequate to meet the needs of "depth" type questions promulgated by the traditional views of man and of therapy. What is sorely needed is more careful thinking about man's complexity, not a continuing plethora of web-spinning theories about inner workings that have never been shown to be right or wrong but only serve to temporize with the harsh realities of living. Although we are all poetically drawn to the wondrous complexity of human behavior, we must never simply yield to this practice in the name of science; poetry enhances, titillates, beckons, but science knows, predicts, understands and controls; and we must cultivate all these virtues—but not confuse them—if we are to become what we are capable of becoming.

When people feel or observe their distressed emotional reactions to the world around them, they "feel" and conceptualize in a manner closely similar to the way they register physical distress and pain; they do not know where it comes from, what it means, or how to make it "go away." As Skinner has so ably pointed out (Skinner, 1974), neither the nervous system nor the "verbal community" has a structure capable of readily knowing what "inner events" mean. Our "innerness" is a social product made possible, to be sure, by our enormously complex nervous system; but how we conceptualize these events and weave them into the larger fabric of life and behavior is often a moot question on which philosophy, not to mention psychology, has divided itself for centuries. Only recently are we gaining the position, the stance, that will probably make possible a really profound understanding of inner events. Thus far in human affairs, inner events have invited the wildest of speculations, where poetry, knowledge, and science, not to mention self-understanding, have all been confused and confounded.

It is fascinating to learn that what we consider our inner, private events spring from a matrix of actually or potentially overtly observable circumstances, open to each of us as self-observers (although this is difficult!) and to others. We begin life, evidently, with this dichotomy between ourselves as "inner-experiencers" and learn only gradually, and sometimes painfully, that others have the "same" innerness and are, indeed, very much like us (see Chapter 6). Patients often miss this point about themselves and others when they ask, naively and plaintively, "Have you ever had a patient with problems and feelings like mine?'' The therapist should, of course, respect first of all where the patient is "coming from" in such a question, but move on to help the patient understand that his or her problems are very much, indeed, part of the human situation and this is an altogether good and constructive and reassuring thing to know and feel. It gives one—or many, that is, both patient and therapist—the confidence to "do" something, rather than just contemplate the realities of human distress and suffering.

Taking a stand that supports a behavioral notion of inner events and the prospect that these events will yield even further to communicable knowledge, does not imply that the behaviorist is either naive or arrogant. Thus far we are often quite humbled by the study of inner events and realize that an enormously fascinating task awaits us, both in regard to understanding and helping patients we work with, but also in cultivating the broader reaches of communicable science and knowledge. What is asserted is that, *in principle,* inner events can be conceptualized by a behavioral position; indeed, that this position gives *more* meaning and connection between these events, subtle as they are, and the more obvious conditions about us that describe our behavior. All these events are of one fabric and support the utter fascination of therapy that seeks to put the pieces together, now and again, with patient after patient, and to reach further into human understanding thereby.

Research strategy and methodology. The entire area of behavior modification and especially operant analysis of behavior has raised to prominence the importance of the individual case. Research strategy is based not on comparing one group with another (experimental versus control groups) but on the consecutive presentation, then removal (or reversal), then re-presentation, of the reinforcement contingency involved in the study of a given behavior. The individual case is compared with itself, wherein the alteration of the reinforcement contingency is the critical methodological strategy (Kazdin, 1973). This type of research strategy, also common in other scientific disciplines, fits more closely with the concerns for demonstrating behavior change in the clinical setting, where the focus is on manipulating the experimental conditions rather than on mean differences between groups. The study of the individual case has, therefore, risen to prominence in the behavior modification literature of the last two decades (Krasner and Ullmann, 1965; Ullmann and Krasner, 1965).

In its simplest features the within-subject design follows this paradigm: an ABAB design, where "A" refers to a "baseline," a free operant or "natural occurrence" of the behavior under study (e.g., a record of the number of times a child cries in a given time frame in a preschool setting, the number of times a person bites his fingernails, or smokes cigarettes, or demonstrates tics, within a given time frame, *prior* to the intervention of any effort to change the behavior in question); where "A" refers also to the experimental conditions, that is, a demonstration of what the probable reinforcement contingency was that was operative (e.g., data taken by observation showing that "attention" on the part of teachers maintained or reinforced crying behavior on the part of a preschool child in a nursery school setting (Harris, 1967); "B" represents a "reversal" of the probable reinforcement contingency operative in "A" by *withholding* "attention" as reinforcement, in the illustrative case of a preschool child's crying behavior suspected as being maintained by adult concern and sympathy; thereby showing the importance of the reinforcer by its experimentally controlled absence but overtly reinforcing alternative (positive problem-solving behaviors); and "A" representing a return to the original reinforcing condition ("attention" in our illustrative case), showing that upon the representation of the contingency of reinforcement, the crying behavior (or whatever behavior we are studying) is again evidenced more frequently. A second return to "B" or further extinction by withholding attention when the child starts to cry (but alternatively reinforcing more mature, problem-solving efforts) results in another decrement in this observed behavior which condition, if continued, will lead to extinction or near-extinction. In the case of the second "B," the environment in a broadly conceived way "takes over" the reinforcement, or, put another way, the new, more adequate social behavior is "generalized" to the environment which reinforces the child through better social contacts with others and through the "fun" and opportunity the child gains where his behavior becomes more consonant with what other children do.

The ABAB design has its importance (or robustness or strength) in showing that a given reinforcement contingency is causally related to an observed behavior both by the presence and the absence of that reinforcement contingency. This is a much more convincing demonstration of the connection between a reinforcement contingency and its consequences than is the effort to determine causality where only group means are compared or where correlation coefficients are used to assess the relationship between two variables.

In applying this strategy to the counseling/psychotherapy situation, the therapist may wish to investigate the extent to which his or her own behavior ("attention") is causally related to the patient's excessive complaining and related lack of effort to carry out an agreed-upon agenda or other assignments. To further study this phenomenon, the therapist may not look at, respond to, or otherwise "attend" to the patient's complaints when they are verbalized in the therapy setting. (In such a case the therapist might not be able to take down the data on his or her own behavior in relation to the patient's behavior, but an observer looking at the therapist–patient interaction through a one-way observation post could make these observations.) The therapist would decide to respond by inattention and by withholding verbal comment when the patient complained. One would, of course, have to define precisely what a "complaint" was: "I really felt down all day Tuesday and so I didn't do anything, didn't even go in to work," might be an example; whereas, "I had a hard time getting here today through the snow and ice and that's why I am late," might be a noncomplaining example, and so on. The therapist would also, correspondingly, respond with attention and verbal comment when the patient reported on actual efforts at solving his or her problems ("I *did* study for two hours last night in spite of my roommate's attempt to get me to play cards with him," and the like). The conduct of such explicit reinforcement administrations and withholdings in therapy and counseling are not as easily come by as in more experimentally controlled situations, but they are nonetheless possible and might well be tried out by therapists in order to obtain a first-hand impression of how important social reinforcement and its withholding can be in therapy. The therapist should, of course, pick rather specific behaviors on the patient's part as the focus for such interpersonal, reinforcement control; this will probably be haltingly tried and may yield a modicum of success the first time or two, but with controlled experience, the effects of selectively applying social reinforcement in the form of attention is likely to yield good therapeutic results. It almost goes without saying that in the writing therapy context it is much easier to respond selectively to what the patient writes than it is to interact with equal precision in the face-to-face counseling situation.

Although the ABAB design has many features to recommend it in terms of research strategy (Kazdin, 1973), for the counseling/psychotherapy situation there are some obvious limitations: The behavior that one is intent upon changing (as agreed upon by therapist and patient) is not likely to be "restored" again (that is, brought back into a higher frequency of occurrence) just to demonstrate the relevance of the reinforcing condition. For example, if a therapist had helped a patient overcome a weight problem through the use of other reinforcers than eating, there would be serious personal, health, ethical, and other problems associated with a return to the eating-as-reinforcement behavior in order to demonstrate the effectiveness of the phenomenon. Sometimes in the natural course of events, circumstances in the patient's life bring about a reversal of the reinforcing conditions and provide informal evidence of the relevance of the control of reinforcement contingencies for the behavior in question. In such a case, the therapist should point up the relevance of the "natural events" for the behavior change effort with the patient.

The nature of the therapist/patient interactions are such that restoration of the baseline or original reinforcing conditions is not possible even if it were desired. The assumption here is that the behavior that has been changed is more flexible and more easily extinguished than may actually be the case. When and as behavior change occurs "for the better," there are many environmental reinforcers available that help to maintain the newly acquired behavior (e.g., a child getting more social invitations to stay overnight, go on camping and outing trips, and the like when he or she has overcome a bedwetting problem) and that render almost impossible a demonstration of how the "old" behavior can be restored again through manipulating the reinforcement contingencies. As the "new" behavior becomes integrated into a variety of environmentally controlled reinforcing contingencies, it may well become highly resistant to extinction (Kazdin, 1973).

Although multiple baseline designs are possible (Kazdin, 1973; Sidman, 1960; Baer, Wolf, and Risley, 1968), it is unlikely that they would be used in counseling and psychotherapy settings; however, one should not go so far as to preclude their use altogether. Conceptually, however, the multiple baseline design is of interest and helps to further extend the notion of within-subject research strategy. For example, two or more behaviors might be observed for one person. Following a stable baseline, only one of the behaviors is subjected to experimental alteration, continuing on with the baseline condition for the other behavior. If, for example, one wanted to alter two behaviors, such as "biting one's fingernails" and "saving money from one's weekly paycheck," in a patient in psychotherapy, the procedure would be to have established baselines for these two (presumably unrelated) behaviors; then expose the first behavior—biting one's nails—to experimental control, allowing the second behavior—saving money weekly—to remain at baseline. When this much procedure has been established at stable rates, one would then set in motion an experimental condition (reinforcement contingency) intended to alter the second behavior. Presumably each separate target behavior changes independently of the other and dependently upon the installation of the reinforcing contingency for that particular behavior. One could, then, extend this procedure for however many behaviors one desired to change. Since each behavior in question (the nail biting and the saving money) is not affected except when an experimental condition is installed, one can conclude that events other than the experimental ones occurring in time are not responsible for the change in the observed behaviors.

Even if a therapist or counselor were unlikely to try to carry out a multiple baseline design with a patient, the conceptualization of the problem of changing multiple facets of a person's behavior and having solid evidence of this change, would be enhanced by following this type of thinking. As we become more sophisticated in conducting psychotherapy and counseling and as technique advances without diminishing the importance of considering emotional factors, we will probably move, as therapists, into more formal efforts to bring about behavior change— perhaps replicating more closely what happens in the laboratory or in well-controlled field studies. One reason we do not carry out this more formal approach, represented by the ABAB and multiple baselines designs, is that we *begin* therapy at a very confused level of exchange between therapist and patient. The tack taken in Chapter 6 emphasizes how far apart therapist and patient might be in their communications and addresses generally the problems of communication in psychotherapy. If we *prepared* the patient more fully (there would presumably be many ways in which we, as therapists, could do this) for therapy by addressing the topics of what behavior change means, how it is achieved, what is expected of the patient, how the patient can hinder or enhance the change effort, and so forth, we could probably eliminate much of the perturbation now characteristic of therapy and counseling, especially at the outset, and increase the effectiveness of the enterprise thereby. Perhaps such a highly structured preparation for therapy would best be tried through writing therapy first, then moving on to face-to-face therapy or counseling when reliable methods appeared evident.

Placing covert processes within the behavioral framework. To the behaviorally uninitiated, the problem of covert processes seems to be the biggest stumbling block against the understanding and use of behavioral psychotherapy and counseling. Defining the environment as including internal processes; allowing self-reports to include data that are observed (however unreliable and untested, at first) by at least one person (the observer also being the observed); relating the covert processes to their observable behavioral consequences; and conceptualizing the whole process so that data from whatever source are, perforce, usable, within the limits of the canons of science, are all problems faced by behaviorists and nonbehaviorists alike. Once people can be clear about these issues, all considerations emanating from the clinic are, perforce, behavioral. If data seem to appear that are both important and too subtle to be brought under scientific control, then we face challenging conceptual, research, and empirical problems. Science grows by such confrontations and challenges, and they are opportunities for which we should be forever grateful. Science generally and clinical practice specifically will be enhanced by open challenges of these sorts.

Not infrequently, however, the reference to covert process as a separate and behaviorally inaccessible domain (even in principle) is proffered as an inexorable reason for considering behavioral principles to be inadequate. The easy dismissal of behavioral or functional analyses of clinical phenomena (especially data from psychotherapy or counseling in favor of easily conjectured inner processes) seems to assuage too many clinicians and allow them to forego the pleasures and challenges inherent in conceptualizing more clearly what they are doing (Maslow, 1968; Jourard, 1971; May, 1971).

The problem with all of us—behaviorists and nonbehaviorists alike—is that *we are all too narrowly wedded to what we think our prerogatives are* and we dismiss others too readily and too easily. Challenges should come from wherever they may come. Let the nonbehaviorist come up with as many observations or hunches or conjectures as possible; the behaviorists will scrutinize and analyze and attempt to functionally relate the phenomena in question. But let the mentalists also know that they cannot get by with conceptual murder and not be taken to task for it. If we work with each other, allowing for weaknesses and strengths alike, we will build a better psychology and a better set of clinical skills.

CHAPTER 9

Cybernetics

Of all the ideas of possible importance to the clinician, cybernetics has probably been the most neglected (Phillips and Wiener, 1966). Cybernetics is a thoroughgoing behavioral system with a set of concepts and propositions of inestimable value to the clinician; but, thus far, its value seems to have lain dormant.

Cybernetics is concerned with *control*. Etymologically the term comes from the Greek word meaning "steersman" (Wiener, 1948). Cybernetics has developed applications to areas of interest to behavioral psychologists in the study of control and communication in human beings, animals, and machines. Perhaps cybernetics has had its most cogent use in aspects of psychology not particularly close to clinical psychology or psychotherapy, namely, human factors study and human engineering where human "systems" are related to mechanical or engineering "systems" (Smith, 1962; Smith and Smith, 1966).

There are several ways in which the concepts and practices of cybernetics are of value to the psychotherapist or counselor. These are now enumerated and explained as they apply to psychotherapy or behavior change.

Possibly the most important concept from cybernetics is that of *feedback*. Feedback is defined by DeLatil (1957, p. 6) as "a device which makes an effect act back on one of its causes, thus enabling this effect to carry out its given aim." Based on the outcome of some action, information (sensory or perceptual information) is fed back to the acting organism (animal, person) or mechanical system (a furnace, for example), this information then steering or directing further outcome. If one were led into a totally dark room and asked to hit a target somewhere in the room, this condition would provide for minimal feedback, and hitting the target would be a matter of chance. On the other hand, when one is threading a needle, one is directed or steered by initial and tentative movements of the thread toward the eye of the needle with many corrections and alterations fed back to the person which influence his or her eye–hand coordination and other matters. Presumably all our behavior is based on some kind of feedback (positive feedback overlapping somewhat with positive reinforcement). When one's sensory acuity is disturbed for some reason, or when a person suffers neurological damage affecting sensory or motor responses, this individual often appears awkward, tentative, "wooden" in behavior, thereby indicating the delay or disruption of feedback. In a more common-sense way, we are guided in part by what we are already doing; thus driving a car, cooking a stew, hanging wallpaper, or painting a picture—from the simplest motor act to the most complicated creative venture—are all guided by the information fed back from our actions up to any given point in time. As with the old adage, "We don't appreciate the water until the well runs dry," we often fail to take note of our utter reliance on feedback until some alteration or prohibition of feedback occurs.

In the counseling and psychotherapy situation, the therapist and patient are each confronted with extremely complex feedback systems. Even the more mundane matters of therapy as envisioned here (setting and carrying out agendas, keeping logs, trying out behaviors in the natural environment, grappling with self-control items in therapy and outside) are examples of feedback to the therapy hour where corrections and extensions of the programs agreed upon are witnessed, as well as feedback on the in-therapy issues related to feelings, facts, fantasy, and behavior toward the therapist, which are abundantly encountered if any communication whatsoever is to take place. The simplest understanding of what the patient has said depends upon feedback.

The notion of feedback includes and is further defined by a description of *loops* (or feedback loops). This draws attention to the fact that the behavior studied can be broken down into loops composed of junctures or connecting points and that the loop patterns repeat themselves in time. If one stops to think of such complex processes as eating, digesting, exercising, sleeping, eating again, and so on, one sees immediately the loop nature of these daily events. All natural processes of biological maintenance are loop processes and each, in turn, is composed of many smaller loops with their junctures and repetitive patterns. Without this redundancy, life could not be maintained. Sometimes the small child observes this process when he or she complains, "Why should I take a bath? I'll just get dirty and have to do it all over again."

When loop processes get out of hand (that is, when they are not maintained on a steady level), they tend to deviate or amplify. This process is called a *deviation amplifying loop,* which refers to the fact that, whatever the starting point of the loop might be, this factor or juncture becomes amplified or exaggerated over time. If loops are positively deviation amplifying, they amplify all junctures in the loop. A person saving money for the bank draws interest in proportion to the amount saved, which, in turn, adds to the principal—the circular process of accumulating money is increased, amplified.

Loops may also have negative or corrective or counteractive elements, such that one or more of the junctures in the loop is contrary to the rest of the loop's goal. A student who fails to concentrate when studying, although other elements in the loop may be present (going to class, taking notes, etc.), may not do well on exams and hence not get the credit sought. Only if all loop elements are positively present will there be a gain; the presence of a negative element in the loop challenges the outcome.

But negative elements also help to maintain stability; otherwise, the deviation amplifying nature of some loops would lead to an "explosion" or to a "running down" of the system. The stock market that keeps going up and up is bound to "break" at some point as the system underlying it, or which it is part of, cannot in all of its junctures "support" the loop; sooner or later the crash comes. The manic individual eventually reaches a limit to his overstimulated reaction to his environment and falls exhausted or becomes depressed and inactive. Corrections that come more modestly in the face of deviation amplifying loops help to maintain stability more than catastrophic counteractive elements or junctures which, when they occur in the face of a rampant deviation amplifying system, cause the whole system to collapse. In common parlance, things just cannot be too good for too long without something happening to "break the spell."

In the case of the person in psychotherapy, uncorrected anger might spin the patient into higher and higher, and more and more intense, emotional rages, until some drastic action occurs. Or, conversely, a deviation amplifying loop that redundantly closes one into smaller and smaller orbits of activity, such as is observed in depression, may end by so isolating the individual that he or she becomes utterly withdrawn and incapable of social interaction. (See the discussion in Chapter 6 on depression in this connection.)

In psychotherapy the therapist will want to identify the elements in these loops and seek counteractive inputs to change the amplifying nature of them. The personal report of patients who say they are "out of control" speaks to the deviation amplifying nature of their subjective experiences or what they are able to observe in themselves in relation to their environment. One can easily translate the complaints of any patient into loop terms. The question is whether such a translation is more than verbal, whether the structure of thinking in cybernetic terms is, itself, able to contribute to the understanding of behavioral processes. The argument here is that, indeed, cybernetics adds some important dimension to the study of behavior, perhaps over and above that offered by learning theory, behavior theory, or operant principles.

The main advantages offered by a cybernetic account of behavior are several: First, the *cyclic* nature of the process (in psychotherapy, the complaint system of the patient) is identified. If a difficulty arose only once it might be unpleasant enough in its own right, but most difficulties have a way of recurring with seeming inexorable regularity, constricting the person so that he or she ends up feeling "unreal," "not in control," and so forth, and, perforce, overtly behaving in the same manner. Processes repeat themselves in time and because of this can be challenged anew each time around. There is considerable hope for change, a prospective, positive viewing of behavior, when we understand clearly its cyclic nature; this is a second reason in psychotherapy to rely somewhat on cybernetic ways of regarding behavior. A third and related asset for cybernetics in this context is that the loop can be entered wherever and whenever a juncture can be spotted allowing for this entry and thereby contributing to a breakup of the presently redundantly amplifying pattern. One might, for example, enter a "vicious circle" loop of a child's bedwetting by altering the amount of highly stimulating or aggressively overt behavior just prior to bedtime (such behavior being one element or juncture in a loop), leaving the child so exhausted during sleep that he or she does not awaken to the usual internal cues of bladder distention. No one item "causes" the resultant behavior; it is a matter of a circular process that shows a repetitive total pattern. One might simply keep the kids from fighting or overstimulating themselves before bedtime because such a ruckus was irritating to the adults and find, serendipitously, that the child had also diminished his or her bedwetting in the process!

Corresponding to the above-cited three advantages of a cybernetic look at behavior, a fourth one emerges, namely, that the loop itself can be viewed as a total causal system. One does not have to look for original or first causes; one is free to manage the loop nature of the interaction of the system with its environment in order to gain a different outcome. The loop is an integral whole; alter its outcome and you alter the behavior in question.

A fifth advantage of a cybernetic look at behavior requires some discussion of the concept of "initial kick" (Maruyama, 1963; Phillips and Wiener, 1966). This concept refers to the occurrence of a slight tendency in a given direction that gets amplified over time, throughout additional junctures in the loop. For example, a slight crack in the wall of a house results in some water and ice getting into the crevice, which further widens the opening, followed by the wind blowing dirt into the crack and seeds starting to grow. The process extends, each juncture resulting in the widening of the crack (unless one repairs the crack as part of the upkeep of the building, the eroding process will continue), which ultimately undermines the wall and the building. This is also a familiar deviation amplifying loop in the sense that all junctures (everything that happens) result in an increase in the size of the crack and the ultimate destruction of the wall. Deteriorating processes in nature are of this type, as is the wear and tear on material objects subject to the ravages of time. Nothing occurs in the initial kick situation that predicts the outcome; the original crack in the wall is not sufficient, without amplification, to account for the outcome. In human lives, untoward events in life—say, some problem in early childhood—probably does not contain the information to account for some drastic outcome in adulthood; rather, the explanation comes from the contribution of the amplification effect of each juncture, not on the basis of the original problem. Many psychological difficulties are of the order of this problem: Small beginnings, through deviation amplifying loops, lead to enormous consequences, far beyond the dimensions calculable from the initial problem (initial kick) itself. Knowledge of this process has two constructive outcomes for psychotherapy in a behavioral/ cybernetic mode: First, it draws attention to the loop and repetitive nature of the process itself, thus taking effort away from finding first causes or uncovering historical origins, all this being quite time-saving and heuristic. Second, it offers a forward-looking view of one's problems, putting the emphasis on aspects of the present environment, the present system of interacting with the environment, and seeks exploratory answers that can be suggested by the loop nature of the interaction and by finding "openings" in the loop subject to counteracting influences.

Another concept of importance in cybernetic thinking is *entropy*. This refers to the running down or disintegration of a system, or the amount of disorder in the system. Over time, systems tend to disintegrate (e.g., the weathering of wood, the spoiling of fruit, aging in a human being, the garden becoming overrun with weeds, and so on). Systems have to be maintained, else they disintegrate. This is an important concept and matches to a considerable extent the operant emphasis on schedules of reinforcement, the latter being a more specific and quantifiable empirical set of relationships. Only operant work and cybernetics give full consideration to the importance of how and under what conditions a system is maintained, a notion as vitally important as those relating to the eliciting conditions and to reinforcement and feedback.

The notion of entropy is important in considering behavior change efforts. Once the behavior is changed—in the clinic, in the classroom, or in some other setting—how is it then maintained? This relates to the generalization of change into wider and wider environmental orbits and to what takes place that makes generalization possible. Too often in traditional psychotherapy the idea has been accepted that once a thoroughgoing analysis of one's problems has been made, the insight will last forever. If it doesn't, then, perforce, one has not been "sufficiently analyzed." In the light of schedules of reinforcement, feedback, entropy, and related notions, the maintenance of change is, itself, an arresting and important problem and certainly not one that can be reduced to making a thoroughgoing analysis of one's problems in the first place, however important that may still be on other grounds.

INTERACTING LOOPS AND COMPLEX PATTERNS

In the above discussion, we view a loop as a single process, but we know full well that humans in their natural orbit of living are involved in a myriad of loops, all going on more or less simultaneously and many of them overlapping, some even contradictory. How, then, does one decipher this complexity in the interest of solving personal problems in the counseling and psychotherapy setting?

Just as with the statement of problems in specific and targeted ways in operant work, one has to identify specific loops and specific outcomes at the beginning of a behavior change effort. Because the therapist *begins* with specifics in order to identify the problem and to gain leverage, does not mean that one ends up with only the same specific outcome. Specifics can always be added to specifics to contribute to a more generalized outcome; identifying and pivoting on behavioral objectives (specifics) is a means to a more generalized end in both operant work and in cybernetics.

Identifying the specific loop and the target behavior (or end point in the loop) is the first order of business. Take, for example, gambling behavior that represents a problem for a person. The gambler has some extra money that he thinks can be parlayed into more money; he takes his extra money and bets on some gambling enterprise (dice, horse racing, etc.). If he wins in a given effort, he is likely to be very encouraged by this (receive positive feedback) and then he increases his bet. Sooner or later, more likely "sooner," he will loose. This negative feedback (loss of money) will not "correct" his behavior because it does not come early enough in the feedback loop and because other factors in the loop continue to support the gambling. The loop's direction, which means the factors or junctures in the loop, has to change to produce an outcome different from the specific factor we can call "loss of money." A loop of the "losing" type may look like that in Figure 14. This loop may be composed of 5, 8, or even 10 or more discernible junctures (or one might

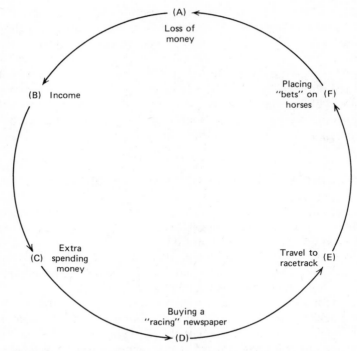

Figure 14. How a gambler repeats each juncture in the loop (there may be more junctures, depending upon circumstances) and ends each time losing money due to betting on race horses.

call them "decision points"); the actual number is not as important as the fact that one juncture leads into the next and tends to complete the whole loop pattern, once started. In therapy, one can discern and get agreement with the patient on the makeup of the loop, then discuss the junctures wherein a change can be installed or attempted. Is it better in the case of the gambler to take the "extra money" at the apparent outset of the loop and put it in the bank? Would this, then, counteract the loop? Or would avoiding buying the newspaper containing racing news be the more pivotal thing to do? Certainly travel-to-the-racetrack should be brought under control since this is closer to the end product (losing the money) we wish to control. Perhaps the train or bus that the person takes to the racetrack is boarded at a station where other trains are available that would take one home or to a sick relative's house; taking the latter route would also break up the "vicious circle" represented in this series of events.

Figure 15 shows how both of these interventions might operate: first, buying some article for a family member in lieu of buying the "racing newspaper"; and second, taking a train from the station different from the one that goes to the racetrack; either of these leading to A', which is an avoidance of the loss of money at the track. In one's behavioral economy, one might find many such interventions possible, but the clinical problem is one of deciding with the patient the *specific* intervention procedure and assessing the probability that the plan can be carried out. If a given plan does not work, then some change must be made: A finer analysis of the loop's junctures, a recognition that a different loop actually prevails, or other measures.

Criteria exist for deciding where to enter the loop. A juncture that is the easiest to control is one criterion. This is probably an individual matter

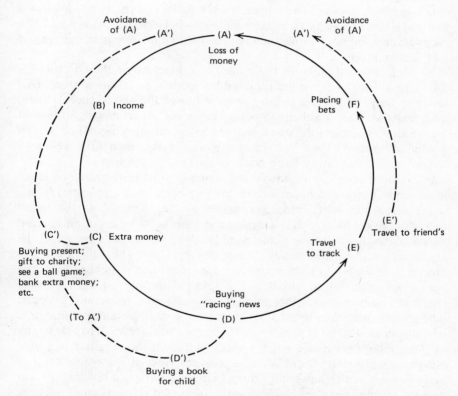

Figure 15. Alternative ways to avoid losing money at the race track: Interrupting at junctures (C) (buying a present, giving to charity, and the like, with extra money), (D), or (E). Any or all of these may bring the problem under control.

with patients and one that would have to be decided between patient and therapist. The patient in the hypothetical case might say, "Well, if I never saw the "racing news" I would probably forget about gambling." Or, "If I just started home in the other direction and didn't even go to the station where I could transfer to the racetrack, I'd be done with it and just not go at all." Or some similar information that would help the patient and the therapist to opt for one or another choice.

A second criterion is that of finding a juncture that has the highest degree of relationship with the target behavior that is up for change. In the hypothetical case cited, this might be actually arriving at the window where bets are placed at the racetrack, allowing for the fact that a person such as we are discussing might say he could go to the track and watch the races for many hours without placing a bet, but that when he does place a bet he "goes all out" and keeps betting, similar to a person who has one drink and then goes off on a binge. Such a patient might aver, "Well, I'll just have to keep away from the windows—if I do that I can watch the races all day and not be influenced to bet—I do it all on paper and get just as big a kick out of it."

A third criterion includes the choice of a juncture or the control of a factor that lies closest to the terminal behavior we wish to control. This juncture may, of course, overlap with either of the above-chosen ones, and might well be, in this hypothetical case, the actual placing of bets at the window. Comparably, one trying to control drinking might find it most pivotal to "not take the first drink at any time" rather than not have booze in the house, stay away from cocktail parties, or the like.

A question arises as to how specific one can get in overcoming some identifiable unwanted behavior. In the gambling case cited above, one could select the actual placing of a bet at the racetrack as the target behavior, in terms of either a cybernetic loop or in terms of an operant approach to the problem. If the gambler does not place a bet at all, he surely will not lose any money. We could intervene cybernetically at this juncture, or we could take an operant viewpoint and possibly "fine" the person for engaging in this behavior (placing the bet) at the racetrack itself; or institute some other aversive consequence. We could have the wife and/or other family members reward the gambler more abundantly when he comes home in preference to going to the racetrack to bet. In any of these interventions we might expect success if the details are carried out reasonably well. But if we take a larger view of the whole orbit of activities supporting and contributing to the gambling and resultant loss of money, we might prefer the cybernetic route as it gives us more options, provides a larger rationale for intervention, can be readily explained and understood by the patient, perhaps allows the patient to "select" his or her own intervention methods, and in no way precludes the use of operant technology with regard to any one juncture or with respect to the whole loop. We can still use any part of the vast range of operant intervention methods (see Chapter 2) but we may have better "advice" on how to apply the technology based on a more integral and patterned analysis of the problem and the possible target behaviors involved.

RELATING OPERANT AND CYBERNETIC CONCEPTS

This brings us to a discussion of how operant and cybernetic principles and concepts may be similar and how they may be different. Information of this type can then give the clinical counselor or psychotherapist more options in conceptualizing the tasks and may well broaden the approach to many behavioral problems. Comparisons will be made in a limited way in terms of the following paired concepts: feedback and reinforcement; initial kick and shaping; entropy and extinction; and loops and chaining.

Feedback and Reinforcement

Feedback is the more general term, covering not only living systems but also machines. If one thinks of going to work daily as the endpoint of a large loop, then starting the car, and all the junctures related to operating a car would appear as mechanical elements, in that each of the junctures would have to interconnect for the car to operate reliably (start motor, engage clutch, propel gas through the carburetor, etc.), and they would occur on an all-or-none basis. Whereas driving to work—involving a "human system," the driver, operating the car on the road—would allow for choice of routes to work, times to depart and arrive, and so on, and all these factors would be subject to reinforcement in the sense that a shorter route would be preferred (more economical on gas), a different route possibly be referred because of picking up passengers or allowing for shopping, and the like. One is locked into the feedback system (a closed loop) in the mechanical analogy; the organism, on the other hand, can modify, through the selectivity of reinforcement, which route to work might be taken (an open loop).

Feedback is often said to give knowledge of results, as with threading a needle; but this behavior is also reinforcing as one may want to learn to sew. Reinforcement often gives knowledge of results, but may not need to do so in all instances for behavior change to occur (Bachrach, 1972, p. 55; Hefferline, 1959).

In the stricter sense of feedback, closed systems require feedback to function (e.g., the operation of a furnace, until the point is reached where it runs out of fuel; hence an "outside-the-system" adjustment has to be made), and reinforcement is not relevant here. In open systems, which characterize living organisms including man, reinforcement provides for a *selectivity* in relating the organism to its environment. Feedback in this case is probably a subordinate issue but nonetheless occurs (the animal listens and is fed back information on the presence of another predatory beast in the vicinity; escape from injury is reinforcing).

Learning depends upon reinforcement being timely—too long a delay reduces the effectiveness of learning or may preclude it altogether. Delayed feedback may also injure the organism's communication with the environment as may be the case with some forms of stuttering, hearing deficits, and motor deficits in humans. No amount of reinforcement will make up for a long-delayed feedback in motor control in a person with sensory-motor or central nervous system damage of a critical type. In such a case, feedback has to "carry" the information within which context reinforcement may be effective in changing or maintaining behavior, and in selecting which behaviors are learned in the first place.

The management of reinforcement influences the rate of learning, the stability of learning, and the maintenance of what is learned; this is a matter of schedules of reinforcement. Feedback, per se, unless it "houses" or includes a reinforcement schedule, probably cannot account for most complex human learning. A retarded child learning to operate an intercom system depends first upon controlling feedback; once this is mastered, what the child learns in the setting and what is communicated to a monitor in the way of learning a task results from reinforcement. In the case of some retardates and some psychotics, feedback must first be established on an ongoing basis before reinforcement efforts can become effective. Sometimes teachers have tried to "reinforce" given behaviors of (say) autistic children before any communication matrix was established (e.g., getting the child's attention through more elementary communication efforts). This is a clumsy way of trying for reinforcement effects without any communication between child and teacher in the first place. When one person does not "hear" or "see" what is being communicated by another person, the results of potential social reinforcement are rendered useless.

Initial Kick and Shaping

"Initial kick" refers to a condition where a slight process once begun accumulates its effect through the operation of a deviation amplifying process, more or less mechanically or automatically. Thus, a small rock may tumble loose on a mountain side, hit and loosen other rocks, overrun bushes and small trees thereby loosening still other rocks and soil, and end in a landslide of enormous proportions. Perhaps some mental health problems represent small beginnings but through interactions at different junctures in one's life accumulate to a much larger effect. There is something fortuitous about this process in the sense that the beginning point does not "intend" or strive for the endpoint. In shaping, on the other hand, change is progressive through small steps, all being reinforced, as they contribute to some larger or more distant goal. The shaping is planned.

What, then, accounts for the disastrous ends some people come to in their lives? Have they been shaped in some way, by intention or not, or have their lives been influenced more by a deviation amplifying condition arising out of an initial kick situation that simply accumulates by way of fortuitous events or chance or "bad luck" reasons? One might need to decide as a therapist which kinds of forces might have been instrumental in producing a presently observed clinical situation in which counseling or psychotherapy are needed. In the university setting, and sometimes in other institutional settings, people end up in trouble seemingly out of accidental characteristics of the system itself; reversing or changing one's direction might be rendered unlikely or impossible because of "red tape" or other exigencies. Students or other members of institutions may be processed out of a setting because of the cumulative effect of an initial kick situation (getting in the wrong course in the first place, or being placed in the wrong job at the outset of employment, and the like).

The point is that not everything in one's life has taken place for "good and discernible reasons." Sometimes we are all victims of circumstances; we need to learn how to avoid and change these circumstances in the future, but the original concatenation that led to where we are now may have arisen wholly or largely out of circumstances over which we had no control (and, indeed, which we may recognize only when the endpoint, decisive as it might be, has been reached). One, then, might need to ask in many counseling and psychotherapy situations: When is a problem a problem?

Changing the endpoint of a series of concatenated junctures producing an untoward effect may, nonetheless, have to come about through shaping procedures. Thus an "understanding" of a fortuitous set of circumstances may help us set up shaping procedures as a restorative measure with more accuracy, help fathom the many ways systems and institutions make mental health problems common, and suggest preventive measures especially where individuals interact to their detriment with large-scale organizations and institutions.

Entropy and Extinction

Although these two terms, as a pair, are less congenial than the other operant and cybernetic terms cited above, they nevertheless point up some interesting similarities and contrasts. Entropy, as has been said, refers to the "running down" of a system, the failure of a system when not supported and maintained by its environmental interactions. Extinction, as used in learning theory and operant principles, represents a systematic study of ways in which behavior can be unlearned; or, in a broader term, it denotes what can be expected by extinction measures in relation to reinforcement schedules. In the manner in which reinforcement and feedback point to similarities and differences in acquiring and maintaining behavior, so do entropy and extinction, emphasizing the "loss" of behavior in a systematic sense. Similarly, as reinforcement and reinforcement schedules explain the acquisition of behavior in some ways more precisely than feedback, so extinction denotes the more specific terms under which behavior is lost compared to the notion of entropy. Feedback and entropy are the broad systemic terms; reinforcement and extinction are the more narrow terms, perhaps each fitting under the two broader terms.

In coping with patients' problems, it is important for the person developing self-control and applying self-regulating principles to understand that large-scale, institutional-based entropic process may overcome or challenge one's efforts to change and to maintain change. The more one deals with large systems and complexly intertwined behaviors (as in the study of institutions and how persons interact with institutions), the more the notion of entropy must be invoked. Students will "forget" how to register for classes from one semester to another unless the registration system is clearly maintained and proper reminders and guideposts provided. One hardly says the students have "extinguished" their how-to-register-for-classes behavior; this kind of behavioral result among students on a campus is more comprehensively and cogently understood as an entropic institutional process for which counteractive efforts have to be forever provided. On the other hand, extinguishing an item of unwanted behavior—for example, nail biting—is not suitably understood in the abstract nor managed in the concrete by talking about entropy. The more the counselor or psychotherapist encounters larger systems of behavioral control—for example, with schools, prisons, recreational centers—and has to deal with them qua systems, as well as in terms of their impact on individual behavior, the more the systemic notions of feedback and entropy seem cogent. One may, of course, as a psychotherapist or counselor, deal simultaneously via the patient with some behaviors requiring extinction and others dealing with an entropic relationship with an institutiohn.

Loops and Chaining

As has been indicated already, loops refer to circular process that "return" to the original juncture in the loop, after going the route of the whole loop. If we pick soiling behavior during free play time in a six-year-old boy as an example, we can note the loop nature of this behavior: eating a meal, going out to play, strenuous play, urge to defecate, suppression of the urge, excitement and hard play leading to a loss of sphincter control, soiling. One can discern such "vicious circle" episodes among children with respect to many items of self-control, habit control, or the like. If this circular process is not brought under control, chances are the process will exacerbate and the soiling will become more common and harder to control. Such process often develop "naturally."

Chaining, on the other hand, represents an operant example of adding on additional responses in sequence; each response becomes the cue for the next one, and so on throughout a complex process. Some of the most interesting examples of chaining in the operant literature come from the work of Bachrach and Karen (1966) and Pierrol and Sherman (1958). These two sets of experimenters trained rats to perform complicated sets of behaviors by chaining the end-product behavior to the critical behavior just prior in time to the end-product, and so on backward in the sequence to some beginning point. Thus the end-product might be pressing a bar to receive food, but prior to that might be jumping over a small hurdle in the rat's cage, and prior to that having the rat go up and down a short stairs or series of steps, and so on back to some beginning point such as walking from one side of the cage to another. At each juncture the act has to be properly executed for the animal to receive reinforcement, and each opportunity to go on in the chain depends upon executing the prior acts properly. There is no explicit attempt here to build a circular process although one could look upon chaining in this way.

Loops appear to have taken place in nature through selective evolutionary and survival means. Many biological processes are examples of loops. Chaining, on the other hand, represents a new set of environmental conditions that make for a complex set of interrelated behaviors, and it demonstrates the power of reinforcement contingencies when arranged in this serial fashion. Chaining represents, although may not necessarily be restricted to, a linear process; loops represent and emphasize circular processes. In applying both concepts and sets of empirical relationships to clinical cases, therapists can ask themselves what kind of a pathological or unwanted process is represented by a given behavioral complex, whether the behavior represents some discernible "vicious circle" or whether it is possibly some more linear process where specific extinction efforts might take hold effectively.

As the arena of behavioral applications moves from the clinic and the consulting room out to wider and wider orbits of life, the use of circular processes as conceptual models will greatly enhance our ability to affect change. Within the larger cybernetic conceptualizations may be placed ever more specific, more or less linear behavioral interventions, in a happy and fruitful marriage between cybernetics and operant principles. Psychological clinicians and counselors, while remaining interested in and skillful with the individual case, will nonetheless move ever more widely into solving problems of an institutional nature, and later those problems related to broad social conditions, in the interest of helping the individual not only solve his or her problems but to extend the solutions to more people and to do incisive preventive work on a broad scale.

CHAPTER 10

Questions and Answers Re Behavioral Therapy

Provocative and innovative measures in any science create uncertainty. Science grows by confrontation as well as by slow, measured progress. In the last two decades, psychology generally, but psychotherapy and counseling specifically, have been challenged to meet the new measures of behavior change provided by behavioral psychology. Reading the record from one vantage point, one wonders why behavioral methods have provoked so much needless controversy—there are always, of course, *legitimate* and interesting and challenging problems to be met—and why behavioral psychology seems to have left such a residue of misunderstanding and negative reactions (Skinner, 1974, pp. 1–8). Nonetheless, there are misunderstandings that have to be cleared up and many of them apply to the more molar areas of counseling and psychotherapy. An excursion into some of the problems will be the purpose of this chapter.

Most of the concerns over behavioral methods apply to the human case. People criticize views toward counseling and psychotherapy that appear to take their position on the basis of experimental work with animals, rather than viewing the work with animals as perhaps prototypic or conceptually clarifying in some useful ways. Science always simplifies and attempts to go to the heart of the problem; science cannot advance without first getting controls from which experimentation and research emanate. This effort is often confused in the mind of the layman, or even among scholarly, trained individuals who, themselves, probably never did an experiment nor thought about how one could research a problem. To the naive the way a problem first appears remains the essential problem; to recast the problem, to search for variables or conditions, seems inimical to the thought processes of those not trained in research and experimentation. Behavioral psychology has been very adept in specifying and defining variables and the conditions under which they occur; this process has taken the examination of human behavior away from the naive (they have no variables!) and placed it in the hands of those technically trained and competent. To talk, then, about variables and the conditions under which variables operate seems to some to be contrary to "humanness" and to proper regard for the complexity of human nature. This, of course, is an unfortunate misunderstanding of science, of how knowledge is obtained, tested, refined, and applied. It is an educational task, in part, of those who espouse more rigorous methods of studying human behavior—the only methods, not coincidentally, that have paid off in terms of reliable knowledge—to "educate" the problem as it generally appears to most people.

The following questions and answers may throw some light on how behavioral psychology can be better understood and applied without continuing restive feelings that "something is wrong with these methods." We begin with the broader theoretical issues first, then go on to practical ones for the clinic.

1. **Question:**   "Does not behavioral psychology (and especially behavioral methods used in the clinic) dehumanize people, treat them as an automatons, as simply acting mechanically?"

Answer: There is a lot of semantic confusion in this question, to say the least. Terms like "dehumanize," "automaton," "mechanical," beg the question. It is like trying to convict a man before he's been tried. The flat out answer to the question is a resounding "No"! Look at the record of behavioral psychology applied to the clinic over the past two decades or so: shorter and more effective psychotherapy; methods of treating the retarded and handicapped that have shown most encouraging results; ability to get "back ward" hospital patients to at least function better in terms of self-care and relating socially to others; the development of improved methods of teaching many kinds of subject matter to an enormously wide variety of students, from the severely handicapped to the superior graduate student; and so on. There has probably been no movement in psychology or, indeed, in any social science that has been so fruitfully applied to so many problem areas as behavioral psychology; it has had a positive influence on education, rehabilitation, psychotherapy and counseling, child development and child rearing, to mention a few instances. How, then, can a dehumanizing approach be so fruitful? One must look at the record, which speaks clearly in terms of positive support for behavioral methods.

2. **Question:**   "Behavioral psychology ignores or denies cognitive processes and thereby leaves out a lot of important data about humans and human functioning generally, does it not?"

Answer: It is as if the accusation of behavioral methods leaving out cognitive factors strikes up the image of one getting ready to go some place and deciding to "leave out" or set aside some of his baggage and go without it. The question seems to imply that standing right there are important cognitive variables that are being denied a place in the study of human behavior. Any science *selects* variables for study; not everything that appears important or useful turns out to be so. When we study the production of green plants we do not concern ourselves with width and breadth dimensions of the plant leaves, the sharpness of the points of the leaves, the distance between leaves growing out of a stalk, or many other variables that might be studied. We study variables that relate to plant growth, reproductivity, the kinds of soils plants grow best in, the longevity and food value of plants, and so forth. These are more *functional* variables, that is, they relate to the usefulness of the plant for some purposes one might have in mind—food for animals or humans, for example.

Humans are very complex. We can select an infinite number of variables. The list of possible traits was once accumulated by Gordon Allport and said to number in the thousands. Can we confront such enormity of variables and use them? No matter what trait variables—just to take this scientifically important matter as an example—one might select from among the thousands available, someone else could say, "You're leaving out the most important traits—what about _____?" One would get nowhere in understanding people in this way; it would only provoke endless polemics.

In selecting variables for study, one sets a number of criteria of importance: Parsimony, replicability, measurability, validity, and so on. The variables then selected meet further criteria as to whether they are "independent," or "dependent" variables, that is, whether they are in some way related to (or a function of) other, more basic variables. The quest goes on and on. There is not a priori some right, finite, definite set of variables that everyone can agree on and proceed from there. Thus, cognitive variables are, or represent, one way of looking at human behavior, especially some aspects of behavior usually termed "perception" and often related to feelings, internal states, and the like. We have seen already that these states or conditions are not eschewed by a behavioral psychology; but they may be looked at differently from the way a "cognitive psychologist" would regard them. What is more important, in the way a behavioral psychologist functions, is to regard the so-called cognitive variables as observable behavior that is the product of some knowable stimulating condition, functionally related to some behavioral consequence. The loci of explanation and description are on the observable behaviors not on some hypothetic inner process, *although the data to which this inner process points is wholly within the interest and technical competence of the behavioral psychologist.* A behavioral counselor or psychotherapist can hardly proceed without acknowledging and using cognitive data but he "gets to" the cognitive data from spoken words (behavior), from reactions to critical or test situations (for example, behavior on structured or unstructured tests), from comparing different sets of data relating to the "same" cognitive states over time, and from observing the consequences of the cognitive state in terms of other behavior. It is primarily a *methodological* difference that separates the behavioral psychologist from the cognitive psychologist working in the clinical domain; they are all beholden to the same data or to any data obtained in reliable and testable ways meeting the canons of science.

3. **Question:**   "Are not intention and purpose denied or overlooked in a behavioral psychology?"

Answer: The answer here is not unlike the one above referencing cognitive variables in the study of humans or in counseling and psychotherapy. Intention and purpose, although part of the daily vocabulary of all of us, present rather formidable problems for science and for understanding humans. The annals of philosophy are full of disputation over the centuries in regard to "purpose." Tolman derived a "purposive behaviorism" viewpoint in psychology. Cybernetic students have grappled with the problem of "purpose" and have proposed solutions similar to the behavioral psychologist (Wiener, 1950; Rosenblueth, Wiener, and Bigelow, 1943).

Behavioral psychology (especially operant psychology) and cybernetics both emphasize the *consequences* of behavior; they both study the "effects" of action (by people, animals, and machines). There are differences, to be sure, between operant psychology and cybernetics (see Chapter 9), but they are closely similar in regard to studying consequences, a position of inestimable empirical importance and of equal philosophical importance. The issue, then, of purpose is enormously complex, ramifying, and involved, and not one that we are prepared to "settle" here. Suffice it to say that purpose or intention or expectation may be *approached* in a behavioral way, as suggested in Chapter 1; but this is not to say that the questions have been answered or that all fears and anxieties are allayed. If we translate "purpose" or "intention" into "expectation," we can derive a possible behavioral analysis of use in counseling and psychotherapy, but this is not to say that the broader issues of these problems are successfully met. Expectations imply previous learning; if this is the case, we are immediately placed on grounds familiar to the behavioral psychologist. The problem is one of translating into observable terms how the expectation is referenced increasingly earlier in time, earlier in a proposed sequence of events; and abstracted (probably verbally) from those events in a way that allows for a kind of personal prediction of what will happen when these circumstances are repeated. It is quite simple and direct in our own immediate experiences that we "expect things to happen" and could, indeed, not function at all if this were not the case; but capturing this complexity in terms of variables and knowable processes is, indeed, a formidable task. The point of the matter is that probably no other area of psychology has grappled any more cogently or convincingly with purpose, intention, or expectations than has behavioral psychology or cybernetics. Just because other psychotherapeutic or clinical persuasions use the term with greater abandon does not, perforce, speak to their superior knowledge in this problem area.

4. **Question:**   "Isn't behavioral psychology all right for animals in the laboratory, but doesn't this constitute an oversimplification if we try to apply this knowledge to people?"

Answer: This is really a two-part question and has to be so answered: The answer is "yes" to behavioral psychology being a laboratory-based science, primarily (historically) using animals as research subjects. The second part of the question concerns the validity of knowledge obtained in the laboratory for application to people in their variegated situations. Throughout this book, one theme has been centered on the problems inherent in extrapolating from the laboratory to the clinic or to the field (see Chapter 1); thus, the problem has not been neglected nor run roughshod over. There is always a problem with extrapolating from the laboratory situation to life, especially with complex behavior such as that encountered in social situations, and in counseling and psychotherapy. However, we have no other choice. We have to proceed first with as much rigor and control as possible, then face the problems of generalizing to more molar settings; this is an intriguing question for science—more demonstrably true for the "human sciences" than for physics and chemistry, although biology insofar as it studies biochemical process in the lab may experience attenuated applications to mankind in matters of food digestion and health, to name but one example—and one that cannot be simply dismissed nor "blamed" on the behavioral psychologist. Much of science faces the test of applying knowledge obtained under more controlled conditions. And a large share of the ethics of science is met in the interface between knowledge obtained and knowledge applied. This, too, embraces a formidable set of problems, questions, and issues not met only by a behavioral psychology.

It must be clearly recognized, in addition, that all psychologists, all counselors and psychotherapists, apply information from other areas of knowledge; they all extrapolate from one area to another. They all select knowledge they think is applicable to a given patient at a given time following a given purpose. The behavioral psychologist does not face this problem alone, but may simply be more cognizant of it than most because the behavioral psychologist appears to be more effective in bringing about change, thereby facing many more problems (including ethical ones) than does the nonbehavioral psychologist.

No test, evaluative procedure, interview, or whatnot, is free from bias; no one of them is extrapolation-free, so to speak. All procedures used by all technology and science, including the most global types of counseling and psychotherapy, are based on knowledge gained, generalized, applied, and reapplied. We all face the same problems here; issues revolve more around how these knowledge limitations and problems are recognized and how they are responded to by concerned parties, than most admit explicitly.

5. **Question:** "Are not facts stressed unduly in behavior therapy to the exclusion or dimunition of feelings and emotion?"

Answer: A science that has had the growth of behavioral psychology, with its abundant applications to therapy over the past two decades, is likely to have grown most rapidly in the accumulation of facts. Some behavioral therapists may have emphasized the factual, more limited aspects of behavior therapy than is desirable. However, in principle, it is not necessary to neglect or deny the role of feelings in a behavioral approach to therapy and counseling. Much of the discussion in Chapter 1 takes on this problem and supports the statements that feelings, too, are behavior and can be regarded, if one wishes to state the matter that way, as fact. One difficulty with feelings, however, is that often (but not always) being covert, they are harder to identify, more subtly woven into the behavioral matrix, and more slippery when it comes to attempts to control them. However, feelings have to be included and some interesting and forward-looking problems are encountered thereby. Many aspects of the development of biofeedback are related to the issue of the role of feelings, in that biofeedback taps inner physiological states that are often the basis of "reported feelings" and taps psychological changes associated with tension reduction. An interesting issue here is that biofeedback seems to bypass or "go beyond" feeling states and pick up physiological processes that may be basic to our sense of well-being as well as to our actual health. Biofeedback demonstrates, as well, that feelings, while important, may not be a good guide to what is actually going on within us, for better or for worse. As we advance more into the realm of relating physiological processes to behavior we may gain a further and more distinct advantage over our present ability to know, control, and effectively use our feelings to our own advantage. Feeling states that now seem so unscientific and so subjective are gradually being brought under a more objective aegis but in this process we are learning more about ourselves, not relegating feelings to limbo.

6. **Question:** "Isn't behavior modification mainly a technology-centered body of knowledge, suitable to young children, retardates, and institutional cases but not for the man-in-the-street, not for people in psychotherapy?"

Answer: This question implies at least some usefulness of behavioral methods with human problems, more than many of the questions above do, but still is skeptical about applying these methods to psychotherapy. The application of behavioral methods to psychotherapy—that is, face-to-face verbal therapy emphasizing the concepts, methods, and principles of behavioral psychology—has not advanced as rapidly as some other area of application. One reason for this is that a far greater number of psychotherapists have been trained in traditional, psychoanalytic-derived methods and in training centers originally started and subsequently maintained by psychoanalytic therapists. Even many of the derivatives of psychoanalytic thinking, such as Gestalt therapy, the interpersonal positions of Sullivan, Horney, Fromm, and others, although parting in some ways from the basic tenets of psychoanalysis, would probably not brook much behavioral psychology insofar as psychotherapy was concerned. Unless psychotherapy positions are pretty explicitly behavioral, they tend to be based on "depth" notions of human behavior, such as the need for the concept of the unconscious, defense mechanisms, and a tendency to divide the functioning person into such notions as id/ego/superego or related ones.

Behavioral psychology has, indeed, been enriching the fields of counseling and psychotherapy, and the main thrust of this book is to demonstrate the general usefulness of a behavioral position for the more global types of problems encountered in counseling and psychotherapy. One of the main issues that this book has emphasized, is the way problems are formulated or *conceptualized*. A person reporting "depression" does not then suggest a label, or a diagnostic state, or an entity of some kind called "depressed." Rather, the behavioral psychologist redefines depression in terms of a number of observable behaviors and observes these behaviors in operation (sluggishness, failure to respond socially to others, and so on) and begins to work on finding out how these behaviors are maintained in the person's environment and how they can be altered, bringing these considerations under the powerful influence of reinforcement contingencies (see Chapter 6).

7. **Question:** "Is not the subjective self, the "I" or "me," the very part of ourselves we seem to know the best, ignored by behavioral psychology?"

Answer: The subjective aspects of one's being are not ignored; it is a matter of how these data are regarded and what, indeed, are data in this realm of experience. In a denotative sense, the "I" is not hard to understand; one uses this pronoun to differentiate oneself from all others. Similarly, this applies to the use of the pronoun "me." The problems arise when we reify the *I* and the *me* into some kind of entity, some homunculus, a wholly autonomous "self" acting independently of any other considerations. This way of thinking and conceptualizing one's own self—the reification—as apart from others, is inimical to behavioral psychology. The opinion here is that there is no loss incurred by disclaiming the "self" as an entity, either for science generally or for the clinical treatment of the individual case. In fact, just the opposite is true: The more one reifies and separates off one's own being, the more difficulty one encounters scientifically and clinically, and the less help one can then offer, therapeutically, to patients.

Two recent cases of psychotherapy will illustrate some problems connected with the self as a reified problem:

John was a 25-year-old beginning graduate student who presented himself for psychotherapy because he could not study or concentrate, and had chalked up a marginal semester in his beginning graduate work in business administration. He had had therapy before: eight different therapists—psychologists, psychiatrists, social workers, religious counselors, and a school psychologist (in high school), each of them being seen for anywhere from 6 to 12 months on a once-a-week or twice-a-week basis, often parallel with a group therapy experience usually once-a-week (although sometimes oftener). His version of what was his difficulty, as he quoted liberally from his past therapist, was that he "had to fail, to show his father he (the patient) needed to depend upon his father, that he couldn't be independent of his father."

Such was the "presenting complaint," briefly summarized. It turned out in the discussion that John was working part-time, going to school part-time, receiving $500–$600 a month gratis from his father to support a failing business. He was unable to give any accounting of how he spent his money, had no schedule for classes, work, study, or recreation, and he often "played all night and slept all day—except for some time on the job," as he put it. He mentioned five or six times in his first interview that he seemed to "want to fail," was "doomed to fail because of his father's influence," and other equivalent statements. It was as if therapy had only to recognize this "failure syndrome" and let it go at that—John would be exonerated for anything he did or didn't do, owing to his "predestined failure."

Therapy with John in the behavioral mode merely acknowledged that he seemed to feel "doomed," but that many things might be considered to alter the situation, and that his relationship with his father would, indeed, be of considerable concern, but we probably didn't need to think the father had some kind of "spell cast over him." We got busy setting up schedules for work, study, play, and a behavioral log of daily events was instituted. John was to relate candidly to the therapist how and where he had trouble keeping himself going as a student, as a businessman, and as a social being relating in a variety of ways to others. It was only about 6–8 weeks before John dropped all reference to his father in the blaming and dependency sense, was able to accumulate some progress in his graduate work (some improved grades on short papers during the semester), and to allow social carousing to play a decreasing role in his life. He said that he guessed he "could do most of the things he needed to do to help himself without relying on or blaming my dad." He evolved a plan of borrowing money from his father in a formal way in order to expand his (John's) business and consulted with his father as a peer in this respect. The "I," the "me," the "self" remained no longer a deranged, dependent, rotted-out entity that separated John from all others and provided an excuse (escape from distress and the requirement of facing up to difficulties) for inaction or poor effort. The therapist did not discuss with John the status of the "I" or the "me" or what the "self" was, nor was there any discussion about how these "factors" figured in John's therapy, past or present. We simply went to work on tangibles (logs, schedules, going to class, setting priorities of sleep–work–class, etc.), which resulted in more self-regard and more positive reinforcement from a number of quarters in John's life; as a result, John began solving his problems and getting a better "self-image." In view of John's therapeutic history, it is doubtful if he could have gained an improved "self-image" by any means other than getting down to specific tasks that had an enormous consequence for him in his daily life—especially in two to three months' time.

Another patient, called "Irene," age 21, was also very "hung-up" on herself, as she put it when she presented herself for therapy. She had "had" a three-year psychoanalysis, as she put it, three or four times a week since near the end of her senior year in high school and nearly through three years of college; only a move of over 3000 miles necessitated the termination of her intensive therapy. She was looking "for another therapist like the one I had who was so good," she averred. She said that she was "beginning to understand how negatively she regarded herself by this time" and was distressed at having to discontinue therapy. Her "negative self-regard" instances were those of spending too much

254 Questions and Answers Re Behavioral Therapy

money on clothes (going on sprees), overrunning her bank account often, having to call upon her parents to cover innumerable financial emergencies owing to exceeding her allowance, and quarrels with her roommate and occasional boyfriends over possessions, promiscuousness in relationships, privileges, shared use of rented quarters, and other logistics of daily living.

Irene was "so negative in my self-image that . . . (I) . . . just have to fight with everyone, everyday, it seems, to protect myself from getting worse, to insure that I am not damaged further—why can't I stop this?" Irene seemed to have little or no grasp, based on her "negative self-image" notion, that she was, in fact, maintaining on a daily basis her reported self-image by her selfish and demanding behavior toward many other people. She was a prima donna wild and on the loose, ready to challenge everyone; she was arrogant, vain, insular and extremely demanding—and had, moreover, a clear history of being reinforced generously by her affluent parents in the self-indulgent swath she was cutting through the life of everyone with whom she came in contact. But she "saw" herself as "possessing" a negative, self-defeated, self-defeating urge, "an urge to destroy herself," as she put it, owing to the way her parents neglected her in her childhood and gave her not love but things.

Irene's "self-image," "depravity," "neglect at the hands of others," "self-destructive urges," and so on were not contested; they were hardly noted, except in passing, but therapeutic matters quickly moved on to ways in which she would report specifically and in some detail on her daily interactions, good and bad, with others (her log); how she spent her time and the attention she gave to her school work (she was bright but excessively undisciplined); and what she actually thought of important people in her life (parents, roommates, male friends, landlord, etc.). At the beginning of the fourth (weekly) therapy session with Irene, she said, "You know . . . I'm beginning to think I may be too demanding and too impatient with some people," and related some specific instances from her log that then became much of the grist for the therapy mill. It was not too long thereafter that Irene began to develop some consideration for others—although it was a struggle for her—and to gain some social reinforcement from interacting more on a mutual basis with others rather than out of contention and arrogance.

The "self" does not make people do things; the "self" is an abstraction, a way of using a noun (or pronoun) to describe a general condition about one's typical way of behaving in regard to one or more aspects of one's life, or in regard to some (or many) relationships one carries out with others. These tendencies, in turn, depend upon reinforcers—

sometimes short-lived with long-range aversive consequences, sometimes not—and upon circumstance after circumstance that maintains the "self-image" in positive or negative terms. The picayune data of daily life are the "self," not some reified, detached (mechanical?) entity that is "running things" (as one patient so aptly put it).

Behavioral therapy with children or retardates does not get into these seemingly philosophical problems—a problem is a problem with the verbally uninitiated. But with introspective adults who can ruminate over and "value" some pretty (seemingly) spurious issues, the behavioral therapist has to be careful not to be caught in a verbal and self-fulfilling quagmire of abstractions that seem to be substantive but really are not. These nonsubstantive issues must be replaced with workable, specific objectives which, in time, subsume the nonspecific issues and allow the person to gain a wider range of positive reinforcement for problem solving. Relationships with others that are, in turn, based on discernible variables, take the place of abstract entities, and may make more specific and enhance the abstract "relationship" itself (Patterson, 1974).

QUESTIONS INVOLVING MORE SPECIFIC CLINICAL REFERENCE

Most of the above-cited questions revolve around broad theoretical issues, issues that have philosophical, conceptual, and related problems connected with them. Attention now is turned to more immediate clinical (i.e., therapeutic) issues, although there is continually a play back and forth between the two sets of considerations.

1. **Question:** "Does behavioral therapy pose more ethical issues than other types of therapy and, if so, how does it propose meeting these issues?"

Answer: This is an extremely broad question, as there are many ethical issues, and one that can only be referred to briefly here. A procedure in science that "works" has consequences and those consequences for the individual and for society must be thoroughly considered. If many therapies in the past have not "worked" well (that is, have not produced reliable and discernible results), then few ethical problems were raised (except the matter of purporting to help others but, over substantial periods of time, reliable change not being evidenced). If behavior can, indeed, be changed, ethical issues will undoubtedly evolve; they must be considered as challenges, not as dangling annoyances we hope will fade out or go away. *Ethical issues will increase as a result of behavioral therapy practice;* we had better get ready for this eventuality. In fact, if not already under consideration, the American Psychological Association, the Association for the Advancement of Behavioral Therapy, regional associations, and similar groups should have on their annual schedules symposia, roundtables, papers, and the like, on ethical issues as a routine matter. It will take all the attention we can possibly give the subject of ethics to begin to address its importance in the behavioral field. We can be the leaders in attending to ethical issues, enhance our own philosophical/ethical/practical skills as a result, and learn how to confront changes in society not intended, foreseen, or promulgated from our efforts (whether these efforts at behavior change are successful or not). The matter of ethics not only concerns individual cases—important as they are—but also considers how practices and "decisions" arising from individual cases have ramifications in society at large. The interface between effective behavioral intervention on the one hand, and its consequences for the individual and for society on the other hand, provides the basis for ethical considerations. These ethical issues must not be neglected; and a catalog of sorts, enumerating and defining ethical issues, must be begun posthaste, reviewed periodically, kept up-to-date, and used in all behavioral education (Stolz, Wienckowski, and Brown, 1975; Woody, 1975).

2. **Question:**   "Is behavior therapy really different from other therapies or is it simply 'old wine in new bottles'?"

Answer: All therapies have a core of similarities, especially if carried on verbally in face-to-face situations. However, differences between therapies tend to emerge the closer we look at the therapist–patient interaction. In behavior therapy, there is more effort to define and point to variables; to locate variables as we have seen in the interaction between the patient and his environment (not in the "psyche" of the patient in the reified sense); to get the patient to take actions designed to change his or her behavior; to have the patient observe himself or herself systematically; to be aware of and actively select reinforcers for the patient designed to encourage, direct, and sustain behavior change; and perhaps other considerations. All therapies probably do some of these things, more or less, often randomly, less systematically; so that when the behavioral therapist reports on how a patient was handled, any therapist of any other persuasion will "hear" things he or she also does and may aver, "Why, that's no different from what I do in _____ therapy!" Although some books have attempted to differentiate between different psychotherapists and psychotherapies (Patterson, 1966, 1973; Loew, Grayson, and Loew, 1975; Jurjevich, 1973, 1974), it is doubtful if any one presently available description foots the bill of clear, extended differentiation. The vast array of available techniques, cited in Chapter 2, has, for example, never been collated and looked at explicitly and systematically as being important in behavioral therapy (except on a limited basis—see Stolz, Wienckowski, and Brown, 1975). Within the therapy setting, desensitization, relaxation, setting and following agendas, role-playing (used in some other therapies), keeping and reporting on logs, making assignments, replaying tapes, and so on are seldom used in any other therapy than behavioral approaches. The active nature of the therapist also distinguishes the behavioral therapist from most other therapists. However, since we are all interacting with human beings and their problems tend to show marked similarities, despite important differences, any therapist listening to the work of another therapist of any persuasion is like to have some déja vu experiences!

3. **Question:** "Does not behavior therapy neglect underlying causes, despite its ability to cope with obvious symptom?"

Answer: Behavior therapy deals with behavior, both subtle and obvious. The notion of "underlying causes" is a construct, not a fact; and it has been discussed amply in this book. As one copes with the problem situation(s) and new or more adequate behaviors result, there is no need to resort to hypothetical entities of an "underlying cause" nature. However, one can never be sure that he or she has covered all facets of a problem—we do not make this requirement in any other department of our lives—hence new aspects may come up or new emphases be entertained; but such cases are not, perforce, instances of "underlying causes" in the hidden, repressed, "depth" sense of the term, but only undiscerned or poorly discerned facets of a problem. It could be argued that as long as one lives, he or she has problems, and life's fulfillment consists in part in continually responding to and solving problems. To say that the job is never done perfectly does not necessarily lead us into the labyrinths of "unconscious, deep, repressed, underlying problems" as an explanation of our unfinished business of living.

4. **Question:** "Is it the therapy technique or the therapist that is 'working' with behavioral intervention?"

Answer: This question can, of course, be asked of any therapist or of any type of therapy. There are good and bad therapists of any persuasion, and one can never neglect nor forget this truism. However, as one develops more and more explicit principles and can communicate and teach and model these principles, the idiosyncracies of the therapist, qua therapist, would seem to diminish; although there are limits in regard to interpersonal behavior which probably are necessary for any exchange between persons to be effective (we do not know much about this kind of problem, and it is one that cries out for research, not only with regard to therapy but with respect to any human interaction). If the behavioral therapist has more techniques that can be brought to bear on problems, this puts an emphasis on the therapist's ingenuity, but also displays the resourcefulness of the therapy approach itself. Presumably physicians who command a greater lexicon of concepts and a greater repertoire of remedial skills are "better" than those without such resourcefulness; are these people, then, better physicians because of *themselves,* qua person/ physicians, or because they can dip into a vaster range of knowledge? It would undoubtedly take far greater resources than any present researchers have to answer questions concerning the contribution of a wide range of therapists, using a broad range of therapeutic persuasions on a typical range of patients.

5. **Question:**   "How long-lasting are behavior therapy results?" Are they superior to the results offered by other therapeutic persuasions?"

Answer: It is impossible to answer this question with any degree of sophistication at this time owing to the sparsity of research on the staying power of any therapy. The answer here is similar to the one above—we need far more comprehensive research on all aspects of this and other problems to offer reliable answers. Suffice it to say, however, that behavior therapy is relatively more economical than most other therapies and, so being, can be "repeated" if necessary at a reasonably minimal effort level; one does not have to be "re-analyzed," taking months or years to accomplish. Behavior therapy is just as straightforward and economical (perhaps even more) the second time around—if this is required for whatever reasons—than the first time.

6. **Question:**   "When is behavior therapy not the treatment of choice?"

Answer: To a behavioral therapist steeped in the art and science of what he or she is doing, there is probably no clear-cut answer to this question. One is challenged to meet new problems and new situations; there is no demarcation line that says behavior therapy stops here (or begins here) and the other side of the line is for other therapies. However, a behavioral therapist may use some of the techniques of other therapies—"reflection" from the Rogerian viewpoint, for example (Phillips and Agnew, 1953). The nonbehavioral therapist might come up with better answers to this question than the behavioral therapist where, so to say, a challenge might be flung at the behavioral therapist. No known instances of this kind of confrontation exist as of this writing (Loew, Grayson, and Loew, 1975).

In further response to this question, answers may turn more on preferred ways of working with patients evidenced by some behavioral therapists, such that certain techniques (e.g., strong aversive measures) may be eschewed. A patient wanting such techniques (e.g., aversive techniques applied to smoking, male homosexual behavior, child molesting behavior) might be bypassed by some behavioral therapists either in favor of other procedures or by referring the patient to another behavioral therapist skilled in using aversive techniques. This is not a delimitation of behavior therapy, per se, but a choice of technique/patient/problem areas allowing for a delimitation of the therapeutic role of a given behavioral therapist at a given time.

7. **Question:**   "Who decides what behavior changes are important?"

Answer: This question is often asked and it seems to represent a misunderstanding of how behavioral intervention proceeds. First, the patient comes for help, expressing a desire to solve certain problems, overcome certain unwanted behaviors, achieve some (frustrated) goals, and so on. Second, the behavioral therapist takes up where the patient allows the therapist to do so. Any therapist of any persuasion whatsoever may "jump the gun," attribute the presenting complaint to some nonapparent or nonexpressed cause or condition. Usually the behavioral therapist is less likely to do this kind of presumptive structuring of the cause of the behavior or attribute it to some underlying condition. Often the behavior change process is a simple one of overcoming the unwanted behavior—this is the patient's "goal" (see Chapter 3 for more discussion); the behavioral therapist is put in this service to the patient, so to speak. However, the behavioral intervention may take many paths, may involve the patient in behavioral efforts not previously thought of by the patient, and so on. The behavioral therapist is not one who takes "answers off the shelf like a merchant in a store" but is more like the architect who fashions and develops with the patient "proposals" as to how to solve the patient's problems in a mutually agreed-upon enterprise. There is lots of give and take, defining and redefining; there is no stencil-like laying-on of a solution to a problem against the patient's judgment (although patient and therapist may differ at times). Techniques may often be tried and abandoned when they do not fit the need, or when the patient demurs; there are usually a large number of techniques or ways to approach problem solving, even though a few techniques may be the preferred treatment. Where most other therapists tend to delimit their techniques to verbal messages, behavioral intervention can call upon many other techniques. Hence the chances of overdetermining the therapist's role by rigid application of narrow techniques is small.

8. **Question:**   "Is a 'symptom' a reinforcer?"

Answer: Strictly speaking and avoiding the medical model, a symptom is not a sign of a more basic disturbance (although any behavior may, in principle, be related to other behavior of a more or less "serious" nature—see Chapter 1), but one or more of several behaviors that one wishes to overcome. The behavior in question has been reinforced by its consequences, if even fortuitously, in the behavioral sequence. Although the unwanted behavior (symptom) is aversive, it may be reinforced, hence maintained, by its consequences; that is, if its occurrence results in some avoidance or escape behavior which removes discomfort or some other aversive condition. One could safely say that many unwanted behaviors (symptoms) are maintained through negative reinforcement (see Chapter 2). The psychotherapeutic problem, then, is not the "symptom" and what it "means" in some deep, repressed sense, but how it functions in a reinforcement sequence in a way that allows it to be continued, and how it can be overcome through some rearrangement of the reinforcement contingencies.

9. **Question:** "Why do people sometimes change their behavior through behavior modification methods, yet still report they do not 'feel better'?"

Answer: This is not a common problem but it does occur. In some cases, very obsessive persons tend to "let go" of some of their compulsiveness, perhaps some of the milder instances, yet retain a considerable amount of general tension, vigilance, and excessive activity. It is with the latter condition that the reported feeling of "still being tense" can be associated; hence the therapy has to move on into other more specific areas of tension, compulsiveness, and the like. Although relaxation methods are often helpful in such cases of compulsiveness (and reported excessive tension feelings), often a much more direct approach to the actual compulsive acts has to be made: For example, in the case of a young college student checking all the wall light plugs he could find, the therapeutic approach might be satiation (checking one plug or a given, limited number of plugs, say, in one room until he was exhausted); then repeating this procedure several days in a row. Or, keeping a record of nonchecking of plugs over time ("I went all morning without checking a single plug," or "I've gone two days now and have not had the urge to check a plug and there are many around the house," and so forth), thereby reinforcing the abstinence or nonoccurrence of the unwanted behavior in some appropriate way. One could consider using an aversive method here (mild electric shock) if the patient concurred and there were no other problems generated thereby. The essential issue, however, is to tackle the specific, nuclear compulsive act and extinguish it, because only then is the vigilance and anxiousness likely to be abated.

Similarly, depressed persons sometimes overcome some aspects of their depressive behavior but retain an overarching apprehension lest they get depressed again for unknown or uncontrollable reasons. They have not yet generalized their problem-solving skills to wider situations, nor have they yet learned a general methodology for solving the problems that have heretofore led to depressive reactions. Again, the more detailed and specific the intervention procedures can become, the more likely is the exact behavior in question to be overcome and, better yet, the more likely a general set of procedures are to be learned which have a preventive as well as a problem-solving outcome. How specific one has to get in order to overcome an unwanted behavior is hard to generalize about; sometimes one is surprised how quickly a "symptom" yields to a pretty obvious and even superficial approach; yet, again, extemely detailed intervention is called for. It is an empirical matter revolving around the patient, the circumstances under which the unwanted behavior occurs, the initiative and independence with which the patient behaves in his or her own behalf, and how the consequences of his or her behavior change might be conceptualized by the therapist and patient in a joint effort.

10. **Question:** "Are behavior therapists 'allowed' to get angry at their patients? If so, how, under what conditions, etc.?"

Answer: Anger, of course, touches all of us. However, in a therapeutic situation, even though the patient seems to be toying with therapy, appears insincere or unusually manipulative, the best tack for the therapist is to state frankly and forthrightly to the patient what he or she, the therapist, thinks is going on. If this is done pointedly and relevantly to the in-therapy behavior, it will allow the therapist to deal with the matter through verbal communication and disallow (or reduce the likelihood of) anger arising out of the therapist's own frustration. The therapist can always say, "When you say or do things like that you make me angry," without, at the same time, displaying anger in the sense of loss of self-control or inability to focus on other aspects of the patient's behavior. Usually such words will suffice, especially if they then lead into further discussion of the patient's in-therapy behavior (how it is also related to out-of-therapy behavior) and what its function is in the patient's life. If the therapist's anger is sufficient to disable him or her in executing the therapeutic role, then the patient begins to set the contingencies and this, in all likelihood, is probably only then another instance of the patient manipulating his or her interactions detrimentally.

11. **Question:** "Does behavior therapy give enough credence to baseline conditions as they might be predictive of future change in the behavior studied?"

Answer: This is a somewhat unusual but interesting question. Are baseline conditions, themselves, predictive of the amount of change that can be expected? There is no known way to generalize on this question, but it would appear that with, say, severely handicapped children or psychotics with many deficits characteristic of their repertoires, changes would be relatively arduous and time-consuming. In Chapter 1, it was proposed that various "rules" about "severity or psychopathology" might be relevant; these, in turn, would appear to cover the instances where baseline conditions were possibly predictive of the amount of change in the target behavior that could be expected. However, the baseline should not be construed as an independent entity being, as it is, a function of the "natural" reinforcing conditions in the environment; when these are appropriately altered, resultant behavior change might be considerable or modest, depending not alone upon the original baseline but upon other conditions as well.

Behavior therapy is not a perfect solution to any problem. It is probably the simplest, most feasible, most easily assessed procedure to be offered to a wide variety of patients/problems/situations. Its inherent flexibility, resourcefulness, objectivity, economy, and manifest reasonableness in the light of recent experiences with an enormous variety of problems certainly recommends it as a serious therapeutic approach to human difficulties. As more data of both clinical and research types are accumulated, behavioral therapies will undoubtedly undergo many changes, refinements, and extensions; this is, fortunately, the course of any science or applied technology. It is an exciting enterprise to be part of this developing process and one that is strongly recommended to all serious students of human behavior.

CHAPTER 11

Summary and Conclusions

This book has attempted to bring to the reader a variety of proposals and working principles in the interest of applying behavioral psychology to the clinic, primarily to counseling and psychotherapy. Although many therapists and counselors work in a behavioral framework, it has not been the purpose of many authors to make a more extensive, while at the same time intensive, application of behavioral management to face-to-face counseling and psychotherapy which is still the most common and perhaps the most needed of all psychological services, especially to adolescent and adult populations.

One difficulty with psychotherapy and counseling in the past—for the most part—has been its derivation from personality theory, mainly from psychoanalysis or "depth" psychology. This condition has brought about a kind of collusion, albeit unintended, between the practice of therapy and the theoretical formulations of Freud and his colleagues and defectors. All in all, Freud's followers and defectors did not change the main structure of psychoanalytic thinking, although many of them (Adler, Horney, Sullivan, Fromm, etc.) stressed the societal context more than Freud. These defectors nonetheless retained the main "depth" structure of human personality and did not learn to think, as we are able to do today with the operant and cybernetic influences, in terms of consequences or effects.

When one changes the locus of causality from inside the person (stated in motivational, cognitive, instinctual, or similar terms) to the environment (where the environment works on and with and in the organism as a set of consequences or effects, arising from the interaction between the organism and the environment), the resultant theory and practice are considerably different. We are thereby freed from looking "inside" the organism for causal notions, for the basis of change, and for understanding what human functioning means in a broad, philosophical sense. We can now take the organism as it is, "inside" and "outside," and meld and mesh the two sets of considerations into the same behavioral study of consequences. The inside–outside, overt–covert dichotomy is artificial in the first place, but we all give some assent to it out of common language usage and because it becomes tiresome and often pedantic to try always to speak precisely about any and every human interaction. I cannot imagine a more boring conversation than one carried on by a behavioral psychologist who disallows himself or herself the use of our common English language, with all its semantic problems, and tries to formulate everything pedantically in behavioral terms. The same can be said for the flip "explanations" of "unconscious motivation" proffered by psychoanalytic thinkers who, too, find our natural language usually stifling. If, however, one wishes to be formal and precise, the use of operant language and/or cybernetic concepts gives one a sturdy leg up on the problem of clear communication which can still remain light, airy, and open.

Counseling and psychotherapy theories (and practices) have been derived in the past, as has been said, mainly from psychodynamic viewpoints. These older formulations have been applied mostly to middle class, intelligent, highly verbal, generally economically secure patients; and applications to the profoundly retarded, the autistic, varieties of so-called brain damage syndrome cases—scarcely to mention problems of senility, problems related to crises in development (as with college students and young adults, and others in change-over positions in life related to divorce, death, separation, job loss, etc.)—have been either relatively poorly conceived or apparently deficient. It is only with a basis in behavioral formulations of problems that really new and exciting change efforts have been applied to these heretofore less popular and less interesting cases. (Maybe it is more interesting to most clinicians to speak with an intelligent college student about his or her "hangups," love life, career decisions, and the like, than it is to teach an institution retardate to dress himself or use a broom to sweep up a mess he has made, regardless of the variety of behavioral techniques one can think of applicable to the latter case.)

As a result of the bias between psychodynamic formulations and the commonest varieties of in-office psychotherapy of the last few decades, not much new thinking—until the advent of operant applications— infiltrated counseling and psychotherapy. This is not to say that many books on behavioral-clinical work have not been published—one can consult the bibliography of this or many other books to show that there has not been a paucity of thought along this line—but most of them are far from the mainstream of influence on counseling and psychotherapy. One reason for this lack of acceptance is a semantic one: we are all used to the older, verbal formulations of problems, and we tend to cast explanations, set therapy goals, and the like in terms of the feeling-states reported by patients and rely too often on the subjective appraisals by patients. In my work in the university setting with dozens of counselor/therapists trained in a wide variety of schools in the United States, I have met very few who can really take the gross, molar–clinical–counseling–psychotherapy context and convert or translate its complexities into behavioral terms and feel comfortable with the translation and exercise a robust change effort with the patient at the same time.

In this book, there has been an effort to eschew the older formulations (except to perhaps quickly touch base with them and then go on to the preferred language and conceptualization) and to try to bring to bear on the reader's discrimination the realization that there are a host of ways to solve personal/social problems that pivot on how the environmental role is conceptualized in producing and maintaining the individual's problem status. This requires attention to technique, a matter that has been implicit in the behavioral literature (most articles have something to say about one or another behavioral technique fitting a particular problem, but too little attention has been given to even a brief survey of a wide variety of behavioral intervention techniques, such as are summarized in Chapter 2). One cannot, however, emphasize technique out of proportion; the technique(s) used should arise out of a cogent statement of the problem. We can, then, learn to conceptualize problems more clearly— which is an important clinical task in its own right—following which we begin to focus on, experiment with, and act clinically on the various techniques. Gradually, as research and clinical experience develop, we will, as a profession, gain some confidence in "assigning" various techniques to various classes of problems, knowing all the while that differences may test or break rules, leading us to gain interesting, new, or provocative information that enhances the profession and increases clinical skills at the same time.

Many traditional problems of the clinic have been eschewed by the behavioral clinician who has characteristically shown little enthusiasm for "inner" events. Although it is true that so-called inner and outer events are not really different worlds of data, requiring different laws, conceptualizations, or techniques, this dichotomy has nevertheless caused trouble for behavioral clinicians and for those of other persuasions. The behaviorists have largely ignored the issues and the nonbehaviorists have overemphasized the alleged inner events, pivoting laborious and often ineffectual therapies in quest of the Internal Holy Grail. I believe no such inner–outer split exists in nature and it is time we recognized this forthwith and did more about it. This book has emphasized several approaches to the problem: First, to realize that the inner–outer, covert–overt dichotomy is artificial, although many subtleties exist as to the accessibility (verbally, experimentally, psychologically) of certain behaviors. If we work on pursuing these subtleties, through clinical observation, physiological studies, and experimentation in a behavioral realm, we will not only gain access to data heretofore overlooked but will show the robustness of the behavioral approach to therapy. We will bring more kinds of problems under the control of the patient–therapist relationship and ultimately under the patient's control. This is a wholly satisfactory goal for all therapists to pursue.

A second outcome of overcoming the inner–outer split (this refers, of course, to overcoming the behavior versus feelings dichotomies) is to emphasize to the behaviorists that they should take data from wherever they may come, examine them, subject them to the usual canons of science, and then rise to the challenge of incorporating the data into the behavioral therapy framework. Perhaps developments in the past decade in the area of "biofeedback" have been the best example of this kind of undertaking and rapprochement.

A third outcome is tutorial—teaching students how to think (conceptualize) in behavioral terms about the many sincere but behaviorally naive statements heard by patients as to what their problems are. Too easily we get locked into the patient's own language concerning his or her difficulties and fail to teach the patient or ourselves that a clearer conceptualization of the problem (asking the right questions about how to change behavior) is an important and far-reaching theoretical and practical problem. These outcomes are advanced, discussed, and tentative solutions proposed in Chapters 1, 2, and 5.

Applying many behavioral principles and conceptualizations to clinical problems has also been an intention of this book. If we take too seriously the old diagnostic categories of depression and the like, we run the risk of reifying these terms and trying to change a condition that is regarded as an entity. We locate these concepts someplace in the psyche and then fail, correspondingly, to realize that we do not treat "depression" as such but a host of specific, interrelated behaviors that are maintained by and through the person's environmental relationships. We thereby learn to include these cues of a so-called internal nature that the patient has learned and incorporated into causal feedback loops in ways that allow a whole process to be triggered off by either some overtly discernible event—what someone says to him—or by not as easily discerned internal events such as "stomach pangs" or a feeling of foreboding. Thus we try to meld the internal referential system, the presenting complaint system of the patient, with what he can discern "within" himself as well as what he can discern in his more easily observed, open environment. It has been alleged that the practical and the conceptual problems inherent in this task can be applied in a variety of ways, some of which are discussed in appropriate chapters in this book (especially see Chapters 3, 4, 6, and 7).

Spinning some larger webs of conceptual structure has taken place in Chapters 7, 9, and 10, wherein the effort was made to stand off and look at the whole matter of extrapolating from the clinic, per se, to larger philosophical, societal, and related problems. For one, I prefer to think that the behavioral movement (including cybernetics) has very, very wide implications for all mankind and for the solution of many societal problems. Thinking of behavior as essentially of "one piece," encourages one to take the observations, principles, and conceptualizations from the clinic—from individual and small-group study—into an ever-widening realm of application. The great ideas of behavior change are not restricted to the microcosm; they belong as well to the macrocosm, and the sooner we attempt these extrapolations in practical and theoretical ways, the sooner we will build a more robust science and technology. A gainful clinical practice will then begin to put behavioral science on a footing with the more mature sciences and raise our skill levels to a point more nearly adequate to meet the demands of our total social and personal being.

References

Ackerman, Nathan W. (Ed.). *Family Therapy in Transition*. Boston: Little, Brown, 1970.

Anderson, O. D., R. Parmenter, and H. S. Liddell. Some cardio-vascular manifestations of the experimental neurosis in sheep. *Pychosom. Med.* **1**:95, 1939.

Anderson, O. D. and R. Parmenter. A Long-Term Study of the Experimental Neurosis in the Sheep and Dog. Washington, D.C.: National Research Council, 1941.

Ayllon, T. Toward a new hospital psychiatry, in G. Abrams and N. Greenfield (Eds.), *The New Hospital Psychiatry*. New York: Academic, 1971.

Ayllon, T. and N. H. Azrin. Reinforcement and instructions with mental patients. *J. Exp. Anal. Behav.*, **7**:327–331, 1964.

Ayllon, T. and N. H. Azrin. The measurement and reinforcement of behavior of psychotics. *J. Exp. Anal. Behav.*, **8**:357–383, 1965.

Ayllon, T. and N. H. Azrin. *The Token Economy: A Motivational System for Therapy and Rehabilitation*. New York: Appleton-Century-Crofts, 1968.

Ayllon, T. and J. Michael. The psychiatric nurse as a behavioral engineer. *J. Exp. Anal. Behav.*, **2**:323–334, 1959.

Bachrach, Arthur J. Direct methods of treatment, in I. A. Berg and L. A. Pennington (Eds.), *Introduction to Clinical Psychology*, 3rd ed. New York: Ronald Press, 1966.

Bachrach, Arthur J. Learning, in A. M. Freedman and H. Kaplan (Eds.), *Comprehensive Textbook of Psychiatry*. Baltimore: Williams & Wilkins, 1967.

Bachrach, Arthur J. *Psychological Research: An Introduction*, 3rd ed. New York: Random House, 1972.

Bachrach, Arthur J. and R. Karen. *Chaining: Complex Behavior*. 16mm film. San Diego: Rodentia Productions, 1966.

Bach-y-Rita, Paul. *Brain Mechanisms in Sensory Substitution*. New York: Academic, 1972.

Back, Kurt. *Beyond Words: The Story of Sensitivity Training and The Encounter Movement*. New York: Russell Sage, 1972.

Baer, D., M. Wolf, and T. Risley. Some current dimensions of applied behavior analysis. *J. Appl. Behav. Anal.*, **1**:91–97, 1968.

Bain, J. A. *Thought Control in Everyday Life*. New York: Frush and Wagnalls, 1928.

Bandura, A. Vicarious processes: A case of no-trial learning, in L. Berkowitz (Ed.), *Advances in Experimental Social Psychology*, Vol. II. New York: Academic, 1965(a), pp. 1–55.

Bandura, Albert. Behavior modification through modeling procedures, in L. Krasner and L. P. Ullmann (Eds.), *Research in Behavior Modification.* New York: Holt, Rinehart and Winston, 1965(b).

Bandura, A. *Principles of Behavior Modification.* New York: Holt, Rinehart and Winston, 1969.

Bandura, A. Psychotherapy based upon modeling principles, in A. E. Bergin and S. L. Garfield (Eds.), *Handbook of Psychotherapy and Behavior Change.* New York: Wiley, 1971(a), pp. 653–708.

Bandura, A. *Social Learning Theory.* Morristown, N.J.: General Learning Press, 1971(b).

Bandura, Albert. Behavior theory and the models of man. *Am. Psychol.,* **29**:859–869, 1974.

Bass, B. A. An unusual behavioral technique for treating obsessive ruminations. *Psychother. Theory Res. Pract.,* **10**:191–192, 1973.

Beck, A. T. *Depression.* Philadelphia: University of Pennsylvania Press, 1967.

Benson, Herbert, John F. Beary, and Mark P. Carol. The relaxation response. *Psychiatry,* **37**:37–46, 1974.

Bergin, A. E. A self-regulation technique for impulse control disorders. *Psychother. Theory Res. Pract.,* **6**:113–118, 1969.

Bergin, A. E. Cognitive therapy and behavior therapy: Foci for a multidimensional approach to treatment. *Behav. Ther.,* **1**:205–212, 1970.

Birk, Lee (Ed.). *Biofeedback: Behavioral Medicine.* New York: Grune & Stratton, 1973.

Bonwit, Kenneth S., E. Lakin Phillips, and David L. Williams. The electric pencil—a device for training in fine motor skills, in *Proceedings: 1972 Cornahan Conference on Electronic Prosthesis.* Lexington, Ky: University of Kentucky, 1972.

Boren, J. J. and A. D. Coleman. Some experiments on reinforcement principles within a psychiatric ward for delinquent soldiers. *J. Appl. Behav. Anal.,* **3**:29–37, 1970.

Boszormenyi-Nagy, I. and J. L. Framo (Eds.). *Intensive Family Therapy.* New York: Harper & Row, 1965.

Brown, J. S. Gradients of approach and avoidance responses and their relations to level of motivation, *J. Comp. Physiol. Psychol.,* **1**:450–465, 1948.

Brush, F. R. (Ed.). *Aversive Conditioning and Learning.* New York: Academic, 1969.

Campbell, Donald T. On the conflicts between biological and social evolution and between psychology and moral tradition. *Am. Psychol.,* **30**:1103–1126, 1975.

Cautela, J. R. Covert sensitization. *Psychol. Rep.,* **20**:459–468, 1967.

Clark, Ronald W. *The Life of Bertrand Russell.* New York: Knopf, 1975.

Davison, Gerald C. and Richard B. Stuart. Behavior therapy and civil liberties, *Am. Psychol.,* **30**:755–763, 1975.

DeLatil, Pierre. *Thinking by Machine: A Study of Cybernetics.* Boston: Houghton Mifflin, 1957.

Dember, W. N. Motivation and the cognitive revolution. *Am. Psychol.,* **29**:161–168, 1974.

Dollard, John and Neal E. Miller. *Personality and Psychotherapy*. New York: McGraw-Hill, 1950.

Dunlap, K. A. A revision of the fundamental law of habit formation. *Science,* **67**:360–362, 1928.

Dunlap, K. A. Repetition in the breaking of habits. *Sci. Mon.,* **30**:66–70, 1930.

Ellis, A. *Reason and Emotion in Psychotherapy*. New York: Lyle Stuart, 1962.

Ellis, Albert. A cognitive approach to behavior therapy. *Intern. J. Psychother.,* **8**:896–900, 1969.

Ellis, Albert. *The Essence of Rational Psychotherapy: A Comprehensive Approach to Treatment*. New York: Institute of Rational Living, 1970.

Eysenck, H. J. (Ed.). *Behavior Therapy and the Neuroses*. New York: Pergamon, 1960.

Ferster, C. B. Behavioral approaches to depression, in A. T. Beck. *Depression*. Philadelphia: University of Pennsylvania Press, 1967.

Ferster, C. B. Clinical reinforcement. *Semin. Psychiatr.,* **9**:101–111, 1972.

Ferster, C. B. A functional analysis of depression. *Am. Psychol.,* **28**:857–870, 1973.

Ferster, C. B., Stuart Culbertson, and Mary C. P. Boren. *Behavior Principles,* 2nd ed. Englewood Cliffs, N.J.: Prentice-Hall, 1975.

Ferster, C. B. and Skinner, B. F. *Schedules of Reinforcement*. New York: Appleton-Century Crofts, 1957.

Fischer, Constance T. Behaviorism and behavioralism. *Psychother. Theory Res. Pract.,* **10**:2–4, 1973.

Fish, Jefferson M. *Placebo Therapy*. San Francisco: Jossey-Bass, 1973.

Gantt, W. H. An experimental approach to psychiatry. *Am. J. Psychiatr.,* **92**:1007, 1936.

Gantt, W. H. *Experimental Basis for Neurotic Behavior*. New York: Paul B. Hoefer, 1944.

Gelfand, D. M., S. Gelfand, and W. R. Dobson. Unprogrammed reinforcement of patients' behavior in a mental hospital. *Behav. Res. Ther.,* **5**:201–207, 1967.

Glasser, Wm. *Reality Therapy*. New York: Harper & Row, 1975.

Goldfried, Marvin R. and Gerald C. Davison. *Clinical Behavior Therapy*. New York: Holt, Rinehart and Winston, 1976.

Goldiamond, I. Self-control procedures in personal behavior problems. *Psychol. Rep.,* **17**:851–868, 1965.

Greenspoon, J. Behavioristic approaches to psychotherapy, in F. J. Shaw (Ed.), *Behavioristic Approaches to Counseling and Psychotherapy*. University, Ala.: University of Alabama Press, 1961.

Greenspoon, J. and A. J. Brownstein. Psychotherapy from the standpoint of a behaviorist. *Psychol. Rec.,* **17**:401–416, 1968.

Haley, Jay and Ira D. Gluck. *Family Therapy and Research: An Annotated Bibliography of Articles and Books, 1950–1970*. New York: Grune & Stratton, 1971.

Haley, Jay and Lynn Hoffman. *Techniques of Family Therapy*. New York: Basic Books, 1968.

Haring, Norris G. and E. Lakin Phillips. *Educating Emotionally Disturbed Children*. New York: McGraw-Hill, 1962.

Haring, Norris G. and E. Lakin Phillips. *Analysis and Modification of Classroom Behavior*. Englewood Cliffs, N.J.: Prentice-Hall, 1972.

Harper, Robert A. *Psychoanalysis and Psychotherapy, 36 Systems*. Englewood Cliffs, N.J.: Prentice-Hall, 1959.

Harper, Robert. *The New Psychotherapies*. Englewood Cliffs, N.J.: Prentice-Hall, 1975.

Harris, Florence R. *Field Studies of Social Reinforcement in a Preschool*. Durham, North Carolina: Durham Educational Improvement Program, 1967.

Haughton, E. and T. Ayllon. Production and elimination of symptomatic behavior, in L. P. Ullmann and L. Krasner (Eds.), *Case Studies in Behavior Modification*. New York: Holt, Rinehart and Winston, 1965.

Hefferline, Ralph F., B. Keenan, and R. A. Harford. Escape and avoidance conditioning in human subjects without their observation of the response. *Science*, **130**:1338–1339, 1959.

Herzberg, A. Short treatment of neurosis by graduated tasks, *Brit. J. Med. Psychol.*, 1941, 19, 36–51.

Hogan, R. A. Implosive therapy in the short-term treatment of psychotics. *Psychother. Theory Res. Pract.*, **3**:25–32, 1966.

Holz, W. C., N. H. Azrin, and T. Ayllon. Elimination of behavior of mental patients by response-produced extinction. *J. Exp. Anal. Behav.*, **6**:407–412, 1963.

Hoon, Peter W. and Ogden R. Lindsley. A comparison of behavior and traditional therapy publication activity. *Am. Psychol.*, **29**:694–697, 1974.

Jacobson, E. *Progressive Relaxation*. Chicago: University of Chicago Press, 1938.

Johnson, Wm. G. Group therapy: A behavioral perspective. *Behav. Ther.*, **6**:30–37, 1975.

Jourard, Sidney. *The Transparent Self*. New York: D. Van Nostrand, 1971.

Jurjevich, Ray M. *Direct Psychotherapy I*. Coral Gables, Fla.: University of Miami Press, 1973.

Jurjevich, Ray M. *Direct Psychotherapy II*. Coral Gables, Fla.: University of Miami Press, 1973.

Jurjevich, Ray. *The Hoax of Freudism*. Philadelphia: Dorrance, 1974.

Kanfer, F. H. The maintenance of behavior by self-generated stimuli and reinforcement, in A. Jacobs and L. B. Sachs (Eds.), *The Psychology of Private Events: Perspectives on Covert Response Systems*. New York: Academic, 1971, pp. 39–59.

Kanfer, F. H. and A. R. Marston. Conditioning of self-reinforcing response: An analogue to self-confidence training. *Psychol. Rep.*, **13**:63–70, 1963.

Kanfer, F. H. and J. S. Phillips. *Learning Foundations of Behavior Therapy*. New York: Wiley, 1970.

Karen, R. L. *An Introduction to Behavior Theory and Its Applications*. New York: Harper & Row, 1974.

Kazdin, A. E. Response cost: The removal of conditioned reinforcers for therapeutic change. *Behav. Ther.,* **3:**533–546, 1972.

Kazdin, Alan E. Methodological and assessment considerations in evaluating reinforcement programs in applied settings. *J. Appl. Behav. Anal.,* **6:**3, 1973.

Kazdin, A. E. Self-monitoring and behavior change, in M. J. Mahoney and C. E. Thoresen (Eds.), *Self-Control: Power to the Person.* Monterey, Calif.: Brooks/Cole, 1974.

Kinkade, Kathleen. *A Walden Two Experiment.* New York: Morrow, 1973.

Kolb, David A., I. M. Reubin, and J. M. McIntyre (Eds.). *Organizational Psychology.* Englewood Cliffs, N.J.: Prentice-Hall, 1971.

Krasner, L. Behavior therapy. *Ann. Rev. Psychol.,* **22:**483–532, 1971.

Krasner, L. and L. P. Ullmann (Eds.). *Research in Behavior Modification.* New York: Holt, Rinehart and Winston, 1965.

Krumboltz, John D. and Carl E. Thoresen. The effect of behavioral counseling in group and individual settings on information-seeking behavior. *J. Couns. Psychol.,* **11:**324–333, 1964.

Krumboltz, John D. and Carl E. Thoresen. *Behavioral Counseling: Cases and Techniques.* New York: Holt, Rinehart and Winston, 1969.

Lazarus, A. A. and S. Rachman. The use of systematic desensitization in psychotherapy. *South Afr. Med. J.,* **31:**934–937, 1957.

Lazaras, A. A., and Serber, M. Is systematic desensitization being misapplied? *Psychol. Reports,* 1968, 23, 215–218.

Lincourt, John M. and Paul V. Olezak. C. S. Peirce and H. S. Sullivan on the human self. *Psychiatry,* **37:**78–87, 1974.

Lloyd, Richard W., Jr., and Herman C. Salzberg. Controlled social drinking: An alternative to abstinence as a treatment goal for some alcohol abusers, *Psychol. Bull.,* **82:**815–843, 1975.

Loew, C. A., H. Grayson, and G. H. Loew (Eds.). *Three Psychotherapies.* New York: Brunner/Mazel, 1975.

McCary, James L. and Daniel E. Sheer. *Six Approahces to Psychotherapy.* New York: Dryden, 1955.

McGinnies, E. and C. B. Ferster. (Eds.). *The Reinforcement of Social Behavior.* Boston: Houghton Mifflin, 1971.

McGuigan, Frank J. and Reginald A. Schoonover (Eds.). *The Psychophysiology of Thinking; Studies of Covert Processes.* New York: Academic, 1973.

Mahoney, Michael J. *Cognition and Behavior Modification.* Cambridge, Mass.: Ballinger, 1974.

Mahoney, Michael and Carl E. Thoresen (Eds.). *Self-Control: Power To The Person.* Monterey, Calif.: Brooks/Cole, 1974.

Maruyama, M. The second cybernetics: deviation amplifying mutual causal processes. *Am. Sci.,* **51:**164–179, 1963.

Maslow, Abraham. *Toward a Psychology of Being,* 2nd ed. New York: D. Van Nostrand, 1968.

Masserman, Jules H. *Principles of Dynamic Psychiatry.* Philadelphia: W. B. Saunders, 1946.

May, Rollo. *Psychology and the Human Dilemma*. New York: D. Van Nostrand, 1971.

Miller, N. E. Learning of visceral and glandular responses. *Science*, **163**:434–445, 1969.

Miller, Neal E. Interaction between learned and physical factors in mental illness. *Semin. Psychiatr.*, **4**:239–254, 1972.

Minuchin, Salvador. *Families and Family Therapy*. Cambridge, Mass: Harvard University Press, 1974.

Murdock, Bennet B. *Human Memory: Theory and Data*. Potomac, Md.: Eslbaum, 1974.

Olson, Paul (Ed.). *Emotional Flooding*, Vol. 1. New York: Human Sciences Press, 1976.

Ornstein, Robert E. *On the Experience of Time*. New York: Penguin Books, 1975(a).

Ornstein, Robert E. *The Psychology of Consciousness*. New York: Penguin Books, 1975(b).

Page, J. D. *Psychopathology*. New York: Aldine, 1971.

Patterson, C. H. *Theories of Counseling and Psychotherapy*. New York: Harper & Row, 1966.

Patterson, C. H. A current view of client-centered or relationship therapy. *Couns. Psychol.*, **1**:1–29, 1969.

Patterson, C. H. *Theories of Counseling and Psychotherapy*, 2nd. ed. New York: Harper & Row, 1973.

Patterson, C. H. *Relationship Counseling and Psychotherapy*. New York: Harper & Row, 1974.

Peck, R. Biofeedback: Fad, fancy or future therapy? *Hosp. Physician*, **5**:38–41, 1972.

Phillips, E. Lakin. *Psychotherapy: A Modern Theory and Practice*. Englewood Cliffs, N.J.: Prentice-Hall, 1956.

Phillips, Ellery L. Achievement place; token reinforcement procedures in a home-style rehabilitation setting for "pre-delinquent" boys. *J. Appl. Behav. Anal.*, **1**:213–223, 1968.

Phillips, E. Lakin. Review of Patterson's "A current view of client-centered or relationship therapy." *Couns. Psychol.*, **1**:67–71, 1969.

Phillips, E. Lakin. Some areas of needed research into autism. Paper presented at the National Society for Autistic Children, Washington, D.C., June, 1974.

Phillips, E. Lakin. When is a placebo a placebo? Review of Fish, Jefferson M., *Placebo Therapy*. *Contemp. Psychol.*, **20**:249–250, 1975.

Phillips, E. Lakin. Three approaches to writing as a therapeutic enterprise. Paper presented at the American Personnel and Guidance Association, Chicago, Ill., April, 1976.

Phillips, E. Lakin and Judith Gershenson. A report on Time-Limited Writing Therapy. In press.

Phillips, Ellery L., E. A. Phillips, F. L. Fixen, and M. M. Wolf. Achievement place: Modification of the behaviors of pre-delinquent boys with a token economy. *J. Appl. Behav. Anal.*, **4**:45–59, 1971.

Phillips, E. Lakin, Ann Raiford, V. Rutledge, and J. Burkhardt. Attrition—A perplexing clinical problem. *Psychol. Rep.*, **20**:26, 1967.
Phillips, E. Lakin and Daniel N. Wiener. *Short-Term Psychotherapy and Structured Behavior Change*. New York: McGraw-Hill, 1966.
Phillips, E. Lakin and J. W. Agnew. A study of Rogers' "Reflection" Hypothesis. *J. Clinical Psychology*, 1953, **9**:281–284.
Pierrol, R., and G. Sherman. *Barnabus, The Barnard Rat: Demonstration*. New York: Barnard College, 1958.
Popper, Karl R. *The Logic of Scientific Discovery*. New York: Basic Books, 1959.
Premack, D. Toward empirical behavioral laws: I. Positive reinforcement. *Psychol. Rev.*, **66**:219–233, 1959.
Premack, D. Reinforcement theory, in D. Levine (Ed.), *Nebraska Symposium on Motivation: 1965*. Lincoln: University of Nebraska Press, 1965.
Premack, D. Catching up with common sense or two sides of a generalization, reinforcement and punishment, in R. Glaser (Ed.), *The Nature of Reinforcement*. New York: Academic, 1971.
Reese, Ellen P. *The Analysis of Human Operant Behavior*. Dubuque, Iowa: Wm C. Brown, 1966.
Reppucci, N. D. and J. T. Saunders. Social psychology of behavior modification: Problems of implementation in natural settings. *Am. Psychol.*, **30**:649–660, 1974.
Rosenblueth, A., N. Wiener, and J. Bigelow. Behavior, purpose and teleology. *Philos. Sci.*, **10**:18–24, 1943.
Rosenthal, R., D. Archer, J. H. Kowumaki, M. R. DiMatteo, and P. L. Rogers. Assessing sensitivity to non-verbal communications: The PONS test. *Division 8 Newsletter*, January, 1974.
Rotter, J. B. *Social Learning and Clinical Psychology*. Englewood Cliffs, N.J.: Prentice-Hall, 1954.
Rubin, G., K. Griswald, I. Smith, and C. DeLeonardo. A case study in the remediation of severe self-destructive behavior in a 7-year-old mentally retarded girl. *J. Clin. Psychol.*, **28**:424–426, 1972.
Sargent, J. Preliminary report on the use of autogenic feedback training in the treatment of migraine and tension headaches. *Psychosom. Med.*, **35**:129–135, 1973.
Satir, Virginia. *Conjoint Family Therapy*. Palo Alto: Science and Behavior, 1964.
Schwartz, G. Biofeedback as therapy: Some theoretical and practical issues. *Am. Psychol.*, **28**:666–673, 1973.
Schwitzgebel, Ralph K. and David A. Kolb. *Changing Human Behavior: Principles of Planned Intervention*. New York: McGraw-Hill, 1974.
Segal, Julius. Biofeedback as medical treatment. *J. Am. Med. Assoc.*, **232**:179–180, 1975.
Seligman, M. E. P. Depression and learned helplessness, in Raymond J. Friedman and Martin M. Katz (Eds.), *The Psychology of Depression: Contemporary Theory and Research*. Washington, D.C.: V. H. Winston & Sons, 1974.
Seligman, M. E. P., and Steven F. Maier. Failure to escape traumatic shock. *J. Exper. Psychol.*, **74**:1–9, 1967.

Shapiro, D., T. X. Barber, Leo V. DiCara, Joe Kamiya, Neal E. Miller, and Johann Stoyva. *Biofeedback and Self-Control*. Chicago: Aldine, 1973.

Shapiro, Deane H., Jr. and Steven M. Zifferblatt. Zen meditation and behavioral self-control:Similarities, differences, and clinical applications. *Am. Psychol.*, **31:**519–532, 1976.

Sidman, M. *Tactics of Scientific Research*. New York: Basic Books, 1960.

Shneidman, E. S. Classification of suicidal phenomena. *Bull. Suicidology,* July, 1968, **1:**1–9.

Shneidman, E. S., N. L. Farberow, and R. E. Litman. *The Psychology of Suicide*. New York: Science House, 1970.

Skinner, B. F. *Walden Two*. New York: Macmillan, 1948.

Skinner, B. F. *Science and Human Behavior*. New York: Macmillan, 1953.

Skinner, B. F. *The Technology of Teaching*. New York: Appleton-Century-Crofts, 1968.

Skinner, B. F. *Beyond Freedom and Dignity*, New York: Knopf, 1971.

Skinner, B. F. *About Behaviorism*. New York: Knopf, 1974.

Smith, Karl U. *Delayed Sensory Feedback and Behavior*. Philadelphia: W. B. Saunders, 1962.

Smith, Karl U. and Margaret F. Smith. *Cybernetic Principles of Learning and Educational Design*. New York: Holt, Rinehart and Winston, 1966.

Solomon, R. L. Punishment. *Am. Psychol.*, **19:**239–253, 1964.

Solomon, R. L. and L. C. Wynne. Traumatic avoidance learning: Acquisition in normal dogs. *Psychol. Monogr.*, **67**(4): 1953.

Sowards, Stephen and E. Lakin Phillips. Social skill deficit as a critical element in depression: A preliminary investigation. George Washington University Counseling Center Paper, June, 1975 (privately circulated).

Staats, Arthur W. *Complex Human Behavior*. New York: Holt, Rinehart and Winston, 1963.

Staats, Arthur W. *Social Behaviorism*. Homewood, Ill: Dorsey, 1975.

Stampfl, T. G. and D. J. Levis. Essentials of implosive therapy: A learning-theory-based psychodynamic behavioral therapy. *J. Abnorm. Psychol.*, **72:**496–503, 1967.

Stolz, Stephanie B., Louis A. Wienckowski, and Bertram S. Brown. Behavior modification: A perspective on critical issues, *Am. Psychol.*, **30:**1027–1048, 1975.

Suppe, Frederick (Ed.). *The Structure of Scientific Theories*. Urbana: University of Illinois Press, 1974.

Task Force Report: American Psychiatric Association. *Behavior Therapy in Psychiatry*. New York: Jason Aronson, 1974.

Test, L. A. A comparative study of four approaches to short-term psychotherapy. Washington, D.C.: George Washington University, 1964.

Tharp, Ronald G. and Ralph J. Wetzel. *Behavior Modification in the Natural Environment*. New York: Academic, 1969.

Thompson, Travis and John G. Grabowski. *Reinforcement Schedules and Multi-operant Analysis*. New York: Appleton-Century-Crofts, 1972.

Thoresen, C. E. and J. J. Mahoney. *Behavioral Self-Control*. New York: Holt, Rinehart and Winston, 1974.

Thornton, Jerry W. and Paul D. Jacobs. Learned helplessness in human subjects. *J. Exp. Psychol.*, **87**:367–372, 1971.

Torrey, E. Fuller. *The Death of Psychiatry*. Radnor, Pa.: Chilton, 1974.

Truax, C. B. Reinforcement and non-reinforcement in Rogerian psychotherapy. *J. Abnorm. Psychol.*, **71**:1–9, 1966.

Ullmann, L. P. On cognitions and behavior therapy. *Behav. Ther.*, **1**:201–204, 1970.

Ullmann, L. P., and L. Krasner. *Case Studies in Behavior Modification*. New York: Holt, Rinehart and Winston, 1965.

Ullmann, L. P. and Leonard Krasner. Methods of change: Behavior modification in Jack T. Huber and Howard L. Millman (Eds.), *Goals and Behavior in Psychotherapy and Counseling*. Columbus, Ohio: Merrill, 1972.

Ullmann, L. P. and Leonard Krasner. *A Psychological Approach to Abnormal Behavior*, 2nd ed. Englewood Cliffs, N.J.: Prentice-Hall, 1975.

Wachtel, Paul L. An approach to the study of body language in psychotherapy. *Psychother. Theory Res. Pract.*, **4**:97–100, 1967.

Wagner, M. K. Comparative effectiveness of behavior rehearsal and verbal reinforcement for effecting anger expressiveness. *Psychol. Rep.*, **3**:77–88, 1968.

Walton, D. and M. D. Mather. The application of learning principles to the treatment of obsessive-compulsive states in the acute and chronic phases of illness, in H. J. Eysenck (Ed.), *Experiments in Behavior Therapy*. New York: Macmillan, 1964, pp. 117–151.

Watzlawick, P., J. Weakland, and R. Fisch. *Change: Principles of Problem Formation and Problem Resolution*. New York: Norton, 1974.

Weakland, John H., R. Fisch, P. Watzlawick, and A. M. Bodin. Brief therapy: focused problem resolution. *Fam. Proc.*, **13**:141–168, 1974.

Wiener, N. *Cybernetics*. New York: Wiley, 1948.

Wiener, N. *The Human Use of Human Beings: Cybernetics and Society*. Boston: Houghton Mifflin, 1950.

Wiener, Daniel N. and E. Lakin Phillips. *Training Children in Self-Discipline and Self-Control*. Englewood Cliffs, N.J.: Prentice-Hall, 1972.

Wolpe, J. *Psychotherapy by Reciprocal Inhibition*. Stanford, Calif: Stanford University Press, 1958.

Wolpe, J. *The Practice of Behavior Therapy*. New York: Pergamon, 1969.

Wolpe, J. and A. A. Lazarus. *Behavior Therapy Techniques*. Oxford, England: Pergamon, 1966.

Woody, R. H. *Psychobehavioral Counseling and Therapy: Integrating Behavioral and Insight Techniques*. New York: Appleton-Century-Crofts, 1971.

Yates, Aubrey J. *Theory and Practice in Behavior Therapy*. New York: Wiley, 1975.

Author Index

Numbers in *italics* indicate the pages on which the references appear.

Subject Index

Numbers in *italics* refer to charts, tables, graphs.

Adequate behavior, 20, 21, 94–95
  eliciting, 177
  hypochondriasis and, 168
  therapist recognition of, 117–119
Agenda setting, 71, 121, 168, 225
  explanation of, 36
  hysteria cases and, 171
  short-term psychotherapy and, 201
  sticking to, 111, 257
Aggressive threats against therapist,
    206–207
Alcoholics Anonymous, 32
Alcoholism, 178
American Psychological Association, 256
Anger, 116, 121, 122, 123
  at patient, 261
  at therapist, 205–206
Animal experimentation, 245, 249
  on depression, 162–163
  shaping in, 66
Antecedent conditions, 72
  stimulus control and, 12, 213–215
Anxiety and tension, 135, 203
  crowding and, 115–116, 118, 123, 130
  escape-avoidance and, 177, 178
  fear of driving and, 115–116, 121, 123,
    124–127, 130
  fear of heights and, 116, 118, 123
  hypochondriasis and, 166
  nonfunctional ways of dealing with, 97
  nonverbal signs of, 88
  obsessive-compulsive cases and, 172,
    173–174, 260
  recognizing, 131, 136

stopgap measures for, 97–99
Approach and avoidance, *see* Escape and
    avoidance
Assertiveness training, 59
  in case studies, 80–81, 117, 118, 119,
    130
  explanation of, 36, 40
  log-keeping and, 91
  self-blame and, 207
  theory-and-practice wedded in, 33
Association for the Advancement of
    Behavioral Therapy, 256
Augmented feedback, 33
Autistic children, 22–23, 264
Aversive consequences, avoidance of,
    see Aversive stimulation
Aversiveness, 196–197, 260
  depression and, 153–154, 155, 158
  escape and/or avoidance and, 161
  nonverbal signs of, 188
Aversive stimulation, 15, 40, 161, 258–259
  hypochondriases patients and, 168–169
  in obsessive-compulsive cases, 173
  shame-aversion therapy and, 65
  thought stopping and, 14, 67, 173
Avoidance, *see* Escape and avoidance

Backward (reverse) shaping, 40–41
Behavior, defining, 1–34, 215–216
  behavior modification characteristics,
    27–29
  covert processes, 13–16
  by environmental versus mentalistic
    causes, 16–17, 24, 28